The Nature of the Transnational Firm

The theory of the transnational corporation is a topic of central importance to economics. Transnational corporations play a key role in the world economy, and their enormous size and power make them the subject of great interest and concern to consumers, producers, nation states and international organisations, as well as to researchers. Understanding the nature of the transnational firm is central to understanding how to attract foreign investment, and how to optimise its impact; it is also central to the nature of international business.

Christos N. Pitelis and Roger Sugden have brought together leading theorists in this area to present a variety of perspectives on the nature of the transnational firm. This unique volume incorporates both orthodox and radical theories, providing new insights and suggesting areas of potential development. This second edition brings its popular predecessor completely up to date by introducing major revisions and a completely new analysis.

The Editors: Christos N. Pitelis is Director of the Centre of International Business and Management, the Judge Institute of Management Studies, and Fellow in Economics and Director of Studies in Management, at Queens' college, both at the University of Cambridge. He has published extensively, is the joint editor of *Frontiers to Political Economy* (with M. Milgate), and editor of the forthcoming *Collected Papers of Edith Penrose*, both published by Routledge. **Roger Sugden** is Professor of Commerce at the University of Birmingham and Director of the Institute for Industrial Development Policy. He has published extensively, being the editor of *Competitiveness, Subsidiary and Industrial Policy*, and co-author of *Transnationals and Governments*, and *Making Transnationals Accountable*, all published by Routledge.

The Nature of the
Transnational Firm
Second Edition

**Edited by Christos N. Pitelis
and Roger Sugden**

London and New York

First published 1991 by Routledge
2 Park Square, Milton Park, Abingdon, Oxon, OX14 4RN

Simultaneously published in the USA and Canada
by Routledge
270 Madison Ave, New York NY 10016

Routledge is an imprint of the Taylor & Francis Group

Second edition 2000

Transferred to Digital Printing 2006

Typeset in Times by Keystroke Ltd

British Library Cataloguing in Publication Data
A catalogue record for this book is available from the British Library

Library of Congress Cataloging in Publication Data
The nature of the transnational firm / edited by Christos N. Pitelis and Roger Sugden,–
2nd ed.
    p.   cm.
  Includes bibliographical references and index.
  1. International business enterprises. I. Pitelis, Christos. II. Sugden, Roger.

HD2755.5.N42 2000
338.8′8–dc21   99–053474

ISBN 0–415–16787–6 (hbk)
ISBN 0–415–16788–4 (pbk)

Publisher's Note
The publisher has gone to great lengths to ensure the quality of this reprint
but points out that some imperfections in the original may be apparent

Contents

Contributors

John Cantwell is Professor of International Economics at the University of Reading.

John H. Dunning is State of New Jersey Professor of International Business at Rutgers University, USA and Professor Emeritus of International Business at the University of Reading.

Edward M. Graham is Senior Research Fellow at the Institute for International Economics, Washington DC.

Jean-François Hennart is Professor of International Management at Tilburg University.

Neil Kay is Professor of Business Economics at the University of Strathclyde.

James Peoples is Professor of Economics at the University of Wisconsin-Milwaukee.

Christos N. Pitelis is Director of the Centre of International Business and Management at the Judge Institute of Management Studies, and Director of Studies in Management, both at the University of Cambridge.

Roger Sugden is the Director of the Institute for Industrial Development Policy (Universities of Birmingham, Ferrara and Wisconsin-Milwaukee) and Professor of Commerce at the University of Birmingham, UK.

Mohammad Yamin is Senior Lecturer in International Business at the Manchester School of Management, UMIST.

Figures and tables

Figures

Tables

1 The (theory of the) transnational firm

The 1990s and beyond

Christos N. Pitelis and Roger Sugden

The introductory chapter of the first edition of this book was written almost a decade ago. At the time we felt that the continuing expansion of the activities of transnational corporations (TNCs), alongside the emergence and swift acquisition of near dominance by the 'internalization' perspective on the TNC, generated a need for: first, recognition by internalization-transaction costs theorists outside the area of the TNC of the important contribution on this issue by contributors in the TNC literature, such as Buckley and Casson (1976) and Hennart (see this volume); second, a redress of the balance to account for the significance of early contributions to the theory, such as Stephen Hymer's advantage cum oligopolistic interaction-based approach, as well as an integration of industrial organization (IO) and internalization-type theory of the TNC; third, filling a gap in the market by presenting all major (and not only) approaches to the TNC in one volume, and by some of their major proponents.

While the volume was not meant to be a textbook *per se*, it appears that it gradually acquired such a role, thus pointing to an apparent success of our third objective as stated above. This second edition is in response to this role.

Nor did our other stimuli and objectives let us down. The 1990s have witnessed an explosive growth of foreign direct investment (FDI), far exceeding the growth of both incomes and international trade. The strategies and locational choices of TNCs have also undergone significant shifts.[1] Arguably, the term 'globalization' (a broad indication of the significance of FDI and TNC activities in the world economy) has been one of the trendiest in the 1990s, and it seems likely to remain so in the next decade.

On the issue of mutual learning, progress has been made, albeit arguably one-sided. Buckley (1990) and Buckley and Casson (1998a) have both acknowledged the need for incorporating advantage and oligopolistic interaction-based issues in their analyses. Learning from the other side seems to have been slower. In the transaction costs literature the Williamsonian, asset specificity-based perspective still seems to dominate the scene, despite extensive criticism; see, among others Demsetz (1995), Holmström and Roberts (1998). In part, this is due to the paucity of any empirical evidence in direct support of the other mainstream perspective, the incomplete contracts theory of Hart and Moore (1990) and Grossman and Hart (1986). Both these perspectives, however, have been slow in incorporating insights from the TNC-related internalization school of the Buckley–Casson type. In this perspective, TNCs internalize markets which fail because of intangible assets exhibiting public goods characteristics. As Kay (1991) observed, these need not be specific assets, in contrast to the Williamsonian approach. The pervasive influence of 'asset specificity' in the Williamsonian theory and its extensive empirical tests (see, for example, Seth and Thomas, 1994), with the associated difficulties of dealing with non-specific assets in this context, may partly explain failure of progress. Similarly slow has been the mainstream IO theory, which, despite acknowledgment of asset specificity and incomplete contract-based perspectives on the firm (see Tirole, 1988), has not been equally open to non-specific assets-based theories. More progress is needed on this front, and we hope this volume will help to contribute in this direction.

At the time of our writing for the first edition, we were able to claim that 'in the theory of the transnational, transaction cost analysis has arguably attained dominance, and has done so fairly quickly' (p. 10). This view is now widely accepted; see, for example, Caves (1996), Dunning (1998), Dunning (this volume). In view of the critiques of the transaction costs model already in place by then, we had felt that 'such dominance was unsatisfactory' (p. 11). Much more criticism has emerged since, as have alternatives justifying this view; see, for example, Kogut and Zander (1993), Demsetz (1995), Dunning (1998), Ostry (1998), among others. As already noted, many proponents of the internalization theory have been open-minded and ready to acknowledge such critiques and alternatives; see notably Buckley and Casson (1998b). However, critiques, alternatives and overall new developments on the theory of the firm in general and the TNC in particular pose challenges to this volume too, which this edition needs to tackle.

First, critiques and alternatives. When writing the introduction to the first edition, some problems and confusion within the internalization school were becoming apparent. One is that there is simply not one internalization approach. As already noted, the Williamson version and Buckley–Casson's are in fact quite distinct. Both have received further criticism. Williamson's almost exclusive focus on specific assets has been criticized by no less than Coase (1993) and Demsetz (1995).[2] Buckley and Casson's version relies on the alleged public good nature of intermediate products, such as technology, know-how and more generally knowledge-related 'intangible assets'. Building on earlier work by Teece (1977), Kogut and Zander (1993) raised doubts about this. In their view, much of knowledge is tacit, and hard and expensive to transfer. This is far from it being a public good. If so, it is arguable that TNCs (exist because they) are better in transferring tacit knowledge than are either markets or other firms. This differential efficiency in the transfer of knowledge can explain TNCs, they claim, not (transaction costs-related) market failure.

Kogut and Zander's (1993) approach to the TNC is most interesting. It reads as very Penrosean, although it has been developed independently (Penrose is not referred to in the paper). Resurrection of the Penrosean contribution to the theory of the firm has surely been the big news of the 1990s. Edith Penrose's classic

The Theory of the Growth of the Firm was published in 1959, although the main arguments behind the book were already in print in Penrose (1955). In her book, Penrose defines the firm as a bundle of resources under administrative co-ordination, producing for profit realized through sale in the market. Among the tangible and intangible resources most important are the latter, notably the human resources and, amongst these, management. The cohesive shell of the administrative structure called a firm gives rise to knowledge through teamwork, learning by doing, learning to work with others, etc. Learning and indivisibilities of resources give rise to endogenous growth. The availability of (firm-specific) managerial resources in particular puts a limit to the rate of growth but not to the size of the firm. Unused resources provide an incentive for expansion but also determine in part the direction of expansion (where such resources are most suitably of use). They also provide an incentive for innovations. There is a dynamic interaction between the internal and external environment, the latter being an 'image' of management's perceptions. This dynamic interaction results in internal and external growth – horizontal, vertical and diversified. Diversification is the natural result of the process of growth. This applies to both intra-national and inter-national diversification. In this sense, the TNC is the outcome of an (endogenous) growth process.

Penrose's focus on endogenous growth and the role of knowledge has currently given rise to an industry of writings in the theory of the firm. Resource, competence and knowledge-based theories of the firm are arguably now dominant, at least in the strategic management literature. While not always drawing explicitly on Penrose, her motherhood of such theories now seems to be very widely acknowledged; see, for example, Foss (1997) for extensive coverage. However, with the notable exception of Kogut and Zander (1993), this extensive literature has found very little application indeed in the theory of the TNC. That was a major issue to be addressed in this edition, and a major objective of it.

One can hazard various reasons why the Penrosean perspective, while arguably dominant on the issue of diversification (see Foss, 1997), has failed to make inroads so far on the theory of the TNC. While Penrose spent a lot of time and effort analysing TNCs, she did not make much effort in showing the links between her analysis of the theory of the growth of the firm and the TNC itself. In part, this is owing to her view that once up and running, a subsidiary could usefully be regarded as a separate entity (Penrose, 1956). In the preface to the 1995 edition of her classic, Penrose suggests that all she said on firm growth is directly applicable to the TNC, leaving it, however, to the reader to perform the task! In addition to the above, as Kay (this volume) observes, Penrose's choice of (the oil) industry was hardly the best case study of her theory of growth, exhibiting scarcely any (internal resource-related) diversification strategies.

There are additional reasons that might explain the failure of the Penrosean approach to make inroads into the theory of the TNC. Arguably, her theory is more amenable in explaining the direction of expansion, but not the mode (see Kay, this volume). When it comes to understanding the mode, transaction costs-related arguments may well be indispensable. Another reason may be the result of strength, not weaknesses. The Penrosean approach is arguably fully compatible with the Hymer story. It complements the latter by providing an endogenous growth theory cum (relatedly) an explanation of the direction of diversification. Other than these, the resource-based related, firm-specific advantages can be easily translated as monopolistic or ownership advantages. This affinity is not really surprising, given Penrose's own recognition of the close links between her work and that of Chandler (1962); see Penrose (1995) and the fact that Hymer's own account of the historical evolution of firms and the related acquisition of advantages drew explicitly on Chandler's work (Hymer, 1972). The link between Hymer's work and that of Penrose is also noted in Buckley and Casson (1998b). Sanna Randaccio integrates Penrose's work with oligopolistic inter-action; see Cantwell (this volume), who also notes the links between the Penrosean perspective and the technological accumulation approach to TNCs. Finally, the links between the Buckley–Casson approach to internalization and the Penrosean theory are simply too obvious to be missed. It could well be that Penrose's theory could prove to be the glue to bind everything together. To that point, however, no explicitly Penrose-based theory of the TNC has yet been developed.

In this edition we address this problem by killing two birds with one stone. In the previous edition there were, in effect, two chapters on internalization: one in favour (Hennart's), one partially critical (Kay's). Whilst in line with the lack of a unified approach on this issue, as already mentioned, that was also rather unbalanced. In this edition, we have asked Neil Kay, who was already working on a resource-based approach to the TNC (see Kay, 1997), to link his work explicitly with that of Penrose, and develop what he considers an explicitly Penrose-based theory of the TNC. Kay's earlier arguments also feature here, while the issue of a potential synthesis with transaction costs-related arguments is also addressed.

Chapter 6 by Kay, then, represents a major change in this edition. Moreover, whilst it is the only explicitly resource-based approach in the volume (and quite independently of any design on the part of the editors), Penrose and resources feature extensively in this edition (in stark contrast to the previous one), notably in the chapters by Cantwell and Yamin, but also in those by Dunning and Pitelis.

The other major development since the last edition concerns the role of inter-firm relations. This also links with Penrose's contribution, but arguably owes more to the work of George Richardson (1960, 1972). In Richardson's now classic 1972 *Economic Journal* article, the conventional distinction between market and hierarchy is put to task, given the 'dense network of *co-operation* and affiliation by which firms are inter-related' (1972: 884, emphasis added). Echoing Penrose, albeit independently, Richardson attributes such inter-relationships to production-side related capabilities, as well as informational interdependence; see Richardson (1999). Co-operation provides an alternative to integration and it is pursued when there exist complementary but dissimilar activities. When activities are complementary but similar, integration is more likely, while weakly complementary activities are more amenable to market co-ordination. The now immense literature on inter-firm relations, joint ventures, alliances, subcontracting, clusters, industrial districts, networks, relational contracting and many such others, arguably owe their modern theoretical justification to Richardson's work.

It is well beyond the scope of this introductory chapter to review developments in this field; for surveys see, among others You (1995), and more recently Holmström and Roberts (1998). For our purposes, such developments as they impact on the theory of the TNC are covered in this volume mainly by Dunning and, from an internalization perspective, by Hennart. For Dunning, the significance of such inter-firm relations today is large enough to have led to what he calls 'alliance capitalism'; see also Dunning (1998). Dunning attributes many of these relationships to the need to acquire complementary capabilities, in line with Richardson.

A particularly significant aspect of inter-firm relations are clusters, networks, webs and/or industrial districts. These represent inter-firm linkages, often with a territorial dimension. They have been hailed in recent years as the major alternative to integration, in that they can achieve unit cost economies, normally associated with large size, through co-operation. At the same time, further such economies can be achieved due to the development of trust (which reduces transaction costs) and 'external economies', which further reduce unit costs. Clusters are also arguably more bottom-up, a seedbed of larger firms and a source of innovation and competition for large firms. Members of a cluster also compete, often fiercely, while maintaining co-operation for joint inputs, marketing and innovation; see, for example, Best (1990), Porter (1990) and, more recently, You (1995), Porter (1998).

There is a particularly interesting aspect of clusters which pertains to this volume. For many years, Dunning was among the very few (arguably lonely) champions of locational factors in explaining the TNC. The resurgence of interest in clusters has greatly facilitated the reappearance of geography and location in economics. Porter (1990) and Krugman (1991), among others, have led this resurgence. Models of the TNC building explicitly on geographical issues have also been developed; see for example Markusen (1995). As Dunning (1998), however, observes, such models still fail to account for multinationalism as opposed to multi-dimensionality; they help explain a different location, but not necessarily a different nation. For this one needs to build also on, at least, ownership and internalization advantages. This takes us back to Dunning's OLI (Ownership–Location–Internalization) paradigm, which is worth rereading in a fresher light. Far from being the poor relative, L may well turn out to be the prince. Dunning (1998) does not quite say as much, but the return of space has certainly done much to vindicate his long-held position. Cantwell (this volume) also covers location-related issues, mainly in the context of OLI.

Whilst resources, knowledge, inter-firm relationships, clusters and location (all related) represent the 'news', much of the most welcome catholicism in the literature of the TNC remains. Indeed, it has gone a step further. Despite repeated claims concerning the difficulties, and for some the impossibility, of constructing a general theory of the TNC (Cantwell, this volume; Buckley and Casson, 1998b), and almost in contradiction to this claim, the 1990s have experienced a (welcome in our view) trend for pluralism and synthesis. Besides Dunning, major contributors in the field have recognized the need for synthesis, e.g. between transaction costs and monopolistic advantages (Buckley, 1990); ownership advantages and capabilities (Kogut and Zander, 1993); resources, capabilities and transaction costs (Buckley and Casson, 1998b); location and ownership advantages (Dunning, 1998); oligopoly and resources (Cantwell, this volume); transaction costs and oligopolistic interaction (Buckley and Casson, 1998a); location and resources (Ostry, 1998). Indeed, much like the 1982 edition, Caves' 1996 edition of his classic book on the TNC reads like a synthesis of resource-based and transaction costs arguments, despite Caves' own phrasing in terms of transaction costs. Last, but not least, and in recognition of the static character of transaction costs economics, Buckley and Casson (1998b) identify 'flexibility' as the hallmark of recent modeling on the TNC. Flexibility is taken to be the ability to reallocate resources quickly and smoothly in response to change. Interestingly, flexibility is claimed to discourage integration, thus partially explaining subcontracting and other neo-market-based firm strategies, notably export over FDI and licensing over internalization. Flexible firms should exploit the relative advantage of market, hierarchy and co-operation. Although it is too early to predict where these new developments will lead, the focus on syntheses and dynamics is most welcome.

The above summarizes what we consider to be the main issues of the 1990s on *The Nature of the Transnational Firm*. Although we have already referred to some of the main additions and changes to the volume, to facilitate reading we also briefly summarize here the philosophy, sequence and main points of the contents of this book.

Following this introductory chapter, Cantwell provides in chapter 2 an updated critical survey of the literature on the TNC. The main additions to the previous version refer to Penrose and resources, their links with the 'technological accumulation' approach to the TNC, and the expanded role of inter-firm relationships.

In chapter 3, Yamin recapitulates the monopolistic advantages cum reduction of conflict approach of Hymer. He goes on, however, to highlight some limitations to the Hymer perspective, drawing on the works of Penrose, Richardson and developments in the resource-based and knowledge-based perspectives. Yamin's main points are that Hymer regarded advantages as tradable, which, following the works of Teece and Kogut and Zander, need not be the case, not always anyway. In addition, he suggests that inter-firm strategies such as alliances may have positive-sum game attributes. This contrasts to battles over market shares of the traditional type, which are arguably zero-sum.

Chapter 4 presents the internalization school. Hennart insists on viewing this as a general theory of the TNC. He points to differences within the internalization school. Going back to Coase's concern with the employment relationship, Hennart suggests that we need more than a market failure to explain firms; we need reasons for firms' success. This he traces in the ability of firms to use hierarchy. This replaces market-based co-ordination with intra-firm hierarchical co-ordination. The result is potentially lower transaction costs, but also higher shirking. This results in a trade-off between market-based and hierarchical organization and points to the need for incentives within hierarchies. TNCs are said to internalize markets, not (just) advantages. They are better than foreign firms in managing foreign labour. The internalization of different markets gives rise to different types of TNCs. Even free-standing firms are explainable in this context, in terms of internalizing the market for capital.

In chapter 5 Dunning presents his by now classic OLI paradigm. He re-emphasizes its role as a framework, not a general theory, and expands it to account for what he calls 'alliance capitalism': the emergence of close inter-firm relationships at the global level, such as strategic alliances. Dunning, moreover, compares and contrasts OLI to different perspectives, while at the same time addressing some points of contention and critique of this perspective.

In chapter 6 Kay tries to build an explicitly resource-based perspective of the TNC. He discusses reasons for the failure of resource-based theory to make inroads into the theory of the TNC, despite some useful earlier attempts. In his version, specialization as a strategy dominates diversification in general, and geographical diversification in particular. In this context, the TNC is a sign of weakness rather than strength. It comes about when richer-linked strategies become unavailable.

In chapter 7 Graham provides a slightly amended version of his previous chapter on the oligopolistic interaction theory. As already noted, the 1990s have witnessed revived interest and recognition of oligopolistic interaction, thus retaining the freshness of the approach. Sugden, in chapter 8, teams in this edition with Peoples, to recapitulate and empirically substantiate his divide-and-rule theory. They find evidence in favour of the hypothesis.

The volume concludes with Pitelis's attempted synthesis of micro-based theories and re-statement of the macro, effective demand-based theory of international production. The macro argument is now put in terms of business cycle–differential location advantages, and empirical econometric evidence is provided. Hymer is synthesized (a) with Penrose to explain endogenous growth and the direction of expansion, (b) with the business cycle to explain geographical diversification and (c) with transaction costs-related arguments to explain the choice of mode.

In all, we hope that much of the exciting new work on this most important and topical issue incorporated in this second edition will prove to be of use to researchers, students and businesspeople alike. As before, new developments are taking place as these words are being written; hinting at the sequel . . .

Notes

1   See Dunning (1998), Ostry (1998) for detailed recent statistics. An important trend, observes Ostry, is the shift of activity outside the OECD to developing and/or emerging economies in the 1990s.

2 Similar considerations apply to Williamson's related concept of opportunism; see, for example, the debate between Foss (1997), Kogut and Zander (1996) and Conner and Prahalad (1996).

References

Best, M. (1990) *The New Competition: Institutions for Industrial Restructuring*, Oxford: Polity Press.

Buckley, P. (1990) 'Problems and developments in the core theory of international business', *Journal of International Business Studies*, 21, 4.

Buckley, P.J. and M.C. Casson (1976) *The Future of Multinational Enterprise*, London: Macmillan.

Buckley, P.J. and M.C. Casson (1998a) 'Analyzing foreign market entry strategies: Extending the internalization approach', *Journal of International Business Studies*, 29, 3: 539–62.

Buckley, P.J. and M.C. Casson (1998b) 'Models of the multinational enterprise', *Journal of International Business Studies*, 29, 1: 21–44.

Caves, R.E. (1996) *Multinational Enterprise and Economic Analysis*, Cambridge: Cambridge University Press, 2nd edn.

Chandler, A.D. (1962) *Strategy and Structure*, Cambridge, MA: MIT Press.

Coase, R.H. (1993) '1991 Nobel Lecture: The institutional structure of production', in O.E. Williamson and S.G. Winter (eds) *The Nature of the Firm*, Oxford: Oxford University Press.

Conner, K.R. and C.K. Prahalad (1996) 'A resource-based theory of the firm: Knowledge versus opportunism', *Organisation Science*, 7, 5, September–October: 477–501.

Demsetz, H. (1995) *The Economics of the Business Firm: Seven Critical Commentaries*, Cambridge: Cambridge University Press.

Dunning, J.H. (1998) 'Location and the multinational enterprise: A neglected factor?' *Journal of International Business Studies*, 29, 1: 45–66.

Foss, N.J. (1997) (ed.) *Resources, Firms and Strategies*, Oxford: Oxford University Press.

Grossman, S. and O. Hart (1986) 'The costs and benefits of ownership: A theory of lateral and vertical integration', *Journal of Political Economy*, 94: 691–719.

Hart, O. and J. Moore (1990) 'Property rights and the nature of the firm', *Journal of Political Economy*, 98: 1119–58.

Hymer, S.H. (1972) 'The multinational corporation and the law of uneven development', in J.N. Bhagwati (ed.) *Economics and World Order*, London: Macmillan.

Holmström, B. and J. Roberts (1998) 'The boundaries of the firm revisited', *Journal of Economic Perspectives*, 12, 4: 73–94.

Kay, N.M. (1991) 'Multinational enterprise as strategic choice: Some transaction cost perspectives', in C. Pitelis and R. Sugden (eds) *The Nature of the Transnational Firm*, London: Routledge.

Kay, N.M. (1997) *Pattern in Corporate Evolution*, Oxford: Oxford University Press.

Kogut, B. and U. Zander (1993) 'Knowledge of the firm and the evolutionary theory of the multinational corporation', *Journal of International Business Studies*, 4th quarter: 625–45.

Kogut, B. and U. Zander (1996) 'What firms do? Coordination, identity, and learning', *Organisation Science*, 7, 5, September–October: 502–518.

Krugman, P.R. (1991) *Geography and Trade*, Cambridge, MA: MIT Press.

Markusen, J.R. (1995) 'The boundaries of multinational enterprise and the theory of international trade', *Journal of Economic Perspectives*, 9, 2: 169–89.

Ostry, S. (1998) 'Technology, productivity and the multinational enterprise', *Journal of International Business Studies*, 29, 1: 85–99.

Penrose, E.T. (1955) 'Research on the business firms: Limits to growth and size of firms', *American Economic Review*, vol. XLV, no. 2.

Penrose, E.T. (1956) 'Foreign investment and the growth of the firm', *Economic Journal*, LXVI, June.

Penrose, E.T. (1959/1995) *The Theory of the Growth of the Firm*, Oxford: Oxford University Press, 3rd edn.

Porter, M.E. (1990) *The Competitive Advantage of Nations*, Basingstoke: Macmillan.

Porter, M.E. (1998) 'Clusters and the new economics of competition', *Harvard Business Review*, November/December.

Richardson, G. (1960) *Information and Investment: A Study in the Working of the Competitive Economy*, Oxford: Clarendon Press.

Richardson, G. (1972) 'The organisation of industry', *Economic Journal*, 82: 883–96.

Richardson, G. (1999) 'Mrs Penrose and neoclassical theory', *Contributions to Political Economy*, Oxford: Oxford University Press.

Seth, A. and H. Thomas (1994) 'Theories of the firm: Implications for strategy research', *Journal of Management Studies*, 31, 2 (March): 165–91.

Teece, D.J. (1977) 'Technology transfer by multinational firms: The resource costs of transferring technological know-how', *Economic Journal*, 87: 242–61.

Tirole, J. (1988) *The Theory of Industrial Organization*, Cambridge, MA: MIT Press.

You, J-I. (1995) 'Small firms in economic theory', *Cambridge Journal of Economics*, 19: 441–62.

2 A survey of theories of international production

John Cantwell

Introduction

In the 1970s and early 1980s it became fashionable to search for general theories of international production which encompassed all the contributions of earlier writers thought to be significant. These were sometimes advanced as general theories of the multinational corporation (MNC), the main institutional agent of international production, or general theories of foreign direct investment (FDI), the major means by which international production is financed.[1] When confronted with evidence on certain types of international production that their 'general' theories did not seem to explain, the proponents of such theories all too frequently seemed to respond either by dismissing the relevance of the evidence or by adapting their terminology to accommodate it. To the extent they succeeded their theories became increasingly cumbersome and less operational (as discussed by Buckley, 1983).

By the late 1980s the limitations of particular theoretical approaches as catch-all explanations of international production seem to have become clearer even to their keenest advocates. This has led work in the field in two directions. First, within each approach there has been an effort to extend or develop theories to broaden their coverage, while allowing for the influence of other factors perhaps better explained by other complementary theoretical approaches. One issue that most schools of thought have identified as particularly requiring attention is the dynamic aspects of international production. This chapter therefore concentrates on theories of the growth of international production, and of changes in its composition, from various different perspectives.

Second, an attempt has been made to avoid fruitless confrontation between alternative theories that set out spuriously to encompass one another, by constructing a general framework of analysis of international production which represents the common ground between different theoretical approaches but is not inextricably wedded to any one of them. It also provides a framework for helping to articulate the real areas of disagreement and to decide between alternative theories where they offer genuinely competing explanations of the same phenomenon. This general framework has been developed by John Dunning, and since it deliberately draws on a variety of theoretical approaches, it is known as the eclectic paradigm (Dunning, 1977, 1981, 1988a). The eclectic paradigm combines elements of quite different approaches to international production, and so it should not be misunderstood itself as another general theory: '[P]recisely because of its generality, the eclectic paradigm has only limited power to explain or predict particular kinds of international production; and even less, the behaviour of individual enterprises' (Dunning, 1988a: 1).

Theoretical diversity is to be expected in the field of economics of international production as much as in any other area of economics. However, it is one of the virtues of the eclectic paradigm that it makes clear that such diversity is attributable not only to a variety of ideological standpoints. There are three additional reasons to expect theoretical diversity in this case. First, international production may be of a resource-based, import-substituting, export-platform or globally integrated kind, each of which raises distinctive considerations and each of which affects home and host counties in different ways.

Second, and related to this, the use of particular theories often reflects the issues addressed and the questions asked. Theories of international production have drawn on six separate branches of economic theory (Cantwell *et al.*, 1986): the theories of international capital movements, trade, location, industrial organisation, innovation and the firm. To give examples of possible approaches, those whose concern is with the MNC *per se* tend to rely on a particular theory of the firm, while those interested in FDI for its own sake may place special emphasis on a theory of international financial flows.

Third, international production can be analysed at three levels: macroeconomic (examining broad national and international trends), mesoeconomic (considering the interaction between firms at an industry level) and microeconomic (looking at the international growth of individual firms). It is quite natural that macroeconomic theories of international production have often relied heavily on theories of trade, location and (in the case of FDI) the balance of payments and exchange rate effects; mesoeconomic approaches tend to be derived from industrial economics, game theory and the theory of innovation and comparative corporate trajectories or strategies; while microeconomic thinking is grounded upon the theory of the individual firm.

Using this distinction between different levels of analysis, the main theories of international production can be grouped under four headings. These constitute four alternative theoretical frameworks, since approaches within each share certain common theoretical foundations. However, each of them can be further subdivided into particular theories or approaches, and they are not always mutually exclusive. The first two are based on alternative theories of the individual firm in its relationships with markets: the market power or Hymer theory of the firm, and the internalisation or Coasian theory of the firm. The third group is macroeconomic developmental approaches, while the fourth is based on the analysis of comparative firm growth in competitive international industries.

It should be noted that, as already suggested above, the eclectic paradigm is not an alternative analytical framework in the same sense, since it incorporates elements from all four types of approach and can be applied equally well at micro or macro levels. It is rather an overall organising paradigm for identifying the elements from each approach which are most relevant in explaining a wide range of various kinds of international production, and the wide range of different environments in which international production has been established.

There now follows a review of the four major types of approach to international production, together with the eclectic paradigm. The next section then examines the relationship between different approaches in the perspectives they offer on the growth of the firm and international competitiveness. This leads into a concluding section on how the various approaches have attempted or are attempting to treat the dynamic aspects of international production, with some speculations on possible future developments in the analysis of international production. Since much of the literature has been concerned to emphasise the role played by technology in the growth of MNCs, this features heavily in the discussion.

A survey of the major theories of international production

The theory of international production dates from 1960 when Hymer, in a doctoral dissertation eventually published in 1976, showed that the orthodox theory of international trade and capital movements did not explain the foreign operations of MNCs (see Cantwell *et al.*, 1986). In particular, it did not explain two-way flows of FDI between countries, and still less between countries with similar factor proportions. His explanation of why firms move abroad and establish international production was based on a theory of the firm and industrial organisation. Since that time, four major theoretical frameworks for the analysis of MNCs have emerged, and a fifth overall framework which attempts to bring strands from each together. The first two are based on particular theories of the individual firm *vis-à-vis* markets, and although their advocates sometimes claim that they are general theories, they are unlike the eclectic paradigm, which is a general, all-encompassing framework which need not be tied to any particular theory of the firm or MNC development. The other two frameworks suggested here also collect together somewhat different approaches, derived from adaptations of the theory of international trade or economic development, and the theory of oligopolistic competition or technological innovation (which has also become associated with a third approach to the firm *vis-à-vis* other firms) respectively.

The first theoretical framework used to analyse international production is that passed down by Hymer, based on a view of the firm as an agent for market power and collusion. It comes in both non-Marxist and Marxist versions, the latter dating back to Baran and Sweezy (1966). Two of the clearest recent statements of this framework can be found in Newfarmer (1985) and Cowling and Sugden (1987).

The second is the internalisation approach, based on a Coasian or institutionalist view of the firm as a device for raising efficiency by replacing markets; it has been advanced as a general paradigm by Rugman (1980), though less extravagant claims are made for a similar approach by Buckley and Casson (1976, 1985), Casson (1987), Caves (1982), Teece (1983) and Williamson (1975), amongst others.

Approaches based on the analysis of competitive interaction in international industries include later (Mark II) versions of the product cycle tradition (Flowers, 1976; Graham, 1975; Knickerbocker, 1973; Vernon, 1974); the technological accumulation approach and the related competence-based approach to comparative firm growth (Cantwell, 1989b, 1994a, 1998a; Kogut and Zander, 1993; Pavitt, 1987); the internationalisation of capital approach (Jenkins, 1987); and in a development context the work of those whom Jenkins terms neo-fundamentalist Marxists (Warren, 1980).

Macroeconomic developmental approaches come in various forms, covering the earliest versions of the product cycle model (PCM Mark I) which trace back to Vernon (1966) and Hirsch (1967); the approach of the Japanese economists Kojima (1978) and Ozawa (1982); the investment-development cycle (Dunning, 1982) and stages of development approach (Cantwell and Tolentino, 1990; Tolentino, 1993); and – though these are rather different – approaches that deal with the role of financial factors in FDI (Aliber, 1970; Casson, 1982; Rugman, 1979).

The final framework is the eclectic paradigm developed by Dunning (1977, 1988a), which, as its name suggests, combines elements of all the other four in such a way that it is compatible with various different theoretical approaches. It can be applied at a macroeconomic or mesoeconomic level, but since it is discussed in the literature in a microeconomic context with reference to theories of the firm, it is reviewed immediately after the first two approaches in the survey that follows.

The market power approach

The earliest articulation of a rounded-out theory of international production separate from the theory of international trade and capital movements can be traced back to Hymer (1976). In the traditional neoclassical approach, economically advanced countries, owing to their relative abundance of capital but scarcity of labour, have low rates of profit or interest but high wage rates prior to international transactions. They therefore tend to export goods requiring capital-intensive production methods to less advanced, labour-abundant countries; or, as a partial substitute for this, to export capital directly through FDI in developing countries. Capital thereby flows from countries in which the interest rate is low (due to the abundance of capital) to those in which it is high (due to capital scarcity).

The traditional classical and Marxist approaches reached similar conclusions, though by following a different line of reasoning. It was argued that there is a tendency for the rate of profit to fall (or in some versions a tendency towards underconsumption) in an advanced capitalist country. This provides an incentive for foreign investment in countries at an earlier stage of development where capital can be employed more profitably. If the rate of profit at home has been driven down due to the intensity of competition, as in Adam Smith's story, then foreign investment in underdeveloped countries serves as an outlet for surplus capital. In Marxist accounts the rate of profit falls either because of a rise in the capital–output ratio (the organic composition of capital) or a fall in the share of profits in income (the rate of exploitation). It then follows that there are likely to be investment opportunities in economically backward countries with low capital–output ratios or which permit a super-exploitation of a weakly organised labour force. Alternatively, foreign investment and trade involve the search for new markets in underdeveloped countries and regions, due to the inadequacy of local consumption or demand.

Although theorists sometimes react only slowly to changes in the reality they endeavour to explain, such traditional explanations could not survive for long without severe adaptation in the period after 1945. It was true that before 1939 the bulk of international trade and investment flows ran between industrialised and developing countries, often in accord with colonial or other historical connections. However, this changed rapidly in the post-war period. In 1950 around three-fifths of the manufacturing exports from Europe, North America or Japan were directed to the rest of the world, but by 1971 this had reduced to just over a third (Armstrong *et al.*, 1991: 215). Even more dramatically, two-thirds of the world's stock of FDI was located in developing countries in 1938, but this had fallen to just over a quarter by the 1970s where it has remained since (Dunning, 1983b: 88). In other words, international production is now organised principally between the industrialised countries.

Clearly, the conventional explanations of international production which were essentially constructed at a macroeconomic level were in need of substantial revision if they were to remain useful. They did not explain cross-investments between countries at an advanced stage of development, let alone the cross-investments within the same industry which became increasingly important from the 1970s onwards. Hymer's response was to apply a theory of the firm within its industry to establish the determinants of internationalisation. The theory of the firm or the industry therefore has a longer heritage in the international production field than in work on international trade, in which area such ideas were only applied from the late 1970s onwards.

Hymer's particular theory of the firm sees it as a means by which producers increase the extent of their market power. A definition of market power can be taken from Sanjaya Lall, whose work at the time was identified with this approach:

> Market power ... may ... be simply understood as the ability of particular firms, acting singly or in collusion, to dominate their respective markets (and so earn higher profits), to be more secure, or even to be less efficient than in a situation with more effective competition ... The concept may, of course, be applied to buyers (monopsonists) as well as sellers.
>
> (Lall, 1976: 1343)

Originally applied to international production by Hymer (1976), this theoretical approach has been used recently by those such as Cowling and Sugden (1987), Newfarmer (1985) and Savary (1984).[2]

The main idea is that in the early stages of growth, firms steadily increase their share of domestic markets by means of merger as well as capacity extension, and that as industrial concentration (and market power) rises, so do profits. However, there comes a point at which it is no longer easy to increase still further concentration in the domestic market, as few major firms remain, and at this stage profits earned from the high degree of monopoly power at home are invested in foreign operations, leading to a similar process of increased concentration in foreign markets.

The notion that firms everywhere seek out collusive arrangements as the major means by which they keep profits high is reminiscent of Adam Smith, but the market power school has gone further. According to Smith, competition between firms remained a spur to increased investment and technological change, whereas for those who have emphasised the role of market power in MNC activity, investment is not so much an independent response to competition as a means of further extending collusive networks. MNCs are believed to invest in foreign operations to reduce competition and increase barriers to entry in their industry, and by increasing the degree of monopoly power they may even (in the longer term) have an adverse effect on the efficiency of foreign plants.

The market power theory of the firm is therefore clearly at odds with the alternative theory that the central objective of the firm is to raise its internal efficiency as the means of increasing profits. To the extent that MNCs raise research and productivity in their foreign operations, and improve efficiency through coordinating different types of plant and different types of technology, the effects on profitability in international industries may be ambiguous. Higher internal efficiency within MNCs may increase competition amongst them, making it more difficult for them to divide markets by agreement, and reducing profitability (or at least offsetting the gains due to greater efficiency). If this continued it might act as a disincentive to a further extension of international production, but in this view greater short-run efficiency is to be understood simply as a source of increased market power, which is likely to reduce the extent of investment in greater efficiency in the future.

The market power approach is often associated with the industrial organisation literature, in which it is commonplace to argue that a more concentrated market structure is allied to greater collusion and a higher rate of profit. It should be noted, though, that in Hymer's original version it was a theory of the firm and of the behaviour of the firm rather than a theory of industrial organisation in the modern sense. In Hymer (1976) the firm appears as an active rather than a passive agent. Hymer followed Bain (1956) in viewing the firm as actively raising entry barriers and colluding with other firms in its industry. In the market power theory the primary causal link runs from the conduct of firms to market structure rather than vice versa. MNCs are seen as building up a position of market power at home, and then in their respective international industries. Their movement abroad is hastened by depression in the home market, which may result in part from their own diminishing incentive to invest due to their ever more extensive market power and collusive agreements.

Kindleberger's (1969) interpretation of the Hymer story placed it more firmly in the industrial organisation tradition, which revolves around a structure–conduct–performance model. In Kindleberger's restatement the MNC was seen as a function of market structure characterised by monopolistic competition between differentiated products, rather than as an agent involved in oligopolistic interaction with other firms. The more recent writings of Newfarmer (1985) and Cowling and Sugden (1987) have moved back towards the Hymer stance, in that while their argument is set in an industrial organisation context, they emphasise the (anti-competitive) impact of MNCs on host country market structure.

The use of an industrial organisation context by more recent authors partly reflects a change in the issues and the institutions under study themselves. Hymer's objective had been to investigate why national firms went abroad, rather than to evaluate the operations of existing MNCs. Today the concern is with the way in which international industries are organised. Cowling and Sugden (1987) contend that internationalisation is undertaken not only as a means of increasing the market power of firms in final product markets, but also to raise the share of profits in two ways. First, the greater ability to shift production between alternative locations strengthens the bargaining power of firms in negotiations over wages and conditions of work. Second, by 'putting out' work previously done within the firm to a network of dependent subcontractors, both locally and internationally, the position of collectively organised trade unions in large plants is weakened. This is then integrated with the 'monopoly capitalism' argument of Baran and Sweezy (1966) or the stagnationist argument of Steindl (1952): a combination of a rising share of profits and an increasing market power (which reduces the incentive to invest) leads to a slower growth of demand, and secular stagnation eventually at an international level.

Within the market power approach, as is the case within all the frameworks considered, differences of emphasis can be detected. In his work, Hymer was concerned with the relationship between the efficiency with which production is organised within the firm and the extent of market power and collusion. By contrast, Cowling and Sugden (1987) make almost no mention of the technological efficiency of production other than with reference to the organisation of work. They are much more concerned with the distribution of income between wages and profits. Indeed, Sugden (1983) suggests that the pursuit of a higher profit share necessarily entails inefficiency, as MNCs geographically spread production as a means of increasing their bargaining power through a 'divide and rule' strategy. Certain of the differences between authors and approaches to international production can therefore be attributed to differences in the issues addressed.

It might be argued that the market power approach has been rendered less relevant by the increasing globalisation in the organisation of economic activity and in the wider diversity of potential sources of supply, since many traditional positions of market power at a national level have been undermined. This would suggest a longer-term reorientation of MNCs away from profits associated with market power, and towards profits through innovation of the kind often linked to the work of Schumpeter (Cantwell, 1999). Rather than seeing the MNC as a network of market power controlled from a corporate centre, the MNC is instead obliged to create an international network for innovation through the looser coordination of locationally dispersed centres of differentiated sources of new technology, a theme emphasised in much recent literature (Cantwell, 1995). From this viewpoint, inter-company alliances between MNCs from different technological traditions are motivated increasingly by cooperation in innovation (Hagedoorn and Narula, 1996; Sachwald, 1998) rather than as a means of fostering mutual market power through collusion. These arguments feature in the technological accumulation approach considered below.

The counter-argument of the market power school might be that recent globalisation has also been associated with the growing influence of finance capital, reminiscent of the categorisation of the economics of imperialism in the early years of the twentieth century by Hilferding. The deregulation of financial markets, and the increasing economic weight of the leading financial institutions, has created a renewed pressure for profits from market power through continual recontracting and the redistribution of income. The question is whether such pressures can generate sustained results over a longer period under the modern conditions of greater difficulty in establishing and holding market power (Cantwell, 1999).

Internalisation

The alternative theory of the individual firm in relation to markets which has been applied to international production derives from the work of Coase and lays emphasis on the efficiency with which transactions between units of productive activity are organised. This modern theory of the 'internalisation' of markets as it is applied in the case of international production (see Buckley and Casson, 1976) is based on Coase's (1937) criticism of neoclassical economics. The framework of analysis is like the neoclassical theory of trade and investment based on exchange between individuals or groups of individuals, but it introduces the transaction costs of such exchange which vary in an arm's-length or market relationship as compared with a cooperative relationship. Where the transaction costs of an administered exchange are lower than those of a market exchange, then the market is internalised and the collective efficiency of the group is thereby increased. Apart from the existence of economies of scope across activities, the direct coordination of transactions may reduce the costs associated with information impactedness, opportunism, bounded rationality and uncertainty (for a summary see Caves, 1982).

It is argued that intangible assets such as technology are especially costly to exchange in arm's-length transactions. By thinking of the exchange of technology as a transaction that is internalised when the firm has a horizontally integrated network of production, horizontal integration is treated by analogy with vertical integration. Firms that invest abroad in R&D facilities are therefore treated in exactly the same way as firms that invest in a venture to extract natural resources and secure supplies of raw materials; both are internalising markets, and it is simply that they internalise markets for different commodities. The analogy between technology and tangible intermediate products depends upon treating technology narrowly as akin to information or potentially public knowledge, which in fact is only one aspect of technology more broadly defined (Cantwell, 1994a). The other integral part of technology is tacit capability, which accrues through collective learning processes within firms and hence becomes organisationally embedded in specific companies. Hence, tacit capability is not directly exchanged or transferred between firms except in the special case of some mergers and acquisitions. The alternative view of the internalisation of technological knowledge is considered later, a perspective which attributes internalisation to the needs of the effective use of the knowledge and the continued generation of new technology (each of which depends upon the complementary development of related knowledge and internal tacit capability) rather than to any characteristics of the potential market for knowledge.

Where markets are internalised through the common ownership and control of the groups that are involved in exchange with one another, the transaction cost approach suggests the appropriate institutional arrangement on which cooperation between the parties is likely to be founded. At one extreme are joint ventures over which the MNC exerts little direct control, or a largely decentralised MNC in which internal markets regulated by transfer prices have replaced external markets, as emphasised by Rugman (1981). Indeed, where the MNC internalises an externality (an external economy or diseconomy), it may create an internal market where no external market existed previously (Casson, 1986a). At the other extreme is the organisational structure stressed by Williamson (1975), that of globally integrated multinationals in which control is centralised and hierarchical. This distinction is discussed in Kay (1983).

Of course, there is an overlap of the spectrums spanned by market and administrative coordination, in that where market exchange is characterised by monopolistic or monopsonistic elements, the MNC may exercise control over its contractual partner without resort to 'internalisation'. Strictly speaking, in the transactions cost approach the firm is defined as the direct organiser of non-market transactions. However, the firm or MNC might equally well be defined as the controller and coordinator of an (international) network of production or income-generating assets (Cowling and Sugden, 1987). If so, the firm may exercise control over production which it has subcontracted out but for which it is the monopsonistic buyer. Transactions are of an external market kind, but production may be controlled and coordinated from a single administrative centre. In this respect, the internalisation framework offers a theory of the choice between different modes of transacting rather than a theory of the (boundaries of) the firm.

To be of use in empirical work this approach needs to be operationalised in a workable model of transaction costs (Buckley, 1983; Casson, 1981), but the variables thought to be especially significant are the regularity of transactions between the parties and the complexity of the technology exchanged. Transaction cost analysis may also require adjustment to take account of the distribution of the gains from exchange under different institutional arrangements (as suggested by Sugden, 1983). Thus, the MNC may not favour the most efficient or lowest cost arrangement if its profit share is higher under another. By the internationalisation of production MNCs may weaken the effectiveness of trade union organisation, and increase the share of profits.

Advocates of the internalisation approach have also recognised the possibility that MNCs may increase profits through the restriction of competition in final product markets, and that this may offset the generally superior allocation of resources associated with MNC activity:

> Welfare losses arise where multinationals maximise monopoly profits by restricting the output of (high technology) goods and services . . . where vertical integration is used as a barrier to entry . . . [or] because they provide a more suitable mechanism for exploiting an international monopoly than does a cartel.
>
> (Buckley, 1985: 119)

However, they believe that even in the presence of monopolistic elements, the creation of new internal markets generates sufficient improvements in efficiency that overall cost minimisation remains the overriding motivation of the growth of the firm. As Buckley (1985: 119) explains, 'The internal market . . . in the long run will stimulate both the undertaking of R&D and its effective implementation in production and marketing. Consequently, dynamic welfare improvement is likely to result.'

Although in the past internalisation theorists and the market power school have claimed theirs as a general theory of the firm (and hence the MNC), they have each addressed rather specific aspects of the firm's operations. Unlike in the market power argument, in the transaction costs approach the structure of the final product market is only of secondary interest. The emphasis is on achieving profit maximisation through the efficient exchange of intermediate products rather than through the exclusion of (potential) rivals in the final product market.

For this reason the counterfactuals with which international production is compared are different. Internalisation theorists have treated the alternative to international production as being the licensing of a local firm (or inter-firm trade in intermediate products), or exports from the home country (and no local production). The market power school has instead treated the alternative as being independent local production, which is driven out or diminished by the direct local presence of the MNC (or, to a lesser extent, by its licensing a local competitor). In this respect it is quite possible for work in the internalisation tradition to take into account influences deriving from competition or collusion in final product markets or the distribution of income, just as certain of the market power group going back to Hymer himself made allowance for efficiency considerations. However, disagreement between these approaches remains in the sense that the choice of theoretical issues on which to concentrate is not arbitrary, but reflects what each camp believes to be the most important historical driving forces underlying the growth of the modern firm.

The eclectic paradigm

The eclectic paradigm grew out of a desire to synthesise elements from the two competing theories of the individual firm in its relationship to markets and certain other approaches to international production considered below. However, it was not intended to be a complete synthesis as it is not possible fully to encompass a set of theories that addresses rather different questions and relies on different views of the world. It was therefore soon acknowledged that it was not itself another theory. It was instead intended to provide an overall analytical framework for empirical investigations which would draw the attention of the analyst to the most important theories for the problem at hand. It also provided a framework for a comparison between theories by establishing the common ground or the points of contact between them, and clarifying the relationship between different levels of analysis and the different questions which theorists have been concerned to address. Thus, for example, internalisation theory may be the most relevant under certain circumstances or when answering certain kinds of questions (such as those related to backward vertical integration into resource extraction), while the determinants of the competitive strategy of firms in their final product market may be more pertinent in other cases (such as technological competition or cooperation).

In the eclectic paradigm it is contended that MNCs have competitive or 'ownership' advantages *vis-à-vis* their major rivals which they utilise in establishing production in sites that are attractive due to their 'location' advantages. According to Dunning, two types of competitive advantage can be distinguished: the first is attributable to the ownership of particular unique intangible assets (such as firm-specific technology), and the second is due to the joint ownership of complementary assets (such as the ability to create new technologies).[3] MNCs retain control over their networks of assets (productive, commercial, financial and so forth) because of the 'internalisation' advantages of doing so. Internalisation advantages arise both from the greater ease with which an integrated firm is able to appropriate a full return on its ownership of distinctive assets, such as its own technology, as well as directly from the coordination of the use of complementary assets, subject to the costs of managing a more complex network.[4]

Dunning (1988a) describes the internalisation advantages that result from the coordination of the use of complementary assets as 'the transactional benefits . . . arising from a common governance of a network of these assets, located in different countries' (p. 2). That such benefits can only be enjoyed through coordination within the firm rather than by market coordination is said to be the result of transactional market failure. Three reasons are given for transactional market failure (Dunning, 1988a, 1988b). First, risk and uncertainty may be significant in transactions carried out across national boundaries. Second, where there are externalities, benefits external to the transactions concerned may not be captured by parties transacting at arm's length. Third, there may be economies of scope through the direct coordination of interrelated activities.

More will be said about ownership advantages in due course, since they have been the subject of considerable debate in the literature. However, there are two points that must be clarified at the outset. First, there may appear to be an overlap between those ownership advantages that are due to the joint ownership of complementary assets and those internalisation advantages that derive from the coordinated use of such assets. In fact, the distinction here is rather like the distinction between the advantages of owning particular assets, such as patented technology and the internalisation advantages of retaining control over their use, in order to ensure that the full return on them is appropriated by the firm that holds proprietary rights.

None the less, while ownership advantages that derive from particular assets can normally (in principle at least) be sold – such as in the licensing of the use of a technology to another firm – there is in general no market for ownership advantages of a more collective kind. Examples of the collective type of ownership advantage are the overall organisational abilities of the firm, the experience and entrepreneurial capabilities of its managers taken together, the reputation and creditworthiness of the firm in international capital markets, its political contacts and its long-term business agreements with other firms. This kind of ownership advantage goes beyond any particular asset or any one individual, and in general cannot be sold outside the firm but is only usable within it. Collective ownership advantages are emphasised in the technological accumulation approach considered below, in which corporate capabilities are created through collective internal learning processes, and then become embodied in organisational routines (Nelson and Winter, 1982).

One such collective ownership advantage is the ability of the firm to generate new technology, which will eventually result in a stream of new ownership advantages of a particular kind. This example will serve to illustrate the distinction between collective ownership advantages at the level of the firm as a whole and the internalisation advantages of the coordinated use of assets that are associated with them. Consider a firm that holds a strong position in a certain branch of the chemicals industry and which uses its innovative potential to expand into the development of a technologically related chemical process. Suppose, for the sake of argument, that to date scientific and technical effort in the related sector has been concentrated outside the home country of the firm, so that its development work in this area is undertaken primarily in a subsidiary located in some foreign centre of excellence for the process concerned. A specialised R&D unit is established in the foreign country which is linked up with the parent firm's R&D facilities.

Now the ability of the firm to set up production in the foreign country and to initiate a new research programme there is due to its initial ownership advantage, which consists of established technology and an innovative strength in chemicals. The firm then gains internalisation advantages through the coordination of R&D in home and host countries which extends its original ownership advantage by increasing its capacity to innovate in both related sectors. In other words there is a progressive interaction between ownership advantages (the possession of technology and the ability to innovate) and internalisation advantages (the international coordination of R&D facilities). Ownership and internalisation advantages increase alongside one another in the case of successful international growth.

The second point that requires clarification at this stage is that the concept of ownership advantages is open to two possible theoretical interpretations. It is apparent from the discussion above that the market power theory of the firm perceives ownership advantages principally as anti-competitive devices which act as barriers to entry against other firms. Meanwhile, the competitive international industry approach considered below sees ownership advantages as competitive weapons which sustain a process of competition between rivals. For this reason ownership advantages are 'sometimes called competitive or [sometimes called] monopolistic advantages' (Dunning, 1988a: 2).

In conventional neoclassical or industrial organisation analyses of market structure, in which competition and monopoly are treated as opposites, to describe advantages as competitive or monopolistic would suggest a contradiction in terms. This is how matters also appear on the whole to the market power school, whose work is one variant of the industrial organisation analysis. In their view, if the larger firms in an industry have stronger ownership advantages, this reduces the number of firms in the sector and increases the extent of collusion amongst those that remain, thereby restricting competition and implying a higher degree of monopoly power. This market structure perspective emphasises profits of the kind that are associated with various different positions of market power.

However, this contrasts with the classical approach to competition which saw it as a process rather than a market structure. In the dynamic view of competition what matters is not the number of firms within an industry but the mobility of resources (within firms, as well as in terms of the entry and exit of new firms) and the balance of forces between firms in an industry. In this context, in an oligopolistic industry Jenkins (1987) argues that competition and monopoly coexist. Firms compete through the continual creation of quasi-monopolistic positions, such as the creation of a new technology ahead of the field. This perspective is akin to Schumpeter's (1934) suggestion of how profits may instead be created through innovation in the establishment and exploitation of new products and processes, by adding new value to the circular flow of economic activity (Cantwell, 1999). It will be necessary to return to this issue in later sections.

As the eclectic paradigm is an overall organising framework rather than a theory, it does not have a definite view of competition built into it. Neither does it depend a priori on a particular theory of the firm. It is capable of providing expression either to the internalisation approach, in which the firm grows by displacing markets that operate in a costly and imperfect way, or to the market power theory, in which it is the growth of the firm which is the essential cause of market imperfections and failure. The eclectic paradigm incorporates elements of both these alternative theories of the firm, since it allows that ownership advantages may act as barriers to entry and sources of market power. However, Dunning himself accords priority to internalisation and supposes that competition is more important than collusion amongst MNCs: 'It is not the orthodox type of monopoly advantages which give the enterprise an edge over its rivals – actual or potential – but the advantages which accrue through internalisation' (Dunning, 1988b: 32). Indeed, the latest terminology in which the eclectic paradigm has been couched (Dunning, 1988a, 1988b), suggesting that the growth of the firm is a function of market failure, owes much to the internalisation approach. While particular ownership advantages and the internalisation advantages of appropriating rents are attributed to structural market failure, collective ownership advantages and the internalisation advantages of coordinating the use of complementary assets are said to be due to transactional market failure.

Despite the priority which Dunning gives to the internalisation over the market power theory of the firm, it would still be wrong to make the eclectic paradigm synonymous with the internalisation approach, as is sometimes done in literature reviews. The more general nature of the eclectic paradigm has already been stressed, and this allows it to give equal weight to theories of macroeconomic locational advantages, and the interaction between the firm and its macroeconomic environment. Thus, 'the theory of foreign owned production stands at the crossroads between a macroeconomic theory of international trade and a microeconomic theory of the firm' (Dunning, 1988b: 19).

In the same way the eclectic paradigm can be used to set out arguments that derive from competitive international industry approaches. In this case interest also switches away from the analysis of the firm or MNC as such towards the impact of the activity of one firm on that of another, and the interrelated development of the firm and its industry. Indeed, in the latest version of the eclectic paradigm, Dunning (1995) has emphasised the current context of 'alliance capitalism'. While one interpretation of the formation of ownership advantages through alliance agreements might rely on a step back to the market power approach, as in many traditional cartel arrangements in which 'monopolistic' advantages are exercised jointly to the exclusion of others – Dunning's argument accords rather with the competitive international industry view of how ownership advantages are generated and are to be understood as still 'competitive'. The continual interaction and mutual reinforcement of business cooperation and competition follow from the association of modern alliance capitalism with technological dynamism (Hagedoorn and Narula, 1996; Loasby, 1998; Sachwald, 1998), and the ability of firms to cope with greater technological complexity due to an increase in interrelatedness and hence fusion between formerly quite separate technological fields which draw upon distinctively different areas of expertise (Cantwell, 1998b).

Again, this new line of argument in the eclectic paradigm is closely linked to the technological accumulation approach, in which firms may cooperate in the combined increase of their ownership advantages or dynamic capabilities. Thus, the eclectic paradigm has now taken on board much of the thinking that has emerged from the technological accumulation or dynamic capabilities approach to competitive international industries, concerning the role played in the growth of the firm by technology-based alliances, and by the steady accumulation of technological assets through internal corporate learning processes associated in the international context with the asset-seeking motive for FDI.

Competitive international industry approaches

Of the theoretical frameworks considered here there are two combinations which have conflicting perspectives, even though ideas from one might be used to qualify the other. The different perspectives of the market power and internalisation theories of the firm have already been discussed; the market power and competitive international industry approaches are similarly opposed, although for slightly different reasons. Both relate to final product markets and are set out in the context of an oligopolistic industry. However, while the market power school supposes that, in general, internationalisation lowers the extent of competition and increases collusion amongst firms, competitive international industry approaches share the view that in general the growth of international production tends to be associated with rivalry and to sustain the process of technological competition amongst MNCs. Also, the latter are genuinely mesoeconomic (industry level) approaches and have given rise to a theory of comparative firm growth as opposed to the more conventional theory of the individual firm in its relationship with markets; they begin from the interaction between firms and the progress of industrial development rather than examining the implications of behaviour inherent in the nature of the firm itself. The comparative firm growth theory (implicitly) places greater weight on profits as a source of growth and an indicator of growth potential which derive from innovation and the generation of corporate competence or dynamic capabilities *vis-à-vis* other companies, in place of the standard interpretations of profit maximisation based on static efficiency and associated market power.

The earliest oligopolistic theories of international production (in the rivalrous as opposed to the market power sense) were the later versions of the product cycle model (PCM), and similar extensions of the product cycle approach. In 1971 Vernon recognised that the original PCM was losing its explanatory capacity, and in 1974 he suggested a modified (Mark II) version which introduced oligopolistic considerations (Vernon, 1971, 1974). After the initial innovatory phase of the product life cycle, established firms were seen as preserving their position through the existence of scale economies in place of technological leadership.

In this case the reason for relocating production abroad (import-substituting investment) as a product matured was no longer a matter of simple profit maximisation in the face of a changing pattern of demand as income levels in other countries caught up. The emphasis shifted towards risk-minimising strategies with the aim of avoiding price warfare in a mature oligopoly. On the assumption of a high ratio of fixed to total costs in an industry characterised by economies of scale, security became a more important consideration for the firm relative to profitability. Vernon argued that this led to cross-investment (that is, intra-industry production) to reduce the threat of subsidiary price-cutting in the domestic market of each large firm, despite the potential cost-minimising benefits of concentrating production in just one or a few locations.

This idea of intra-industry production as an 'exchange of threats' became crucial to the work of Graham (1975, 1978, 1985, 1998). According to Graham, oligopolistic interaction between firms in an industry increases as firms grow, since (following product cycle reasoning) the capital-intensity of production rises and economies of scale become more important as the product line matures. As the ratio of fixed to total costs rises, the consequence of rivals adopting aggressive price-cutting strategies becomes potentially more damaging, and so each firm increasingly takes account of risks as well as returns. In doing so it may have to accept some trade-off between security and profitability (Rothschild, 1947).

The notion of the search for security is also at the heart of the market power theory of the firm, although in this case it is achieved through monopolisation and collusion and is generally supposed to be in line with profitability (Cowling and Sugden, 1987). Indeed, Hymer and Rowthorn (1970) had argued on this basis that the leading firms in each industry would aim to have a similar geographical distribution of sales or production, at which point collusive agreements to ensure security would reach a peak. However, in Graham's (1975) historical account, while industrial stability and an avoidance of price warfare had been typically maintained before 1914 by collusive agreements and cartels, the exchange of threats was seen as a non-collusive alternative, which since 1960 had become the more usual means of reducing risk. With an exchange of threats competition is preserved, but in a stable rather than a cut-throat form.

To emphasise the difference with the analysis of the market power school, Graham (1985) goes beyond the product cycle framework and suggests that intra-industry production (IIP) involving the cross-investments of MNCs in the same sector will generally act to accelerate new product development and introduction. He therefore reaches the very opposite view to that of Hymer and Rowthorn (1970) or Cowling and Sugden (1987): '[I]nterpenetration of national markets by MNCs based in different countries – assuming that no merger of major rivals results – acts to reduce the likelihood that collusion can be successfully under-taken globally' (Graham, 1985: 82).

The notion of oligopolistic interaction can also be combined with various other nonproduct cycle ideas on the firm. Sanna-Randaccio (1980) combined oligopolistic interaction with Penrose's (1959) theory of the growth of the firm. She hypothesised that the ability of a firm to gain an increasing share of an individual market through local production was a function of the share of that market already held. Firms with a smaller existing market share would be able to grow rapidly with a lower risk of setting in motion a damaging competitive warfare. To allow a stable competitive process to continue to run smoothly, it was therefore in the interests of US firms to switch resources away from domestic growth and towards the expansion of their European production (starting from a smaller base), just as it was in the interests of European firms to expand their US operations.

Meanwhile, returning to the exchange of threat view of oligopolistic inter-action, Casson (1987) has attempted to integrate this with the internalisation theory of the firm. In this case, in order to examine the implications for rivalry of different relative market shares, Casson's model makes the determinants of long-run market share exogenous. Depending upon the relative strength of firms, an exchange of threats (establishing a foothold in the major markets of rivals) may be used to preserve price stability.

In recent years work has also begun on technological competition between the MNCs in an international industry rather than on the effect of oligopolistic rivalry on price competition. The quotation from Graham above suggests a connection between technological competition and the rise of IIP. Cantwell (1989b) shares Graham's view that the increasing internationalisation of manufacturing production has helped to sustain technological competition between MNCs. Following the idea that MNC expansion can be linked to a process of technological accumulation within the firm (Cantwell, 1989b, 1994a; Pavitt, 1987), innovation and the growth of international production are seen as mutually supportive.

The term 'technological accumulation' encapsulates the view that the devel-opment of technology within a firm is a cumulative process. That is, the creation of new technology is to be understood as a gradual and painstaking process of continual adjustment and refinement, as new productive methods are tested and adapted in the light of experience. In any firm, there is a continual interaction between the creation of technology and its use in production. For this reason, although a group of firms in a given industry is likely to have similar lines of technological development (similarities which may be increased through collaborative R&D projects, through drawing on the results of publicly funded research, and through imitation), the actual technological path of each is to some degree unique and differentiated. The acquisition of new skills, and the generation of new technological capacity, partially embodied in new plant and equipment, must be a goal of every firm in an oligopolistic industry, if it is to maintain and increase its profits. Even where new technology is acquired from outside the firm, it must be gradually adapted and integrated with its existing production methods.

The notion of technological accumulation is consistent with the ideas of Rosenberg (1976, 1982), Usher (1929), and the earlier work of Marx on techno-logical change through systematic adaptation. More recently, Atkinson and Stiglitz (1969), Nelson and Winter (1977) and Stiglitz (1987) have spoken of 'localised' technological change in the context of the previous technological evolution and learning experience of the firm.

While the product cycle theory supposed that an individual act of technology creation was then diffused abroad, in the technological accumulation approach the use of technology in new environments feeds back into fresh adaptation and (depending upon the state of local scientific and technical capability) new inno-vation. When production is located in an area that is itself a centre for innovation in the industry concerned, the firm may gain access to research facilities which allow it to extend technology creation in what are for it previously untried directions. In recent years technological accumulation has frequently been organised in international networks, or in other words integrated MNCs. At one time MNCs may have been simply the providers of technology and finance for scattered international production; today they have become global organisers of economic systems, including systems for allied technological development in different parts of the world.

The technological accumulation approach therefore addresses the question of why it is that technology is developed in international networks, rather than in a series of separately owned plants. Part of the answer is provided by internalisation theory, which focuses on why MNCs as opposed to purely national firms have come into existence. That is, if the initiating firm is to appropriate a full return on its technological advantage, and if it is to coordinate the successful introduction of its new technology elsewhere, then it must exercise direct control over the network as a whole. However, this may be not so much a feature of the market for technological knowledge, which is the focus of internalisation theory, as a feature of the very nature of technological development itself. In the alternative evolutionary view, technological knowledge is not an immediately usable inter-mediate product in its own right, but is rather an input into the collective corporate learning process by which tacit capability and hence technology as a whole is generated. As such, it is an input that normally has its greatest relevance to the learning process of the firm that created it and set the problem-solving agenda to which it represents a response, and thus it is likely to be of the greatest value to the originating company (Cantwell, 1991, 1994a).

The different focus of attention in these two accounts may be understood in terms of the two views of profits described earlier. The standard internalisation approach addresses concerns over individual opportunism and rent-seeking behaviour in the context of conventional profit maximisation, the objective being to find the organisational mode that minimises the transaction costs associated with problems of this kind. In the evolutionary technological accumulation approach, firms search instead for higher profits through innovation (Nelson and Winter, 1982), and by generating new value-creating technological capabilities. From this perspective the firm's incentive to invest is a (usually positive) function of the intensity of technological competition, which implies that the industry-level interaction between firms regulates the investment behaviour of each company, rather than simply a set of internal transaction cost calculations under 'make or buy' alternatives. The key indicator of inter-company differences of potential for firm growth is the ability of each firm to generate tacit capability or corporate technological competence (Cantwell, 1991). While this approach to comparative firm growth became established in the MNC field by around 1990 (Cantwell, 1989b, 1991), it has since become very fashionable in the form of the competence-based theory of the firm in economics and the resource-based view of the firm in management strategy (e.g. Chandler *et al.*, 1998; Foss, 1993; Hodgson, 1998; Loasby, 1998; Nelson, 1991; Teece *et al.*, 1997), just as Buckley and Casson's (1976) work on the MNC preceded a wave of fascination with transaction cost economics from the 1980s onwards.

Suppose for a moment that the act of exchanging technological knowledge between firms does not present a problem, in that a reasonable price for such an exchange can always be readily agreed, such as in a framework of cross-licensing agreements. Now consider an international industry in which constituent firms produce more or less identical products for the same international markets. However, each firm has its own quite specific process technology, derived from a distinct technological tradition (say, different chemical processes with a similar end result). In this situation, if technological accumulation is continuous in each firm, raising its productivity or lowering its costs along a given line of technological development, then no existing firm would abandon its existing pattern of innovation and buy in all its technological knowledge from a competitor. It would be far more costly, and perhaps even infeasible, for an existing firm to switch into a completely new line of technological development, in comparison with the costs of the potential seller of technology simply extending its own network. It is because technology is differentiated across countries even within the same firm, but especially between different firms, that technology transfer is a costly process (as demonstrated by Teece, 1977). Some exchanges of technological knowledge between existing firms will take place, since alternative lines of technological accumulation in the same industry are often complementary to one another, and so spillovers occur and may be facilitated through intercompany alliances in which knowledge is exchanged and occasionally jointly developed. However, where technological knowledge is bought in, it must be adapted to the specific context of the firm's own tacit capability (the other necessary component of any operational technology) and then incorporated into an existing stream of innovation, and this adaptation becomes part and parcel of the ongoing process within an established firm of generating its own technology.

In the case outlined, the retention of technology within each firm has little to do with any failure or malfunctioning of the market for technological knowledge, but everything to do with the close association between the generation and the utilisation of a distinctive type of technology within each firm. By extending its own network, each firm extends the use of its own unique line of technological development; and by extending it into new environments, it increases the complexity of this development. The expansion of international production thereby brings gains to the firm as a whole, as the experience gained from adapting its technology under new conditions feeds back new ideas for development to the rest of its system. For this reason, once they have achieved a sufficient level of technological strength in their own right, firms are particularly keen to produce in the locations from which their major international rivals have emanated which offer them access to alternative sources of complementary innovation. This offers one explanation of the increase in IIP in the industrialised countries (Cantwell, 1989b).

The notion that the geographical dispersion of technological development enhances innovation in the network of the MNC as a whole is founded on the belief that innovation is location-specific as well as firm-specific (Cantwell, 1989b). The scientific and technological traditions of each country, the shared experience of its researchers and production engineers and the communication between them across companies, the nature of its educational system, and its common business practices all contribute to the distinctiveness of the path of technology development undertaken in each location (Nelson, 1993, 1995). By drawing on innovations of various kinds, depending upon the conditions prevailing in the relevant local research centre, MNCs develop a more complex technological system. The attractiveness of locations for other research-related investments may well be strengthened in the process. The involvement of foreign MNCs in research in centres of innovation has a direct effect on broadening the scope of local technological capability, and an indirect effect through its competitive stimulus, encouraging other firms to extend their local research programmes. The process helps to establish locational poles of attraction for research-related activity. The increased role of locationally dispersed sourcing of technology from the major centres of excellence through the international networks of more globally integrated MNCs (Cantwell, 1995) has led to a growing interest in the asset-acquiring motive for FDI (Cantwell, 1989b; Dunning, 1992, 1995, 1996; Kogut and Chang, 1991; Pugel *et al.*, 1996), and in the greater decentralisation in the management of international R&D to capture 'home-base augmenting' benefits (Kuemmerle, 1999; Pearce, 1997; Pearce and Singh, 1992).

The technological accumulation approach suggests two major reasons why the growth in international production has been associated with sustained technological competition between MNCs in manufacturing industries. First, internationalisation has supported technological diversification since the form of technological development varies between locations as well as between firms (Cantwell and Janne, 1999; Cantwell and Piscitello, 2000). By locating production in an alternative centre of innovation in its industry, the MNC gains access to a new but complementary avenue of technological development, which it integrates with its existing lines. By increasing the overlap between the technological profile of firms, competition between MNCs is raised in each international industry, but so also are cooperative agreements as the number of knowledge spillovers between firms increases as well. Spillovers occur where technological knowledge is created by a firm which lies outside its own major lines of development, but which may be of greater use within the main traditions of another firm.

Second, and partly because of the first factor, today there are a growing number of connections between technologies that were formerly quite separate. This greater technological interrelatedness has brought more firms, and especially MNCs, into competition with one another. These two elements have been associated with the growth of what are sometimes called 'technological systems' in MNCs. Where MNCs in a competitive international industry are all attracted to certain centres of innovation to maintain their overall strength, then research and research-related production may tend to agglomerate in these locations (Cantwell, 1987). Closely allied to these arguments, recent literature has examined the emergence of the multi-technology corporation to take advantage of increased technological interrelatedness (Cantwell and Fai, 1999; Cantwell and Santangelo, 2000; Gambardella and Torrisi, 1998; Granstrand, 1998; Granstrand and Sjölander,

1990; Granstrand *et al.*, 1997; Kodama, 1992; Pavitt *et al.*, 1989; Piscitello, 1998); and a rise in the number of technologically motivated inter-firm alliances reflecting the need of companies to draw on a more diversified knowledge base (Loasby, 1998; Mowery *et al.*, 1998; Sachwald, 1998; Teece, 1996).

Some similar themes appear in the internationalisation of capital approach of Jenkins (1984, 1987). In his view the growth of international production is just one aspect of a trend towards a more integrated world economy. As a result of this trend, in each industry products and processes have become increasingly standardised across countries, while firms safeguard their competitive positions through the continuing differentiation of products and technology. Once again, the growth of MNCs is seen as part of a competitive process, in which each firm attempts to gain competitive advantages through innovation, and only in certain circumstances do they enter into (for a time) collusive arrangements.

According to Jenkins, if nationalistic governments in LDCs prevent the entry of MNCs, this only reduces the speed of adaptation to the requirements of international competition, but does not allow them to avoid such adaptation altogether. Marxists such as Warren (1980) go further and argue that FDI helps to promote local capitalist development and economic advance. They emphasise oligopolistic competition between MNCs of different national origins. They reject the idea that MNCs provide host LDCs with inappropriate technology, and contend that this is simply a defence of economic backwardness (Emmanuel, 1982).

In the opinion of Jenkins (1987), the emphasis that Baran and Sweezy (1966) and the Marxists that followed them placed upon monopoly, and their downplaying of oligopolistic competition between MNCs, can be traced back to a time when the USA and her firms held a hegemonic position in the world economy. Since then newer MNCs from Europe, Japan and now the Third World have been growing rapidly. The increasing internationalisation of R&D also suggests that MNC growth has helped to sustain technological competition. The use of the market power approach as a *general* theory of international production therefore has a somewhat dated feel about it.

However, competitive international industry approaches allow for cooperation and collusion between firms, and for the weakening of local firms as a consequence of MNC expansion under certain circumstances. Inward investment may have competitive or anticompetitive effects on host country industries (Cantwell, 1989b). It has been argued that in modern international industries, a competitive impact from MNC growth in one location and an anti-competitive effect in another are two sides of the same coin (Cantwell, 1987). Where indigenous firms enjoy a strong technological tradition in the sector in question, the growth of international production provides a competitive stimulus which encourages an increase in local research-related activity. However, while where such a tradition is weaker, the research of local firms may be displaced by simpler assembly types of production organised by foreign MNCs. The faster growth and upgrading of activity in one location is then achieved at the direct expense of the downgrading of another, as different stages of production become geographically separated. The positive case in which a field characterised by a stronger indigenous technological tradition is more likely to be associated with beneficial knowledge and hence productivity spillovers between foreign-owned and local companies has recently attracted much attention (Blomström, 1989; Cantwell and Iammarino, 1998; Kokko, 1994; Kokko *et al.*, 1996; Perez, 1997, 1998).

Macroeconomic developmental approaches

It was argued above that the earliest neoclassical and Marxist macroeconomic theories of foreign capital movements could not deal satisfactorily with the growth of international production between industrialised countries at a similar stage of development. The more modern macroeconomic theories of international production which address this question are currently at a rather more rudimentary stage of development than are microeconomic or mesoeconomic theories (for a survey see Gray, 1982). They have tended to attract less attention than theories of the firm since the demise of the product cycle model or PCM (Giddy, 1978; Vernon, 1979). However, their origins go back to the same period, the early 1960s. They emerged as a result of criticisms of the traditional theory of international trade, just as Hymer's work represented a criticism of the traditional theory of international capital movements.

The product cycle idea itself was in the first instance a purely microeconomic one which had been familiar for some time in business schools, but which was applied by Vernon (1966) to topical discussions on patterns of international trade and the balance of payments. Vernon's criticism of conventional trade theory also called attention to the rapid rise of international production amongst US firms in Europe at that time. In the Heckscher–Ohlin–Samuelson (H–O–S) theory, trade (or FDI, where capital movements substituted for trade) should be greatest between countries whose proportional factor endowments are most dissimilar. This could not explain the tremendous post-war expansion of trade and investment in manufacturing industry between the US and Europe. Neither could a theory which assumed that trade automatically balances in accordance with comparative advantage offer any assistance in explaining regular US trade surpluses in the 1950s.

The role of technological factors in addressing these issues had already been clear to some authors in the 1950s. As is well known, Leontief (1954) referred to the significance of skilled labour in US export industries. Meanwhile, in linking trade imbalances with the monetary side of the balance of payments, Johnson (1958) suggested that the persistence of a dollar shortage in Europe after the Second World War may be explained by the lag with which innovation in Europe followed that in the USA. Then in the early 1960s two important papers on trade theory appeared. Posner (1961) pioneered a 'technology gap' theory of that part of trade based on innovating and learning faster than others; the link with the problems confronted by Leontief and Johnson are evident. At around the same time Linder (1961) argued that the main motor of trade was a similarity of income levels and patterns of demand, suggesting that trade flows are greatest between countries with similar factor endowments.

The PCM attempted to combine elements from both the Posner and Linder theories of international trade, and to do so in such a way that the growth of US FDI in European manufacturing became part of the story. The essential argument is that high incomes and demand in the USA fostered innovation, especially in consumer durables produced by labour-saving techniques. This gave US firms a competitive lead which they exploited initially through exports and then through import-substituting investment in the region (Europe) catching up. Eventually, as products matured, trade in the sectors concerned would return to a cost-determined comparative advantage pattern, with MNCs losing technological advantages and having to rely on barriers to entry in marketing and distribution instead.

Apart from the original work of Vernon (1966) and Hirsch (1967), the PCM is explained clearly by Wells (1972) and in the studies of Hufbauer (1965, 1970). Detailed critical summaries can be found in Cantwell (1989b), Vernon (1979), Giddy (1978) and Buckley and Casson (1976). One reason for the demise of the PCM is that the technological leadership enjoyed by the USA in the 1950s and early 1960s gave way to a more balanced technological competition between the USA, Europe and Japan. Indeed, it is now Japan which has a regular trade surplus and whose firms are investing heavily in US manufacturing. Another reason is that the PCM deals only with import-substituting investment, but since the 1970s the global integration of affiliates within MNCs has become steadily more important.

In his criticism of the PCM, Kojima (1978) relied heavily on the distinction between import-substituting (trade-displacing) and offshore or export-platform (trade-creating) types of investment. An unfortunate pro-Japanese, anti-American slant was given to his argument by a presumption that through their effects on trade, import-substituting investments damaged welfare while export-platform investment improved it, and by his labelling the former 'American-type' and the latter 'Japanese-type'. Apart from the fact that there are many US firms with export-platform investments in SE Asia, and many Japanese firms with import-substituting investments in Europe and the USA, there is no reason why import-substituting investments must reduce the overall extent of trade at a macro-economic level (as opposed to the level of the individual firm) unless certain restrictive assumptions are made (see Cantwell, 1994b for a survey of the general relationship between international trade and international production). Moreover, there is evidence to suggest that export-platform investments are more likely to be of an enclave kind with little technology diffusion to host country firms (Cantwell and Dunning, 1991), and therefore they may play a lesser role in host country industrial adjustment and welfare.

Kojima's position owes much to his interpretation of FDI (unlike Vernon) within an H–O–S model. Import-substituting investment was therefore seen as a replacement of trade in accordance with comparative advantage (investment emanating from an advantaged home country), while export-platform investment involved firms in an industry comparatively disadvantaged in the home country. As an extension of this argument, Kojima and Ozawa (1985) claim that global welfare is increased where international production helps to restructure the industries of each country in line with dynamic comparative advantage.

The underlying developmental processes described by Vernon and Hirsch and by Kojima and Ozawa have many similarities despite the broader nature of the Kojima–Ozawa argument, and despite the differences in the theories of trade they employ. The Kojima–Ozawa approach applies particularly to a country that is growing rapidly, such as in recent years Japan, Germany or the newly industrialising countries. As local firms innovate and steadily upgrade their domestic activity, they have an interest in relocating their less sophisticated types of production in countries at an earlier stage of development. Although they still possess the technological and organisational know-how to sustain this simpler production, it may be more profitable to do so abroad, and to concentrate on higher value-added activities in the now more developed home environment. In other words, as in the PCM, firms relocate 'mature' or 'maturing' lines of production in countries that are still a step behind the home country.

Apart from export-platform investments, Ozawa (1979, 1982) pays particular attention to resource-based investments. Again, in a country experiencing rapid industrial growth, and especially in a 'Ricardian' one such as Japan lacking in natural resources, the rate of domestic expansion is likely to be constrained by resource availability. Home country MNCs then have a direct interest in investing in resource-related development abroad as a means of supplying their own domestic markets. As they develop their manufacturing operations at home and in other industrialised countries, they may wish to move basic resource processing and simple manufacturing activities close to the site of resource extraction. In this case, the objectives of MNCs are in line with the development strategies of host countries.

This is an interesting idea, particularly when it is not assumed to be peculiarly true of Japanese MNCs alone, and once it is stripped from the intellectual straitjacket of the H–O–S model in which Kojima had confined it. Today, Japanese MNCs are at least as concerned with oligopolistic investments in the USA and Europe as with resource-based and export-platform investments in less developed countries (LDCs). It is now the newer Third World multinationals that are especially oriented to LDCs.

The major problem with Kojima's use of the H–O–S model is that it cannot be assumed that the industries in which a country has its greatest innovative potential are those in which it currently enjoys a comparative advantage (Cantwell, 1989b; Pasinetti, 1981). This indeed is the lesson of Japan's own post-war history, in which she successfully encouraged local technological development in sectors in which she began with a comparative disadvantage. With the assistance of foreign MNCs through licensing agreements (Ozawa, 1974), some comparatively disadvantaged industries were transformed into comparatively advantaged ones.

Moreover, it was precisely Vernon's point that import-substituting investment need not emanate from a sector in which the home country has a comparative advantage (unlike in the H–O–S model). A country that holds technological leadership may be a net exporter in some comparatively disadvantaged as well as in comparatively advantaged industries, owing to the technological edge of its firms. This is what gives it a regular trade surplus. If the innovative lead is lost (in the PCM as products mature), then production is relocated in accordance with underlying cost-determined comparative advantage. Kojima should also welcome this type of industrial adjustment if his argument were to be applied consistently.

A more general macroeconomic approach is the investment-development cycle, advanced by Dunning (1982), and subsequently extended by Narula (1996) and Dunning and Narula (1996). This is based upon the proposition that the level of inward and outward direct investment of different countries, and the balance between the two, depends upon their national stage of development. The poorest countries have very little inward or outward FDI, and consequently a level of net outward investment that is close to zero. Countries at somewhat higher levels of development attract significant amounts of inward direct investment, but as the outward investment of their own firms is still limited, they register negative net outward investment. Past some point outward direct investment takes off, and for countries at yet higher levels of development, net outward investment begins to increase, until for the most developed countries it returns to zero and beyond this becomes positive.

Empirical evidence for the period since the mid-1970s presented by Tolentino (1993) and Hobday (1995) suggests that this formulation may now require some qualification. Countries now seem to be embarking on outward direct investment more rapidly and at a much earlier stage of development than they once were. Apart from the fast growth of MNCs from Japan and Germany, a wide range of smaller industrialised and Third World countries have become significant sources of outward direct investment. The increasing internationalisation of production has become a general phenomenon.

Dunning (1986) has elaborated upon the investment-development cycle by arguing that the character and composition of the outward direct investment of a country's firms (as well as its level) vary with the national stage of development. Early foreign ventures are frequently resource-based, but as firms mature they move beyond investment in a single activity or product and adopt a more international perspective on the location of the different types of production in which they are involved. Such MNCs are increasingly responsible for directly organising an international division of labour in place of markets, and so the character of their activity and their ownership advantages become further removed from the conditions of their home countries.

Cantwell and Tolentino (1990) have extended this idea to argue that the outward direct investment of countries itself tends to follow a developmental course over time. Beginning from resource-based activity with fairly limited technological requirements, MNC involvement shifts towards gradually more sophisticated types of manufacturing. For the mature multinationals of Europe and the USA, such an evolution has been going on for over a hundred years. The changing industrial composition of investment is associated with a changing geographical composition as well; resource-related investment in LDCs has been overtaken by research-related investment in industrialised countries.

The evolution of Japanese multinationals since the 1960s has been compressed into a much shorter timespan. Investments in resource-related activity in SE Asia led the way in the 1960s and early 1970s, but today interest has shifted to the manufacturing investments of Japanese firms in Europe and the USA. Kojima (1978) had claimed that Japanese MNCs were to be distinguished from US MNCs by their comparative lack of technological advantages, and by their orientation towards developing country resource development and industrialisation rather than oligopolistic competition with other developed country multinationals. This now appears to have simply been a reflection of the early stages of development of Japanese multinationals.

Although Third World MNCs are nowhere near as advanced as the modern Japanese multinationals, the sectoral and geographical composition of their activity is also evolving much more rapidly than did the investments of the traditional source countries (Cantwell and Tolentino, 1990). There has been a general trend towards the internationalisation of business which is common to the firms of all countries. As a result, Third World MNCs have tended to embark on multinational expansion at an earlier stage of their development than did industrialised country firms.

The arguments of Cantwell and Tolentino (1990) and more recently Ozawa (1990, 1991, 1992, 1998) have established a linkage between competitive international industry and macroeconomic approaches to the growth of international production. It is suggested that the types of industries involved in international expansion vary with the characteristics of a country and the stage of development which it has reached. In turn, the industrial composition of international production influences its macroeconomic consequences.

Considering a stylised example, industrialisation in a resource-scarce country may lead local manufacturing firms into backward vertical integration abroad. These investments may be thought of as supply-side driven, though their effect is to promote faster growth in the home country. Import-substituting investments in manufacturing in other industrialised countries may follow, attracted by foreign demand (as in the PCM), but quite possibly helping to stimulate (further) outward investments from the host countries concerned in due course. The eventual result may be a system of interlocking investments in each major industry, in which supply-side factors come to regulate the composition of activity in each location and the international division of labour. The geographical concentration of research activity may become cumulative over time (Cantwell, 1989b); while Ozawa (1992) suggests that restructuring in Japan has reached a Schumpeterian phase in which research-led industries are to the fore, within which Japanese firms establish research-related foreign operations to tap into cultural diversities and creative human resources in Europe and the USA.

Macroeconomic developmental approaches relate the investment position of national groups of firms to the industrial progression of their home country. They may be demand-side or supply-side driven; in the PCM the growth of demand leads the relocation of production, while in the arguments of Kojima and Ozawa or Cantwell and Tolentino the emphasis is on supply-side opportunities and constraints in the course of industrial restructuring. However, in each case the underlying development process has both demand-side and supply-side aspects to it.

As alluded to above, it is also possible to trace out the macroeconomic effects of international production that are likely to result within the market power approach. If international collusion between MNCs rises over time, it would create a stagnationist tendency at a macroeconomic level (Cowling and Sugden, 1987). In addition to this, Pitelis (1986) argues that an increasing concentration of market power in the largest MNCs, together with the growing importance of pension funds and other such financial institutions, has led to a steady rise in the economy-wide propensity to save, creating a further demand-side pressure towards stagnation. While this is a description of the macroeconomic effect of MNCs in the market power framework, it does not provide an alternative macroeconomic explanation of the growth of international production. It is true that Marxist writers, particularly around the turn of the century, had argued that a lack of demand in the industrialised countries would lead to imperialist investments in the search for new markets to alleviate the effects of the concentration of capital at home. However, as noted above, this early kind of macroeconomic explanation cannot account for a rapid growth of cross-investments between countries which are all alleged to suffer from the same slackening of investment opportunities.

Macroeconomic theories of international production can also be extended to take account of financial influences on FDI. Part of the original product cycle idea was that a country whose firms became innovative leaders would establish a strong export position, accompanied by outward direct investment to support the international growth of the country's firms. This was true of Britain in the nineteenth century, of the USA in the early post-war period and of Japan and Germany more recently (Cantwell, 1989a). A country in this position may be expected to sustain an overall balance of payments surplus (before short-term capital movements) and hence a strong currency. The strength of the domestic currency then provides an additional motive for outward direct investment by local firms. It can thus be argued that longer-term movements in exchange rates reflect underlying trends in industrial competitiveness, reinforcing the effect of real influences on the growth of international production.

As Europe and Japan caught up with the USA in the 1960s, her export position weakened, and the US dollar ceased being a strong currency in short supply. However, under the terms of the Bretton Woods pegged exchange rate system, the dollar was not allowed to depreciate in response to balance of payments difficulties. As a result the dollar was widely viewed as being overvalued. This overvaluation contributed to yet higher outward investment, since US interests were able to buy up European firms and assets more cheaply in dollar terms, which offered a secondary, financial explanation for the high level of US FDI (emphasised by Aliber, 1970).

Matters are not so clear-cut in the period of general internationalisation across the firms of many countries in the 1980s. European and Japanese MNCs have expanded their US operations throughout the last decade. Inward direct investment in the USA remained buoyant when the US dollar was strong between 1982 and 1985, just as when it was weaker in the early 1980s and late 1980s. However, there is some evidence to suggest that inward direct investment was particularly high (rising above an upward trend) in 1979–82 and since 1986. For this reason, Dunning (1988b) argues that events in international currency markets can affect the timing of FDI but not its long-term trend. Aliber's theory of FDI, emanating from strong currency areas offers 'some interesting ideas about the *timing* of FDI and particularly that of foreign takeovers; and of fluctuations around a long term trend' (Dunning, 1988b: 15). Yet he also rightly notes that 'in many respects, it is a better extension of the traditional portfolio capital theory to incorporate market failure than a theory of FDI *per se*' (ibid.).

In other words, Aliber's approach represents a return to the traditional theory of international capital movements, from which Hymer's (1976) work had led a departure. In the traditional theory, currency valuation and relative interest rates determine foreign investment flows, but factors related to the growth of firms and industries do not. The general trend towards internationalisation, the substantial interpenetration of MNC activity in one another's domestic markets, and changes in the sectoral composition of international production can only be explained by the newer theories which have been emphasised here.

The various approaches to modelling the growth of international production differ over their choice of focus for a driving force underlying this expansion, related to the level of their analysis. In the technological accumulation approach it is the conditions for technology creation and its effective and efficient use in production. In the market power approach it is the widening of collusive networks and the restriction of competition in each national market. For internalisation theorists, whether international production expands or contracts depends upon changes in the transaction costs of operating in a wider set of markets (including the market for technology), relative to the costs of the direct coordination of transactions. In most macroeconomic approaches it is the developmental position of countries and their firms. For theorists that focus on the foreign direct investment flows associated with international production rather than international production itself (such as Aliber, 1970), it is the functioning of currency and financial markets. For business economists whose method is to provide a series of case studies of MNCs (such as Stopford and Turner, 1986), the driving force is individual managerial or entrepreneurial strategies. These approaches are not always mutually exclusive, and the next section examines some points at issue between them.

Points at issue between the different theories of international production

To a large extent the differences between the approaches outlined above can be accounted for by the fact that they have addressed different questions, and in doing so different levels of analysis have been appropriate. The recognition of this variety of interest has led to a retreat from the search for a general theory of international production as remarked upon at the start. Perhaps the most important distinction is that theories of the individual firm *vis-à-vis* markets have naturally been interested in the existence of the firm or the MNC in itself, and issues related to it, while competitive international industry and macroeconomic approaches have been concerned with a broader set of issues, focusing on the interaction between the growth of the firm and the location of production. This distinction, together with the possibility of combining insights gained from these alternative perspectives, is considered below. The implications for the ways in which different authors have interpreted the existence and growth of the firm are examined in the earlier part of this section. The role attributed to the interplay between the growth of MNCs and the changing location of production is considered below, while some suggestions for a cross-fertilisation between approaches are set out in the final section.

First, in comparing different views on the existence and growth of the firm, it is necessary to refer to an area of residual or unresolved debate between the alternative schools of thought on international production. On the face of it, the debate concerns the place of ownership advantages in the growth of the firm or MNC. However, this disguises disagreements (or differences of emphasis) over the role of efficiency considerations in the organisation of the firm, and over the significance of competition between firms in their final product markets. In a nutshell, competitive international industry approaches suppose that ownership advantages that raise the efficiency of the firm are a necessary condition for its survival *vis-à-vis* its rivals in an oligopolistic market. A strengthening of its ownership advantages relative to these rivals will enable it to increase its market share, or in other words to grow faster than its competitors. Internalisation theorists have instead examined the efficiency of firms in terms of how the exchange of intermediate products is organised, in which process ownership advantages and inter-firm competition in final product markets are secondary questions. The market power school also takes the view that ownership advantages associated with greater efficiency need not be regarded as a necessary condition for the existence of the firm or MNC, but for different reasons. They emphasise the conditions prevailing in final product rather than intermediate product markets, but deny that firms necessarily raise efficiency; moreover they think of oligopolies in terms of a gradual extension of collusion, with the establishment of ownership advantages as barriers to entry.

To illustrate the difference, in the technological accumulation approach each firm in an industry internally generates a succession of innovations or ownership advantages, which constitute the basis of both their domestic and their international production. The ability to innovate in a growing sector is itself an ownership advantage which is a function of the past technological experience of the firm. These ownership advantages are oligopolistic advantages, essential to survival in an international oligopoly. The most innovative firms in an industry create a faster stream of more effective ownership advantages, and in so doing they increase their international production more rapidly and raise their world market shares. The weakest firms lose market shares, and if a firm lost all owner-ship advantages it would be quickly driven out of both domestic and international markets. However, firms with the fewest or weakest ownership advantages in general hold their position more easily in domestic markets than in international markets owing to government support, consumer loyalty, the closeness of local business contacts and so forth.

Ownership advantages are defined with reference to the (oligopolistic) final product market. They are advantages which lower the unit costs and raise the profit margins of given firms relative to others in the same industry. A firm with weak ownership advantages, and certainly one with none at all, has high unit costs relative to others in its industry, and consequently suffers consistent losses. A firm with strong ownership advantages (measured, for example, by a high share of patenting activity) will have a larger market share; moreover if its ownership advantages become stronger (its share of patenting rises), then its market share increases. Empirical investigation of competition between the world's largest firms has confirmed that companies whose share of international patenting is greater than their international market share in their industry at a given point in time, experience a faster rate of growth and hence a rising market share in the ensuing period (Cantwell and Sanna-Randaccio, 1993).

Firms that lose ownership advantages face higher unit costs and lower profits, and a reduction in their market share. In the limit, a firm with no ownership advantages at all (though it is difficult to imagine such an extreme case in any existing industry) would lose market share until it was taken over or driven out altogether. Firms or MNCs therefore require ownership advantages as a necessary condition of their continued existence, and the stronger are their advantages, the faster the rate of international growth they are able to sustain.

Against this, it is sometimes claimed by writers in the internalisation tradition that ownership advantages are not necessary for the existence of MNCs and international production, apart from the advantages created by internalisation itself (Buckley and Casson, 1976; Casson, 1987). By this they mean that firms may grow relative to intermediate product markets where producers trading with one another merge their operations, irrespective of the ownership advantages of the productive units concerned. Hence they are referring strictly to the transition from national firms combining to form multinational firms, by means of the internalisation of the intermediate product markets which previously linked them.

However, to conclude from this that ownership advantages are not a necessary condition for international production is a very misleading way of putting matters. At least one of the individual productive units that combine to form an MNC must have ownership advantages, so that the MNC does too. For firms to grow relative to their competitors in final product markets, or indeed simply to retain their share of final product markets, ownership advantages are necessary. The generation of ownership advantages, achieved mainly through innovation, is necessary for competitive success and indeed survival. Firms that fail to accumulate technology and related ownership advantages are either driven out of business, or taken over by firms that have the capacity to do so.

The ownership advantages of each firm represent its particular differentiated area of strength as against its major rivals in turn which determines the level and rate of change of its market share. Ownership advantages relate to production costs while internalisation relates to transaction costs, though there is an inter- action between the two. The internalisation of intermediate product markets may complement ownership advantages, but it is not a substitute for them. A group of firms, each of which has no ownership advantages and therefore makes losses, will not suddenly become profitable merely by organising transactions among themselves more efficiently. They will only reduce their losses. In any event, the benefits of internalisation tend to be greater where each participating affiliate begins with strong ownership advantages, due to the potential for economies of scope, technological complementarities and so forth. Just as compatible owner- ship advantages may encourage internalisation, so internalisation may serve to increase (or in some cases to decrease) the firm's subsequent capacity to innovate or its ownership advantages. The existence of such interaction, though, does not make the concepts logically inseparable from one another.

The need for ownership advantages applies to both national firms and MNCs, although it is especially true of MNCs, since inefficient firms may be able to survive longer in their own domestic markets. Moreover, the most innovative firms whose ownership advantages are strongest are more likely to take over firms whose ownership advantages are weak than vice versa. The international networks of MNCs expand directly through the independent establishment and extension of their own ventures, together with takeovers or mergers with firms whose technological activity (ownership advantages) is complementary. Once MNCs are created, they may gain additional advantages from the international coordination of activity, in part through the enhancement of their technological strengths by way of a more geographically and industrially diversified research programme. The international coordination of research and production is therefore supportive of technological advantages, not a substitute for them, nor a sufficient condition for their generation.

The debate over the necessity or otherwise of ownership advantages is largely a discussion that has proceeded at cross-purposes, since as discussed above, differ- ent approaches have been set up to answer different questions. Internalisation theory endeavours to explain why firms displace intermediate product markets, or why MNCs displace international trade in intermediate products, in which it is not necessary to refer to ownership advantages. The existence of ownership advantages on the part of firms plays no role in the Coasian theory in deriving the existence of firms themselves, the joint ownership of assets being explained by the replacement of markets.

However, while this is a sufficient theory of the existence of firms in place of intermediate product markets without reference to any final product market (in place of atomistic competition), it is not a sufficient theory of firms *vis-à-vis* other firms. To explain why one firm displaces another or why, for example, Japanese MNCs have grown at the expense of US firms, then relatively stronger ownership advantages are necessary. The relative strength of technological ownership advantages is in general the principal determinant of variations in unit costs or productivity across firms (particularly in industrialised countries). Variations in unit costs are in turn necessary to explain why certain firms grow faster than their competitors in a given final product market. In this respect, internalisation theory has addressed a different issue from those of competitive international industry approaches; it is concerned with the extent of firms as opposed to intermediate product markets (or what might be thought of as the degree of concentration of ownership), rather than the process of competition between already existing firms. For a firm in competition and cooperation with others, ownership advantages are a necessary condition for establishing and preserving international production.

To appreciate how the role attributed to ownership advantages varies among theories, it is useful to draw a distinction between a theory of the firm in its relationship with markets and the separate development of theories of the growth of the firm in comparison with one another. In the theory of the growth of the firm as developed by Penrose (1959), internally generated growth associated with firm specific ownership advantages is central. The growth process is inherent to the firm, which directs its internal resources toward expansion:

> While external inducements and difficulties have been widely discussed, little attention has been paid, in a systematic way at least, to the equally important internal influences on the direction of expansion ... both an automatic increase in knowledge and an incentive to search for new knowledge are, as it were, 'built into' the very nature of firms possessing entrepreneurial resources of even average initiative ... I have placed the emphasis on the significance of the resources with which a firm works and on the development of the experience and knowledge of a firm's personnel because these are the factors that will determine the response of the firm to changes in the external world and also determine what it 'sees' in the external world ... Unused productive services are, for the enterprising firm, at the same time a challenge to innovate, an incentive to expand, and a source of competitive advantage.
>
> (Penrose, 1959: 66, 78, 79–80, 85)

The purpose of this rather lengthy quotation is to clarify the difference between the theory of the growth of the firm, in which internal ownership advantages are critical, and the Coasian theory of the firm, in which they are not. The Coasian theory of the firm emphasises the conditions of exchange of intermediate products initially in markets external to the firm which lead firms to internalise the markets in question. Internalisation thus offers a theory of the extent of the firm and its boundaries rather than its in-built mechanisms for growth, except in as much as any static theory can be made dynamic by referring to changes in levels. Thus, despite the claim that the 'original objective of the approach adopted by Buckley and Casson (1976) was to use the concept of the internalisation of markets to develop a model of the growth of the firm' (Buckley, 1988: 182), it is not inherently a theory of growth in the way that the Penrosian theory and the allied competitive international industry approaches based on internal ownership advantages are.

Given this distinction between theories of the internally generated growth of the firm in competition with others, and the internalisation theory in which the motive force for growth lies outside the firm, it is not surprising that internalisation writers have tended to treat ownership advantages as given. At least until now, internalistion theory has concentrated on the issue of technology transfer and the institutional form it assumes, rather than variations between firms in their ability to generate technology. Even when considering oligopolistic interdependence in the form of an exchange of threats, Casson (1987) assumes constant long-run market shares or, in other words, fixed and exogenous ownership advantages in the way they have been defined here.

A similar downplaying of the role of ownership advantages can be found in Kojima's work on Japanese MNCs and in some recent literature on Third World MNCs, in which it is sometimes claimed that investments in LDCs require no ownership advantages on the part of the firms that make them. It is certainly true that it may be the smaller, relatively weaker firms in an international industry which make export-platform investments in labour-intensive production, while the more advanced firms invest in research-related production in the industrialised countries. However, this need not be the case in the Kojima–Ozawa story, since it may be the same firms which upgrade their production at home while redeploying less sophisticated types of activity in countries at an earlier stage of development. Even if it is the case, all that this entails is that the ownership advantages of such smaller, newer MNCs lie in a simpler type of manufacturing and in their access to commercial outlets, not that they have no ownership advantages at all. It is simply that the more sophisticated types of international production require stronger ownership advantages (a stronger technological base) than other types, which is scarcely surprising.

Note also that ownership advantages are not always necessary in the specific sector in which investment takes place. Consider, for example, a diversified takeover by an international conglomerate. Ownership advantages are therefore to be understood as providing a firm with a general capability to expand, and the stronger are these advantages, the faster the speed of international expansion that it is able to sustain. It is true that where a conglomerate chooses to move into an unrelated sector, its motive is essentially of a financial kind, and may be better explained by a theory of FDI (such as that of Aliber, 1970, or Rugman, 1979) than a theory of international production. The ownership advantages of such firms may well be of a financial rather than a technological kind.

Where firms rely on technological ownership advantages, they invest in production in areas related to their existing strengths. Of course, where they produce in foreign centres of innovation, they may also gain access to a new stream of complementary technological developments. Investment may be motivated mainly by the objective of strengthening their ownership advantages. In such cases the original ownership advantages of firms are built upon, consolidated in their existing fields and extended into new areas. There is a progressive interaction between the growth of international networks and the strength of ownership advantages.

The other confusion about ownership advantages that is often found in the literature is that, as noted above, they are frequently described as monopolistic advantages. Perhaps a further reason why internalisation theorists have insistently criticised the concept of ownership advantages is because of this interpretation, associated with the market power approach. The origins of this terminology go back to Kindleberger (1969), who recast Hymer's work to associate MNCs with the existence of a particular market structure, that of monopolistic competition (within which each participating firm has some monopolistic advantage). Hymer himself believed that firms actively sought to raise barriers to entry and to collude with other firms in their industry, and that market structure was a product of their behaviour and the extent to which they succeeded in making lasting collusive agreements rather than the other way around. In Kindleberger's restatement the MNC was seen as a function of a market structure characterised by monopolistic competition between differentiated products rather than as an active agent engaged in oligopolistic interaction with other firms.

In Hymer's approach the strength of ownership advantages amongst the leading firms reflects the degree of monopoly power in a sector. However, strictly speaking, even in his framework ownership advantages should be thought of as oligopolistic and not monopolistic advantages.[5] This is even more true in competitive international industry approaches, such as those based on technological accumulation. Firms accumulate differentiated but overlapping technologies, irrespective of whether they produce identical or different final products. MNCs are therefore involved in technological competition with other members of an international oligopoly. Where it suits them, they may arrive at certain cooperative arrangements, such as in cross-licensing agreements. Each participant in the international oligopoly has certain specific advantages based on their own previous technological experience. The relative strength of the ownership advantages of each firm determines both their rate of growth *vis-à-vis* their competitors, and their attitude towards cooperative arrangements with other firms in the same sector. In this view the extent of collusion is a less important determinant of profits and growth than the strength of advantages, and is instead essentially also a product of the latter. Collusion comes and goes as the balance of advantages between firms changes.

The different perspective that the various approaches have as to the operation of locational influences can now be considered. The dividing line here is essentially between the two theories of the firm which tend to treat location as exogenous (to be determined by some other theory), and the macroeconomic and mesoeconomic approaches in which locational factors are themselves influenced by the growth of firms. To give an illustration of a process of continual interaction between ownership and location advantages, consider the case of a modern global manufacturing industry in which MNCs benefit from direct access to any of the main locationally advantaged centres of technological development. By investing in research and production in these sites, they increase their own competitiveness (ownership advantages), as well as the competitiveness of production in the countries concerned and their attractiveness to other firms (location advantages). In this case ownership and location advantages are not independent.

Looking back historically, the location advantages of countries also helped to determine the pattern of technological specialisation of each country's firms, or in other words the sectors in which they had the greatest capacity for generating ownership advantages. For example, Rosenberg (1976) has shown that US firms emerged from the industrial revolution with advantages in woodworking technologies due to the plentiful availability of local timber supplies, while British firms developed advantages in metal working and coal-related technologies due to local coal deposits.

Internalisation theorists have tended to take location advantages and technological ownership advantages as given and exogenous, in order to focus attention on the form of linkages between plants. Neoclassical trade and location theorists have gone even further, and in many cases simply assumed away technological ownership advantages (all firms have access to the same technology) in order to focus on purely locational factors. The market power school treats technological advantages as barriers to entry while typically taking location as exogenous.

This is not to say that the market power and internalisation approaches have ignored locational factors. Hymer (1975), for example, suggests that firms locate activities in accordance with a hierarchy, with high-grade activities in industrialised countries and low-grade activities in LDCs. Newfarmer (1985) and Bornschier and Chase-Dunn (1985), who take a market power view, similarly distinguish between central and peripheral locations in an international industry. While retaining the internalisation perspective, Casson (1986b) has also suggested a model of the international division of labour. Indeed, internalisation theorists have recognised that the growth of the firm may influence location; for example, 'internalisation allows international transfer price manipulation that will bias location towards inclusion of low tax locations' (Buckley, 1988: 182). It is simply that those who have analysed the growth of international production from the viewpoint of the theory of the firm have not, on the whole, attached very much significance to the interaction between the growth of the firm and the changing location of production. For this reason they have often disregarded those elements of macroeconomic explanations that have attempted to do just this, as exemplified by Buckley (1988: 186): 'Elsewhere I have attempted to show that even this macro explanation must rely on micro aspects to achieve its explanatory cutting edge.'

This contrasts with the product cycle approach, the Kojima–Ozawa analysis and the various competitive international oligopoly theories, which have all stressed the interaction between the growth of the firm and the location of production, and the consequences for the structure of industrial production and trade. Macroeconomic theories of international production make location advantages depend on macroeconomic factors related to countries and their level of development, while mesoeconomic approaches emphasise the locational factors specific to an international industry (see Gray, 1982, for a discussion of whether location advantages can be treated as purely macroeconomic). Naturally, the focus of interest and the level at which analysis is conducted affect the treatment of location in theories of international production.

The development of a dynamic analysis of international production

As a rule, macroeconomic and competitive international industry approaches to international production are by their very nature dynamic, as they have usually been concerned to describe a process over time. Theories of the firm *vis-à-vis* markets, although until recently they have attracted a greater literature, have addressed only certain types of question on the dynamics of international production. The internalisation approach has asked why firms (the visible hand) have expanded relative to markets (the invisible hand). The particular issue that has attracted most attention is the idea of an evolution in the business of firms from exports (through a sales agent), to licensing a foreign company, to the establishment of international production (Buckley and Casson, 1981, 1998; Nicholas, 1986; Teece, 1983).

This section considers how theories of the firm in its relationship to markets may be extended or adapted to take account of the wider evolution of international production linked to the cumulative development of technology through the international networks of MNCs. The technological accumulation approach emphasises the connection between the generation of technology and the growth of production, both within the firms and in terms of the distinctive geographical pattern of innovation and research-related production that develops in each industry. This evolutionary view of the growth of international production and the associated competence-based theory of comparative firm growth may be usefully combined with insights from the transaction cost theory of the individual firm in its relationship with markets.

Two possible extensions of internalisation theory might be considered which would broaden the approach. First, attention can be given to the interrelationship between the growth of the firm and the changing location of production, which has already been raised in the context of other approaches, as suggested in the previous section. Second, the transaction cost framework might be usefully combined with a theory of entrepreneurship, innovation or the changing technology and organisation of production within the firm, as in the competence-based approach to the firm. In recent years various writers have envisaged a possible interchange between the transaction cost and dynamic capabilities approaches (Langlois, 1992; Loasby, 1991; Silverman, 1999; Teece *et al.*, 1997).

Whereas the theory of cumulative technological change, like the work of the classical economists, is a theory of production (and the changing technology of production), as it stands the Coasian theory of the firm, like the neoclassical economic thinking of which it is a criticism, is a pure theory of exchange. Exchange takes place under a variety of institutional arrangements, in markets or within the firm. It is worth noting that Nelson and Winter (1982) make use of certain aspects of the work of Williamson and others in developing their evolutionary theory of economic change. However, in order to make the Coasian theory of the firm itself evolutionary, it would be necessary to specify how transaction costs are themselves influenced by the growth and technological innovation of firms.

As Casson (1986a) has pointed out, while transaction cost theory specifies conditions under which non-market institutional arrangements will obtain (for example, within the firm), it does so at present to the exclusion of any active role for managerial strategy. In other words, while a theory of the MNC, couched in an exchange framework, can explain the existence of the MNC or the firm, it has still left the firm itself as a passive reactor to transactional circumstances. As remarked above, it relates to the external influences on growth, and not to the internal sources of growth which make the firm inherently dynamic when under competition in its final product market. Changes in the organisation or control of production are merely a response to changes in the costs of various exchange relationships in markets or otherwise. This procedure may be justified if one is concerned only with the internalisation of intermediate product markets actively replacing trade between independent parties.

However, difficulties are encountered when this approach is applied to the historical evolution of, say, import-substituting international production; take, for example, the growth of investment by US firms in Europe in the 1950s and 1960s. Part of the reason is that locational factors were responsible (faster growth in Europe). While this helps to explain the initial direction of the investment, it does not explain how manufacturing MNCs steadily grew in the post-war period. Nor does a change in political risk provide a complete explanation. It might be suggested that where markets in intangible assets such as technology become in some sense more imperfect, that the transaction costs of market exchange rise, and horizontally integrated MNCs tend to grow. But it seems most implausible to argue that any international markets were operating more imperfectly in the late 1950s and the 1960s by comparison with the 1930s.

Within this framework, the explanation is presumably in part that the transaction costs of cooperative relationships fell even faster than the costs of using the market mechanism. Yet one of the main reasons for this was the growing experience of firms in international production in the industrialised countries, initially of US firms in Europe. To avoid falling into a static tautology (that is, that international transaction costs fell because of the growth of the MNC, and the MNC grew because of lower internal transaction costs), this must be set in a dynamic framework whereby the interaction between transaction costs and the growth of firms is set out. Transaction costs depend upon the technological and productive activity of the firm. The international growth of firms is part of an evolutionary process. This also helps to call attention to other aspects of the explanation: in this case, the generation of strong technological ownership advantages by US firms, and the greater locational advantage of producing in Europe in the 1960s.

Internalisation theory when taken independently is at its strongest when discussing vertical integration, such as the backward integration of manufacturing companies to secure raw material supplies including natural resources (Casson *et al.*, 1986), or their forward integration into distribution or sales agencies (Nicholas, 1983, 1985). When it comes to the international expansion of manufacturing production itself, a pure theory of exchange is on weaker ground. It has been claimed that the horizontal integration of manufacturing plants can be explained by the transaction costs of exchanging technology at arm's length (Buckley and Casson, 1976). However, technology may accumulate within the firm not so much because of the characteristics of the market for technology once it has been created, as because of the conditions under which it is most easily generated and used in production. Technology is then difficult and costly to transfer or exchange between firms precisely because it tends to be associated with the research and production experience accumulated within a particular firm, rather than vice versa. Armour and Teece (1980) take a step in this direction in recognising from a transaction costs perspective that vertical integration may increase R&D and the rate of technological change.

It seems reasonable to suppose that the accumulation of technology and the growth of production within the firm will affect the transaction costs of exchange. The transaction cost theorist has instead tended to start from exchange in a market which gives way to more consciously organised control where it is relatively inefficient. Coase (1937) stressed the market conditions which lead to a reorganisation or an extension in the organisation of the firm. However, the nature and extent of a firm's transactions and cooperative arrangements with other firms, as well as its market share, also depend upon its innovative capacity *vis-à-vis* other firms. As paths of technological development become established within each firm, this is likely to affect the conditions of technology transfer between them which has been the focus of much of the internalisation literature.

A similar criticism can be made of the conventional structure–conduct–performance paradigm of industrial organisation theory which is essentially static and does not deal with industrial dynamics or evolution (Carlsson, 1987). Once again, the firm appears as a passive reactor to changes in market structure. This is rather unfortunate, since early analysis of the growth of the firm in the 1950s (such as Penrose, 1959) had appeared to fit in nicely with treatments of imperfect competition, and the emergence of the study of industrial economics. Indeed, as noted above, Hymer's theory of the growth of the MNC was based precisely on this combination of an active firm increasing the extent of its market power and colluding with others to raise what Bain (1956) termed barriers to entry or new competition.

However, there are problems with the market power theory of the firm if it is used as a general explanation of the growth of international production, especially in the context of the technological competition that exists today between the firms of the major industrialised countries. In most industries the level of expenditure on research and development has been rising in recent years. Countries have become increasingly concerned about their technological competitiveness, while firms have been under steadily more pressure to maintain and build upon their major sources of innovative strength. It is necessary for all theories of the dynamics of international production to come to terms with this. The implication of the market power view is that profitability is usually seen as being raised through a restriction of output and of the number of firms competing. In fact the steady generation of ownership advantages through technological accumulation, rather than serving as barriers to potential new entrants, may increase competition amongst firms already in the international oligopoly, causing them to expand their own research and production. Research-intensive lines of activity are generally known not for their lack of competition in world markets, but for quite the reverse.

In an industry with rapid technological accumulation, the high profitability associated with the existence of strong ownership advantages is not due to a restriction of output, a lack of competition and a high degree of industrial concentration as a feature of market structure. It is rather accounted for by the greater scope that innovation provides for productivity improvements, and with them the faster growth of output. Competition is more intense in terms of the creation of new products and processes.

Yet the market power theory of the firm as used by Hymer may be relevant to certain types of MNC activity, even if it does not provide a general explanation of MNC growth. Firms are more likely to seek out cooperative agreements or collusion with other firms where they are in a weak position *vis-à-vis* other firms in their industry, or where competition is very intense. Where they are relatively weak, the licensing of technology is liable to run in just one direction, but where they are a leading member of an international oligopoly, cross-licensing arrangements are to be expected. Increasing overlaps between firms in their technological development (as technological interrelatedness rises) are also likely to lead to an increase in cross-licensing as well as greater technological competition. There may therefore be new areas of business cooperation within an essentially competitive environment. Collusion between MNCs is quite possible, but it is generally to improve the relationship between their international production networks rather than being an explanation of them.

Analysing trends in technological competition (and cooperation) between MNCs in the future is likely to be of considerable interest. One question that has been raised is the extent to which the recent upsurge in the internationalisation of production is leading to an increasing locational concentration of research activity. This, in turn, has effects on the competitiveness of both firms and countries. Work on international industrial dynamics of this kind is still at a relatively early stage, but similar work on cumulative patterns of technological change is already attracting increasing attention in other fields. Further explorations of the relationship between technological innovation and the production of MNCs will, it is hoped, make a distinctive and important contribution. As Dunning has suggested,

> It is to be hoped that a next generation of scholars will give more attention to issues of innovation and entrepreneurship as they impinge upon the

internationalisation of business. We believe that if a new breakthrough in our understanding of foreign production occurs, it will be in this direction.

(Dunning, 1988b: 36)

Notes

1 Alan Rugman (1980) invoked internalisation as a general theory of the MNC-cum-FDI, while Robert Aliber (1970, 1971) made international currency valuation the cornerstone of what he seemed to think of as a general theory of FDI-cum-MNC.
2 That Cowling and Sugden do not seem to identify themselves with the Hymer tradition need not be of concern here.
3 Dunning (1983a, 1988a) refers to these as ownership advantages of an asset kind, and ownership advantages of a transaction cost minimising kind, or, following Teece (1983), ownership advantages of a governance cost minimising kind.
4 Although the distinction between appropriability and coordination remains an important conceptual one, in practice where the firm controls complementary assets it may be difficult to differentiate between the two. The significance of this division is discussed further by Teece (1990).
5 They are monopolistic only if they are based entirely on product differentiation. If firms have advantages that are related to production – scale economies, patented technology, or high start-up costs – then they need not have monopolistic control of (segments of) the final product market. Their monopoly power is a result of collusion, which is made easier by such barriers to entry, but is exercised jointly rather than individually. It might still be said that each firm has a quasi-monopolistic position in the everyday sense that each exercises a monopoly over the use of its own patented technology or large-scale plants (Jenkins, 1987). However, if they do not sell the use of such technology or plants in an external market, then they are not monopoly sellers; hence the term *quasi*-monopoly. The market they actually serve is oligopolistic, even if it is divided by collusive agreement.

References

Aliber, R.Z. (1970) 'A theory of direct foreign investment', in C.P. Kindleberger (ed.), *The International Corporation: A Symposium*, Cambridge, Mass.: MIT Press.
—— (1971) 'The multinational enterprise in a multiple currency world', in J.H. Dunning (ed.), *The Multinational Enterprise*, London: Allen & Unwin.
Armour, H.O. and D.J. Teece (1980) 'Vertical integration and technological innovation', *Review of Economics and Statistics*, 62.
Armstrong, P., A. Glyn and J. Harrison (1991) *Capitalism since 1945*, Oxford: Basil Blackwell.
Atkinson, A.B. and J.E. Stiglitz (1969) 'A new view of technological change', *The Economic Journal*, 79, 3, September.
Bain, J.S. (1956) *Barriers to New Competition*, Cambridge, Mass.: Harvard University Press.
Baran, P.A. and P.M. Sweezy (1966) *Monopoly Capital*, New York: Monthly Review Press.
Blomström, M. (1989) *Foreign Investment and Spillovers: A Study of Technology Transfer to Mexico*, London: Routledge.
Bornschier, V. and C. Chase-Dunn (1985) *Transnational Corporations and Underdevelopment*, London: Greenwood.

Buckley, P.J. (1983) 'New theories of international business: Some unresolved issues', in M.C. Casson (ed.), *The Growth of International Business*, London: Allen & Unwin.

—— (1985) 'The economic analysis of the multinational enterprise: Reading versus Japan?', *Hitotsubashi Journal of Economics*, 26, 2. December.

—— (1988) 'The limits of explanation: Testing the internalisation theory of the multinational enterprise', *Journal of International Business Studies*, 19, 2, Summer.

Buckley, P.J. and M.C. Casson (1976) *The Future of the Multinational Enterprise*, London: Macmillan.

—— (1981) 'The optimal timing of a foreign direct investment', *The Economic Journal*, 91, 1.

—— (1985) *The Economic Theory of the Multinational Enterprise: Selected Papers*, London: Macmillan/New York: St Martin's Press.

—— (1998) 'Analyzing foreign market entry strategies: Extending the internalization approach', *Journal of International Business Studies*, 29, 3: 539–62.

Cantwell, J.A. (1987) 'The reorganisation of European industries after integration: Selected evidence on the role of multinational enterprise activities', *Journal of Common Market Studies*, 26, 2, December; reprinted in J.H. Dunning and P. Robson (eds, 1988), *Multinationals and the European Community*, Oxford: Basil Blackwell.

—— (1989a) 'The changing form of multinational enterprise expansion in the twentieth century', in A. Teichova, M. Levy-Leboyer and H. Nussbaum, (eds), *Historical Studies in International Corporate Business*, Cambridge: Cambridge University Press.

—— (1989b) *Technological Innovation and Multinational Corporations*, Oxford: Basil Blackwell.

—— (1991) 'The theory of technological competence and its application to international production', in D. McFetridge (ed.), *Foreign Investment, Technology and Economic Growth*, Calgary: University of Calgary Press.

—— (1994a) 'Introduction', in J.A. Cantwell (ed.), *Transnational Corporations and Innovatory Activities*, London: Routledge.

—— (1994b) 'The relationship between international trade and international production', in D. Greenaway and L.A. Winters (eds), *Surveys in International Trade*, Oxford: Basil Blackwell.

—— (1995) 'The globalisation of technology: What remains of the product cycle model?', *Cambridge Journal of Economics*, 19, 1: 155–74.

—— (1998a) 'Knowledge, capabilities, imagination and cooperation in business: Introduction', *Journal of Economic Behavior and Organization*, 35, 2: 133–37.

—— (1998b) 'Technology and the firm: Introduction', *Research Policy*, 27, 5: iii–v.

—— (1999) 'Innovation as the principal source of growth in the global economy', in D. Archibugi, J. Howells and J. Michie (eds), *Innovation Policy in a Global Economy*, Cambridge: Cambridge University Press.

Cantwell, J.A. and J.H. Dunning, (1991) 'MNEs, technology and the competitiveness of European industries', *Aussenwirtschaft*, 46, 1: 45–65.

Cantwell, J.A. and F.M. Fai, (1999) 'The changing nature of corporate technological diversification and the importance of organisational capability', in S.C. Dow and P.E. Earl, (eds), *Contingency, Complexity and the Theory of the Firm: Essays in Honour of Brian J. Loasby*, Cheltenham: Edward Elgar.

Cantwell, J.A. and S. Iammarino, (1998) 'MNCs, technological innovation and regional systems in the EU: Some evidence in the Italian case', *International Journal of the Economics of Business*, 5, 3: 383–408.

Cantwell, J.A. and O.E.M. Janne, (1999) 'Technological globalisation and innovative centres: The role of corporate technological leadership and locational hierarchy', *Research Policy*, 28.

Cantwell, J.A. and L. Piscitello, (2000) 'Accumulating technological competence – its changing impact on corporate diversification and internationalisation', *Industrial and Corporate Change*, 9, forthcoming.

Cantwell, J.A. and F. Sanna-Randaccio (1993) 'Multinationality and firm growth', *Weltwirtschaftliches Archiv*, 129, 2: 275–99.

Cantwell, J.A. and G.D. Santangelo (2000) 'Capitalism, innovation and profits in the new technoeconomic paradigm', *Journal of Evolutionary Economics*, 10, forthcoming.

Cantwell, J.A. and P.E.E. Tolentino, (1990) 'Technological accumulation and Third World multinationals', University of Reading Discussion Paper in International Investment and Business Studies, no. 139, May.

Cantwell, J.A., T.A.B. Corley and J.H. Dunning, (1986) 'An exploration of some historical antecedents to the modern theory of international production', in G. Jones and P. Hertner, (eds), *Multinationals: Theory and History*, Farnborough: Gower.

Carlsson, B. (1987) 'Reflections on "Industrial Dynamics": the challenges ahead', *International Journal of Industrial Organisation*, 5, 2, June.

Casson, M.C. (1981) 'Foreword', in A.M. Rugman, *Inside the Multinationals: The Economics of Internal Markets*, London: Groom Helm.

—— (1982) 'The theory of foreign direct investment', in J. Black and J.H. Dunning (eds), *International Capital Movements*, London: Macmillan.

—— (1986a) 'General theories of the multinational enterprise: A critical examination', in G. Jones and P. Hertner (eds), *Multinationals: Theory and History*, Farnborough: Gower.

—— (1986b) 'The international division of labour' in M.C. Casson, *et al.*, *Multinationals and World Trade*, London: Allen & Unwin.

—— (1987) *The Firm and the Market: Studies in Multinational Enterprise and the Scope of the Firm*, Oxford: Basil Blackwell.

Casson, M.C. *et al.* (1986) *Multinationals and World Trade: Vertical Integration and the Division of Labour in World Industries*, London: Allen & Unwin.

Caves, R.E. (1982) *Multinational Enterprise and Economic Analysis*, Cambridge: Cambridge University Press.

Chandler, A.D., P. Hagström, and Ö Sölvell, (eds) (1998), *The Dynamic Firm: The Role of Technology, Strategy, Organization, and Regions*, Oxford: Oxford University Press.

Coase, R.H. (1937) 'The nature of the firm', *Economica*, 4, 4, November.

Cowling, K. and R. Sugden (1987) *Transnational Monopoly Capitalism*, Brighton: Wheatsheaf Books.

Dunning, J.H. (1977) 'Trade, location of economic activity, and the MNE: A search for an eclectic approach' in B. Ohlin, P.-O. Hesselborn and P.M. Wijkman, (eds) *The International Allocation of Economic Activity*, London: Macmillan.

—— (1981) *International Production and the Multinational Enterprise*, London: Allen & Unwin.

—— (1982) 'Explaining the international direct investment position of countries: Towards a dynamic or developmental approach' in J. Black and J.H. Dunning (eds), *International Capital Movements*, London: Macmillan.

—— (1983a) 'Market power of the firm and international transfer of technology', *International Journal of Industrial Organisation*, 1, 1, December.

—— (1983b) 'Changes in the level and structure of international production: The last one hundred years', in M.C. Casson (ed.), *The Growth of International Business*, London: Allen & Unwin.

—— (1986) 'The investment development cycle and Third World multinationals', in K.M. Khan, (ed.), *Multinationals of the South: New Actors in the International Economy*, London: Frances Pinter.

—— (1988a) 'The eclectic paradigm of international production: An update and a reply to its critics', *Journal of International Business Studies*, 19, 1, Spring.

—— (1988b), 'The theory of international production', *The International Trade Journal*, 3, Fall.

—— (1992) *Multinational Enterprises and the Global Economy*, Wokingham: Addison Wesley.

—— (1995) 'Reappraising the eclectic paradigm in an age of alliance capitalism', *Journal of International Business Studies*, 26, 3: 461–91.

—— (1996) 'The geographical sources of the competitiveness of firms: Some results of a new survey', *Transnational Corporations*, 5, 3: 1–29.

—— Dunning, J.H. and R. Narula (1996) 'The investment development path revisited: Some emerging issues', in J.H. Dunning, and R. Narula (eds), *Foreign Direct Investment and Governments: Catalysts for Economic Restructuring*, London: Routledge.

Emmanuel, A. (1982) *Appropriate or Underdeveloped Technology?*, Chichester: John Wiley & Sons.

Flowers, E.B. (1976) 'Oligopolistic reaction in European and Canadian direct investment in the US', *Journal of International Business Studies*, 7, 2, Fall/Winter.

Foss, N.J. (1993) 'The theory of the firm: Contractual and competence perspectives', *Journal of Evolutionary Economics*, 3, 2: 127–44.

Gambardella, A. and S. Torrisi, (1998) 'Does technological convergence imply convergence in markets? Evidence from the electronic industry', *Research Policy*, 27, 5: 445–64.

Giddy, I.H. (1978) 'The demise of the product cycle model in international business theory', *Columbia Journal of World Business*, 13, 1, Spring.

Graham, E.M. (1975) 'Oligopolistic imitation and European direct investment', PhD dissertation, Harvard Graduate School of Business Administration.

—— (1978) 'Transatlantic investment by multinational firms: A rivalistic phenomenon?", *Journal of Post-Keynesian Economics*, 1, 1, Fall.

—— (1985) 'Intra-industry direct investment, market structure, firm rivalry and technological performance' in A. Erdilek (ed.), *Multinationals as Mutual Invaders. Intra-Industry Direct Foreign Investment*, London: Croom Helm.

—— (1998) 'Market structure and the multinational enterprise: a game-theoretic approach', *Journal of International Business Studies*, 29, 1: 67–83.

Granstrand, O. (1998), 'Towards a theory of the technology-based firm', *Research Policy*, 27, 5: 465–90.

Granstrand, O. and S. Sjölander, (1990), 'Managing innovation in multi-technology corporations', *Research Policy*, 19, 1: 35–60.

Granstrand, O., P. Patel and K.L.R. Pavitt (1997) 'Multi-technology corporations: Why they have "distributed" rather than "distinctive core" competencies', *California Management Review*, 39, 4: 8–25.

Gray, H.P. (1982) 'Macroeconomic theories of foreign direct investment: An assessment', in A.M. Rugman (ed.), *New Theories of the Multinational Enterprise*, London: Croom Helm.

Hagedoorn, J. and R. Narula (1996) 'Choosing organizational modes of strategic technology partnering: International and sectoral differences', *Journal of International Business Studies*, 27, 2: 265–84.

Hirsch, S. (1967) *Location of Industry and International Competitiveness*, Oxford: Oxford University Press.

Hobday, M. (1995) *Innovation in East Asia: The Challenge to Japan*, Aldershot: Edward Elgar.

Hodgson, G.M. (1998) 'Competence and contract in the theory of the firm', *Journal of Economic Behavior and Organization*, 35, 2: 179–202.

Hufbauer, G.C. (1965) *Synthetic Materials and the Theory of International Trade*, London: Duckworth.

—— (1970) 'The impact of national characteristics and technology on the commodity composition of trade in manufactured goods', in R. Vernon (ed.), *The Technology Factor in International Trade*, New York: Columbia University Press.

Hymer, S. (1975) 'The multinational corporation and the law of uneven development', in H. Radice (ed.), *International Firms and Modern Imperialism*, Harmondsworth: Penguin Books.

—— (1976) *The International Operations of National Firms: A Study of Direct Investment*, Cambridge, Mass.: MIT Press.

Hymer, S. and R. Rowthorn (1970) 'Multinational corporations and international oligopoly: The non-American challenge', in C.P. Kindleberger (ed.), *The International Corporation: A Symposium*, Cambridge, Mass.: MIT Press.

Jenkins, R. (1984) *Transnational Corporations and Industrial Transformation in Latin America*, London: Macmillan.

—— (1987) *Transnational Corporations and Uneven Development: The Internationalisation of Capital and the Third World*, London: Methuen.

Johnson, H.G. (1958) *International Trade and Economic Growth*, London: Allen & Unwin.

Kay, N. (1983) 'Review article: Multinational enterprise', *Scottish Journal of Political Economy*, 30, 3, November.

Kindleberger, C.P. (1969) *American Business Abroad: Six Lectures on Direct Investment*, New Haven, Conn.: Yale University Press.

Knickerbocker, F.T. (1973) *Oligopolistic Reaction and the Multinational Enterprise*, Boston, Mass.: Harvard University Press.

Kodama, F. (1992) 'Technology fusion and the new R&D', *Harvard Business Review*, July–August: 70–78.

Kogut, B. and S.J. Chang (1991) 'Technological capabilities and Japanese foreign direct investment in the United States', *Review of Economics and Statistics*, 73: 401–13.

Kogut, B. and U. Zander (1993) 'Knowledge of the firm and the evolutionary theory of the multinational corporation', *Journal of International Business Studies*, 24, 4: 625–45.

Kojima, K. (1978) *Direct Foreign Investment: A Japanese Model of Multinational Business Operations*, London: Croom Helm.

Kojima, K. and T. Ozawa, (1985) 'Toward a theory of industrial restructuring and dynamic comparative advantage', *Hitotsubashi Journal of Economics*, 26, 2, December.

Kokko, A. (1994) 'Technology, market characteristics and spillovers', *Journal of Development Economics*, 43: 279–93.

Kokko, A., R. Tansini and M.C. Zejan (1996) 'Local technological capability and productivity spillovers from FDI in the Uruguayan manufacturing sector', *Journal of Development Studies*, 32, 4: 602–11.

Kuemmerle, W. (1999) 'The drivers of foreign direct investment into research and development – an empirical investigation', *Journal of International Business Studies*, 30, 1: 1–24.

Lall, S. (1976) 'Theories of direct foreign private investment and multinational behaviour', *Economic and Political Weekly*, 11, 31–33, August.

Langlois, R.N. (1992) 'Transaction cost economics in real time', *Industrial and Corporate Change*, 1, 1: 99–127.

Leontief, W.W. (1954) 'Domestic production and foreign trade: The American capital position reexamined', *Economia Internazionale*, 7, 1, February.

Linder, S.B. (1961) *An Essay on Trade and Transformation*, New York: John Wiley & Sons.

Loasby, B.J. (1991) *Equilibrium and Evolution: An Exploration of Connecting Principles in Economics*, Manchester: Manchester University Press.

—— (1998) 'The organisation of capabilities', *Journal of Economic Behavior and Organization*, 35, 2: 139–60.

Mowery, D.C., J.E. Oxley and B.S. Silverman (1998) 'Technological overlap and interfirm cooperation: Implications for the resource-based view of the firm', *Research Policy*, 27, 5: 507–24.

Narula, R. (1996) *Multinational Investment and Economic Structure: Globalisation and Competitiveness*, London: Routledge.

Nelson, R.R. (1991) 'Why do firms differ, and how does it matter?', *Strategic Management Journal*, 12, 1: 61–74.

—— (ed.), (1993) *National Innovation Systems: A Comparative Analysis*, Oxford: Oxford University Press.

—— (1995) 'Co-evolution of industry structure, technology and supporting institutions, and the making of comparative advantage', *International Journal of the Economics of Business*, 2, 2: 171–84.

Nelson, R.R. and S.J. Winter (1977) 'In search of a useful theory of innovation', *Research Policy*, 5, 1.

—— (1982) *An Evolutionary Theory of Economic Change*, Cambridge, Mass.: Harvard University Press.

Newfarmer, R.S. (ed.) (1985) *Profits, Progress and Poverty: Case Studies of International Industries in Latin America*, Notre Dame, Ind.: University of Notre Dame Press.

Nicholas, S.J. (1983) 'Agency contracts, institutional modes, and the transition to foreign direct investment by British manufacturing multinationals before 1935', *Journal of Economic History*, 43.

—— (1985) 'The theory of multinational enterprise as a transactional mode', in P. Hertner and G. Jones (eds), *Multinationals: Theory and History*, Farnborough: Gower Press.

—— (1986) 'Multinationals, transaction costs and choice of institutional form', University of Reading Discussion Papers in International Investment and Business Studies, no. 97, September.

Ozawa, T. (1974) *Japan's Techonological Challenge to the West, 1950–1974: Motivation and Accomplishment*, Cambridge, Mass.: MIT Press.

—— (1979) *Multinationalism, Japanese Style: The Political Economy of Outward Dependency*, Princeton, NJ: Princeton University Press.

—— (1982) 'A newer type of foreign investment in Third World resource development', Rivista Internazionale di Scienze Economiche e Commerciali, 29, 12, December.

—— (1990) 'Europe 1992 and Japanese multinationals: Transplanting a subcontracting system in the expanded market', in B. Bürgenmeier and J.L. Mucchielli (eds), *Multinationals and Europe 1992*, London: Routledge.

—— (1991) 'Japan in a new phase of multinationalism and industrial upgrading: functional integration of trade, growth and FDI', *Journal of World Trade*, 25, 1: 43–60.

—— (1992) 'Foreign direct investment and economic development', *Transnational Corporations*, 1, 1: 27–54.

—— (1998) 'Manufacturing paradigm and international business: Toward a milieu-based theory of production'. Paper presented to the European International Business Academy Annual Conference, Jerusalem, December.

Pasinetti, L.L. (1981) 'International economic relations', in *Structural Change and Economic Growth: A Theoretical Essay on the Dynamics of the Wealth of Nations*, Cambridge: Cambridge University Press.

Pavitt, K.L.R. (1987) 'International patterns of technological accumulation', in N. Hood and J.E. Vahne (eds), *Strategies in Global Competition*, London: Croom Helm.

Pavitt, K.L.R., M. Robson and J. Townsend (1989) 'Technological accumulation, diversification and organisation in UK companies, 1945–1983', *Management Science*, 35, 1: 81–99.

Pearce, R.D. (1997) *Global Competition and Technology: Essays in the Creation and Application of Knowledge by Multinationals*, London: Macmillan.

Pearce, R.D. and S. Singh (1992) *Globalising Research and Development*, London: Macmillan.

Penrose, E. (1959) *The Theory of the Growth of the Firm*, Oxford: Basil Blackwell.

Perez, T. (1997) 'Multinational enterprises and technological spillovers: An evolutionary model', *Journal of Evolutionary Economlcs*, 7, 2: 169–92.

—— (1998) *Multinational Enterprises and Technological Spillovers*, Chur: Harwood.

Piscitello, L. (1998) 'Corporate diversification, coherence, and the dialectic relationship between technological and product competencies', PhD thesis, Politecnico di Milano.

Pitelis, C.N. (1986) *Corporate Capital: Control, Ownership, Saving and Prices*, Cambridge: Cambridge University Press.

Posner, M.V. (1961) 'Technical change and international trade', *Oxford Economic Papers*, 13.

Pugel, T.A., E.S. Kragas and Y. Kimura (1996) 'Further evidence on Japanese direct investment in US manufacturing', *Review of Economics and Statistics*, 78: 208–13.

Rosenberg, N. (1976) *Perspectives on Technology*, Cambridge: Cambridge University Press.

—— (1982) *Inside the Black Box: Technology and Economics*, Cambridge: Cambridge University Press.

Rothschild, K. (1947) 'Price theory and oligopoly', *The Economic Journal*, 57.

Rugman, A.M. (1979) *International Diversification and the Multinational Enterprise*, Lexington, Mass.: Lexington Books.

—— (1980) 'Internalisation as a general theory of foreign direct investment: A reappraisal of the literature', *Weltwirtschaftliches Archiv*, 116, 2.

—— (1981) *Inside the Multinationals: the Economics of Internal Markets*, London: Croom Helm.

Sachwald, F. (1998) 'Cooperative agreements and the theory of the firm: Focusing on barriers to change', *Journal of Economic Behavior and Organization*, 35, 2: 203–28.

Sanna-Randaccio, F. (1980) 'European direct investments in US manufacturing', M.Litt. thesis, University of Oxford.

Savary, J. (1984) *French Multinationals*, London: Frances Pinter.

Schumpeter, J. (1934) *The Theory of Economic Development*, Cambridge, Mass.: Harvard University Press.

Silverman, B.S. (1999) 'Technological resources and the direction of corporate diversification: Toward an integration of the resource-based view and transaction cost economics', *Management Science*, 45.

Steindl, J. (1952) *Maturity and Stagnation in American Capitalism*, Oxford: Oxford University Press.

Stiglitz, J.E. (1987) 'Learning to learn, localised learning and technological progress', in P. Dasgupta and P. Stoneman (eds), *Economic Policy and Technological Performance*, Cambridge: Cambridge University Press.

Stopford, J.M. and L. Turner (1986) *Britain and the Multinationals*, Chichester: John Wiley & Sons.

Sugden, R. (1983) 'Why transnational corporations?', Warwick Economic Research Paper, no. 222.

Teece, D.J. (1977) 'Technology transfer by multinational firms: The resource costs of transferring technological know-how', *Economic Journal*, 87, 2, June.

—— (1983) 'Technological and organisational factors in the theory of the multinational enterprise', in M.C. Casson (ed.), *The Growth of International Business*. London: Allen & Unwin.

—— (1990) 'Capturing value from technological innovation: Integration, strategic partnering and licensing decisions', in F. Arcangeli, P.A. David and G. Dosi (eds), *Modern Patterns in Introducing and Adopting Innovations*, Oxford: Oxford University Press.

—— (1996) 'Firm organisation, industrial structure and technological innovation', *Journal of Economic Behavior and Organization*, 31, 2: 193–224.

Teece, D.J., G. Pisano and A. Shuen (1997) 'Dynamic capabilities and strategic management', *Strategic Management Journal*, 18, 7: 537–56.

Tolentino, P.E.E. (1993) *Technological Innovation and Third World Multinationals*, London: Routledge.

Usher, A.P. (1929) *A History of Mechanical Inventions*, Cambridge, Mass.: Harvard University Press.

Vernon, R. (1966) 'International investment and international trade in the product cycle', *Quarterly Journal of Economics*, 80, 2, May.

—— (1971) *Sovereignty at Bay*, Harmondsworth: Penguin Books.

—— (1974) 'The location of economic activity', in J.H. Dunning (ed.), *Economic Analysis and the Multinational Enterprise*, London: Allen & Unwin.

—— (1979) 'The product cycle hypothesis in the new international environment', *Oxford Bulletin of Economics and Statistics*, 41, 4, November.

Warren, B. (1980) *Imperialism: Pioneer of Capitalism*, London: Verso.

Wells, L.T. (ed.) (1972) *The Product Life Cycle and International Trade*, Boston, Mass.: Harvard University Press.

Williamson, O.E. (1975) *Markets and Hierarchies: Analysis and Antitrust Implications*, New York: Free Press.

3 A critical re-evaluation of Hymer's contribution to the theory of the transnational corporation

Mohammad Yamin

Introduction

In Yamin (1991), we provided a reassessment of Hymer's contribution to the theory of the transnational corporation (TNC) shaped largely by the debate in the mid-1980s relating to the nature of market imperfections that were held to be the drivers of the TNC. Dunning and Rugman (1985) and Casson (1987), for example, had criticised Hymer for over-emphasising structural market imperfections at the expense of transaction costs, although even in his doctoral dissertation, Hymer (1960, published in 1976) did not totally ignore transaction costs (Yamin, 1991: 74). Furthermore, in a paper written in 1968 (that came to light in 1990) he explicitly utilised Coase's framework. Partly as a result of the discovery of this paper, it is now generally acknowledged that Hymer is *the* pioneer of the economic theory of the multinational company (Horaguchi and Toyne, 1990). It is significant that John Dunning, commenting on the early theoretical work on TNCs, has recently remarked that 'considering Hymer's work as a whole, he has probably come nearest to identifying the ingredients of a general theory' (Dunning, 1996: 33).

Controversy over which type of market failure (transactional or structural) underpins the TNC has clearly subsided and most scholars of the TNC would now view that debate as sterile. Buckley (1990: 658) has summed up the issue succinctly: 'the internalisation and the market power explanations of the [TNC] should not be viewed as mutually exclusive or competing theories but should be combined to give a full and rich explanation of the growth of multinational firms'.

A key issue in current debates on the TNC is whether market failure *per se*, and irrespective of its forms, is necessarily as pivotal a concept as has hitherto been supposed. Kogut and Zander (1993), in particular, question whether market failure and hence 'internalisation' is necessary to explain the TNC. This view is highly pertinent to any re-assessment of Hymer's contribution, as market failures were central to Hymer's analyses of the TNC.

Hymer's thesis (1976) incorporated two explanations of what he called 'international operations'. One emphasised the possession of advantages by firms and the other the removal of conflict between them. Both explanations were heavily premised on the prevalence of structural market failures. For a number of reasons – some of which were discussed in Yamin (1991) – during the 1970s and 1980s, the advantage explanation proved highly influential while the removal of conflict explanation was virtually ignored. In Yamin (1991) it was argued that the latter explanation was likely to be the more enduring aspect of Hymer's contribution. As explained below, in the section entitled 'Removal of conflict', subsequent developments seem to have confirmed that expectation. This is not to argue, however, that this aspect of Hymer's analyses did not suffer from any weaknesses or that it can be applied without any major alteration to current issues or problems in the world economy. On the contrary, this chapter argues that *both* aspects of Hymer's contribution suffer from an over-reliance on the concept of market failure. However, this is more acute in the case of the advantage explanation.

The section that follows provides a brief review of Hymer's overall contribution (for a more detailed exposition, see Yamin 1991). It explains the fundamental aspects of Hymer's contribution: namely, that the exercise of control is the defining feature of direct foreign investment (DFI) and that the need for control arises from market failure.

The subsequent section, 'A critical evaluation of the advantage theory', sets out two related arguments. First, we argue that Hymer's concept of advantage is too narrow: it focuses only on proprietary assets that are tradable and, as a consequence, fails to provide an adequate explanation of a firm's ability to operate in foreign countries. Second, we argue that, as in internalisation theory, Hymer implicitly views the firm as arising *only* in response to market failure. As a consequence, he fails to appreciate that 'control' – the key difference between portfolio capital flows and international operations such as DFI – not only may be due to market failure but may also arise to facilitate the transfer of the advantage across borders. In other words, 'control' may simply be a manifestation of organisational 'replication' – the expansion of the organisation across borders.

Three points are stressed in the subsequent section 'Removal of conflict'. First, this is a general explanation which does not rely on the possession of specific assets. Oligopolistic interdependence and rivalry are clearly important drivers of international operations, even in the absence of transactions involving firm-specific advantages. Game theoretic analyses have reinforced and formalised Hymer's insights in this respect. Second, we argue that, as oligopoly structures become more international and as oligopolists adopt new forms of relationships and alliances, Hymer's removal of conflict framework remains relevant but in a modified form. Third, the downside of Hymer's framework is its *exclusive* reliance on *oligopolistic* interdependence. Due to ever-increasing integration and globalisation in the world economy, the barriers to international operations have now fallen significantly. Consequently, transnationality is no longer the exclusive preserve of large and powerful oligopolists. This does not necessarily invalidate the removal of conflict framework. It does, however, suggest that the framework needs to be adapted to incorporate a broader rationale for interdependence between firms, such as that provided by Richardson (1960).

The final section of this chapter sets out a number of concluding remarks.

A review of Hymer's contribution: market imperfections and the need to exercise control

The fundamental contribution of Hymer's thesis can be summarised in two inter-related statements. First, DFI cannot be explained as inter-country flows of 'capital' responding to interest rate differences. Second, in order to explain DFI, it is necessary to explain why firms find it profitable to *control* firms in other countries. The problem with interest rate differential theory was precisely that it could not accommodate the significance of control. The importance of the concept of control in Hymer's thinking about DFI and the TNC cannot be overstated. Hymer regarded DFI as one form of what he called 'international operations', by which he meant the various ways (full or partial equity ownership, licensing, formal cartels or tacit collusion) in which firms of one nationality can control the decision-making of another (Hymer 1976: 32).[1] Movements of capital associated with DFI were thus not a response to higher interest rates in 'host' countries but took place in order to finance international operations. In order to explain DFI it was necessary, therefore, to explain control. The exercise of control, in turn, was strictly linked with the prevalence of market failure. Hymer identified two reasons for control, one relating to the firm's exploitation of advantages and the other based on the removal of conflict between firms. Both explanations for control rely exclusively on market failure.

So far as the advantage explanation is concerned, Hymer argued that whilst the possession of an advantage is a sufficient condition for international operations, it is not a necessary one. In the absence of some sort of failure in the market for the advantage, there will be no gains from controlling the firm wishing to 'buy' the advantage and, hence, international operations will not take place. An arm's-length market transaction would enable the firm with the advantage to utilise it in other markets without incurring a profit penalty.

Hymer observed that 'if a firm of one country possesses an advantage over firms of all other countries in a certain line of activity, that does not necessarily mean that the firm will have its own enterprises in foreign countries' (1976: 47). In particular, it would be necessary to explain why a firm would choose to use the advantage itself instead of licensing it. His answer was that 'decentralised decision making – the free market – is defective when there are certain types of interactions between the firms; that is if each firm's behaviour noticeably affects the other firms' (p. 48). Thus, the main reason for preferring DFI to licensing was that the market for the advantage was typically one where there were only a few buyers of the advantage in foreign countries; DFI would remove oligopolistic competition and increase joint profits. In addition, the fact that there may be 'a conflict of evaluation' with regard to the worth of the advantage would create difficulties in setting up a licensing agreement. Finally, a contractual arrange-ment such as licensing may fail effectively to protect the property rights of the licensor: 'a reluctance to license may arise from the inherent danger of losing the advantage' (p. 51).

The removal of conflict reason for control also relied on market failure. Hymer pointed out that enterprises are frequently connected to each other through markets across national boundaries. They compete by selling in the same markets or one firm may sell to another. In such a situation profits may be increased if one firm controls all the enterprises rather than having separate firms in each country. In other words, it is profitable to substitute centralised decision-making for decentralised decision-making. Whether this takes place will depend on whether markets are perfect. In particular, if there is duopolistic or oligopolistic interdependence between the firms involved in horizontal relationships, some form of collusion will increase joint profits, and once again integration or merger is possibly the most effective form of collusion. However, if there are many firms, or if entry is easy, then there is not much point in trying to control the market and international operations will not take place. A similar analysis will apply if the interdependence between firms is vertical. Again, as long as there are only a few buyers and sellers, integration or any other effective form of cooperation between the firms will increase joint profits. In neither the horizontal nor the vertical case is it necessary for one of the firms to possess an advantage over the others, although they are likely to be leading members of their respective national oligopolies. The only consideration is whether the increased profits from cooperation/collusion are more than sufficient to offset the costs of international operations. The important point is that international operation is no longer synonymous with the exploitation of some form of firm-specific asset under the firm's own control.

A critical evaluation of the advantage theory

The nature of advantages: some ambiguities in Hymer's analysis

Hymer was strongly influenced by Bain's analysis of the advantages of incumbent firms as compared to new entrants in industries with significant barriers to entry. But he was interested in barriers to entry 'not as they apply to new firms but as they apply to firms *of a different nationality*' (Hymer, 1976: 42–43, emphasis added). As such, however, advantages could stem from location or nationality rather than reflect skills or capabilities unique to an individual firm. For example, Hymer observed that American firms would have easier access to the US capital market compared to their foreign rivals. Similarly, skilled American workers might be willing to work for the subsidiary of an American company but not for locally owned firms in a foreign country. More generally, foreign firms will not have the same access as American firms to the general fund of skill and ability available in abundance in the USA. In Dunning's parlance, such advantages are source-country 'locational advantages'; they are not 'ownership' advantages if that is meant to describe skills or capabilities unique to a particular firm.

Hymer's rather brief and rudimentary treatment of the nature and the kind of advantages needed to support international operations betrays a confusion between locational and ownership categories. His narrative suggests that he viewed advantages as possessing the attributes of an 'item of property' –

something that, potentially at least, could be bought and sold. In fact, his analysis of the choice between licensing and DFI requires the assumption that advantages are potentially sellable assets. He was inclined to the view that such assets would normally not be traded in the market as these were highly imperfect. However, the possibility that some advantages may be inherently non-tradable was not considered. This creates an inconsistency in relation to his own description of the sources of a firm's advantage. As we have seen, some advantages mentioned by Hymer are locational in nature and it is rather problematic to treat them as items of property as, by definition, they are enjoyed by *all* firms of a given nationality (e.g. American) over firms of other nationalities.

More importantly, setting aside Hymer's confusion between locational and ownership advantages, it is doubtful whether all, or even most, ownership advantages can be treated as sellable assets. In the barriers-to-entry framework, which was the key influence on Hymer, only *some* aspects of the 'absolute-cost' and 'product differentiation' categories of entry barriers can be viewed as 'items of property', of which patents, trademarks and brand names are the main examples of sellable or tradable assets that come to mind. Presumably, Hymer would argue that tradability of ownership advantages is a matter of degree. Some, such as patents and trademarks, would be more tradable (involving, *inter alia*, a lower degree of 'conflict of evaluation') compared to a non-codified asset such as 'know-how'. However, this still leaves open the question of how a non-codified asset can be traded at all and, more importantly, *why* some assets are non-codified. Hymer does not seem to have appreciated the significance of the difference between tradable assets and non-tradable skills and capabilities; he frequently referred loosely to a firm 'selling' its skills and advantages (pp. 47, 49). We develop this point more fully below.

A firm's ability to overcome the costs of international operations is significantly strengthened by combining its tradable assets with its non-tradable skills. In fact, some authors have suggested that tradable and non-tradable elements are strictly complementary (Cantwell, 1995). In Hymer's analysis, international operations appear to be narrowly restricted to the various forms in which tradable assets or advantages are exploited across borders, where what is traded is essentially the legal right to use an asset. But legal access is not always tantamount to obtaining the capability of using the asset in a production system unless the 'buying' enterprise can also gain access to the non-tradable skills or combine the traded asset with its own know-how. At least in the context of less developed countries, where domestic enterprises may lack such skills, the advantage of foreign investors may reside more in their non-tradable skills than in their tradable assets (Davies, 1977).

Explaining the boundaries of the firm: organisational replication versus control

Hymer unambiguously adopted the view that 'the firm is a practical institutional device which substitutes for the market. The firm internalises or supersedes the market' (p. 48).[2] This view assumes that the function of the firm is merely to coordinate a set of activities that could in principal be coordinated by the market. In Hymer's words: '"the firm" is a *particular form* of relating various activities in the economy' (p. 68, emphasis added).

From this perspective, the main question in the theory of international operations is how 'the various relationships between enterprises in one country and enterprises of another' should be organised – through the market or through centralised control exercised by the firm possessing the advantage. In this analysis, control plays only *one* role, namely, to resolve the potential conflict in the distribution of benefits in favour of the investing firm. Hymer assumes, implicitly, that the object of an inter-firm transaction (that is, the physical transfer of an advantage from firm 1 in country A to firm 2 in country B) is itself a technically trivial issue. However, the transfer issue is trivial only if the firm's advantages have the property of a public good. Although there is no explicit reference to this in Hymer's thesis, a public good assumption is strongly implied by his analysis, in the absence of which there would be an analytical difficulty. Thus, given the extra costs of operating in foreign countries, the firm may not enjoy a net cost or revenue differential over its domestic rivals, if its advantages cannot be deployed at zero or a low marginal cost in the host country.

As we noted in the previous section, however, the advantages that underlie international operations, particularly through DFI, cannot be fully described in terms of tradable assets. Thus, for example, although a patent itself is a tradable asset, the complementary skills and knowledge associated with it are not. There are normally elements in such knowledge that are 'firm specific' in the sense that the relevant knowledge or skill cannot be *fully detached* from the firm and be traded separately. Dunning (1993: 81) provides a fairly comprehensive list of 'owner-ship' advantages. Included in the category of asset ownership advantages are the 'resource structure of the firm', 'organisational and marketing systems', 'innova-tory capacity', 'organisation of work and a bank of human capital experience'. While these are all assets in the sense of being capable of generating an income stream, none can meaningfully be regarded as 'items of property'.[3] It follows, *a fortiori*, that these aspects of a firm's knowledge cannot be treated as a public good if that is meant to imply that they can be transferred to another organisation at a low, let alone a zero, marginal cost. Teece (1977), in a seminal contribution, provided convincing evidence that technology, which is often considered to be the key monopolistic advantage held by TNCs, is far from being a public good. He showed that there were significant costs associated with technology transfer. These costs mainly arose from the difficulties involved in conveying and obtaining knowledge across organisational boundaries.[4] But transfer costs are not obviously increased by transaction costs (such as legal costs or the dissipation of technology) (see also Kogut and Zander, 1993).[5]

If we conceive of advantages as including firm-specific elements rather than as purely tradable assets, then we must allow a role for 'control' in facilitating the transfer process of firm-specific knowledge. Transfer costs analytically, if not practically, arise prior to 'transaction costs'. If the firm's advantages are deeply embedded within its internal structures and thus totally undetachable, then inter-firm transaction of these advantages is impossible and only through internal transfers via DFI can they be exploited in another country.

More generally, 'control' of the transferee by the transferor may be a technical necessity without which transfer may be either impossible or more costly. The function of control would not be to circumvent bilateral interdependence, to protect against opportunistic behaviour or to resolve the conflict of evaluation with regard to the worth of an advantage. Even if these problems were somehow to be resolved, the actual transfer of individual skills and routines (the organisational equivalent of skills; see Nelson and Winter, 1982) across a firm's boundaries would remain a task that is far from trivial. The fact that internal transfers, which by definition do not involve an exchange of ownership and hence do not incur costs associated with protecting property rights, are also costly indicates the relevance of 'transfer costs' as an independent category *vis-à-vis* 'transaction costs'.

There is good reason, however, to expect that external transfers may incur a higher marginal cost compared to internal transfers, even controlling for trans-action costs. The reason why internal transfers may incur a lower cost is rooted in the heterogeneity of firms. The notion of firm heterogeneity was first fully articulated by Penrose (1959) and is now central to the resource-based theories of the firm (Foss, 1997). In these theories, what is distinctive about firms is that their internal capabilities – the things they know how to do – cannot be readily assembled through the market; the firm is 'a domain for organising activities in a non-market-like fashion' (Teece *et. al.*, 1997: 269; see also Kogut and Zander, 1997). In this sense, each firm is unique as it generates a differentiated set of capabilities and hence advantages. Unless firms make a conscious effort to codify their knowledge, in order perhaps to facilitate its transfer to other firms, much of what they know will be uncodified to other firms simply because the internal codes by which knowledge is transmitted and transformed within firms are different.

Thus transfer may take place within the firm (through DFI), not, as Hymer would argue, because it is necessary to control the 'other' (in this case, notional) party to the transaction. Rather, internal transfer may be *dictated* by particular characteristics of the advantage (such as, for example, its lack of codifiability). DFI is a particular form of 'organisational replication' (Nelson and Winter, 1982). By definition, this is a process through which an organisation enacts its *existing* routines and standard operating procedures in a new productive entity. For this reason, organisational replication is an effective conduit for the transfer of firm-specific knowledge across borders.[6] By contrast, when knowledge has to be transferred across firms, which, inevitably, have diverse routines and operating procedures, the effectiveness of the transfer suffers.[7] Interestingly, Nelson and Winter note that 'the replication assumption in evolutionary models is intended primarily to reflect the advantages that favour a going concern to do more of the *same* as contrasted with the difficulties that it would encounter in doing something else' (1982: 119, original emphasis). Thus when technology is transferred across the boundaries of different firms, both parties, to an extent, are encountering 'something else' – that is, the unfamiliar and poorly understood work practices of the other party. This creates a difficulty that internal expansion can avoid.

Removal of conflict: its relevance and its limitations

The logic of the removal of conflict explanation

Hymer's logic in relation to the removal of conflict explanation for international operations was straightforward. Firms in particular industries that encounter one another in markets across national boundaries are likely to be few in number. This is because there are significant barriers to cross-border business and only the largest and most powerful firms are likely to have the resources to overcome them. Inevitably, cross-border contact meant oligopolistic or even duopolistic interdependence. Whether and how such interdependence was resolved would determine the pattern and form of international operations. For example, if firms are able to collude effectively, they may arrive at a market-sharing agreement. Accordingly, each firm may be allotted a market in which it can invest without competition from the other firm(s). Alternatively, the colluding firms may set up joint ventures in a number of markets. On the other hand, if collusion fails, there may be competitive investments in all markets.

Hymer's analysis was informal and he illustrated these possible scenarios through two case studies. One, which he took from Dunning's early study of American investment in Britain (Dunning, 1958), was the tobacco industry. The case explained the development, after an initial period of cut-throat competition, of a market-sharing agreement according to which Imperial Tobacco obtained a monopoly in Britain and Ireland, while the US and dependent markets were to be supplied by American Tobacco. The other and contrasting example was the meat-packing industry. Both American and British firms had established meat-packing plants in Latin American countries. Bitter competition ensued, but, unlike the tobacco case, there was no successful resolution of the conflict. Both sets of firms continued to operate independently in Latin American markets.

The important feature of Hymer's insight is that the removal of conflict explanation does not require the possession of advantage by one member of the oligopoly group *vis-à-vis* others. Thus, whilst his advantage explanation was premised on the assumption that 'firms are unequal in their ability to operate in a particular industry', the removal of conflict explanation assumed, implicitly, that the firms in question would possess roughly comparable resources and capabilities. He clearly envisaged that they would be leading members of national oligopolies (we return to this issue below).

Hymer's analysis, though informal, showed that the existence of oligopolistic interdependence between firms across markets created a process of dynamic interaction which could, by itself, generate various patterns of international operations – an insight that has been confirmed by more formal game theoretic analyses. As examples, Dixit and Kyle (1986) show that strategic interdependence between firms in two countries can result in cross-investments even when this may not be the optimal solution for either, while Hargreaves-Heap and Hughes (1990) show how multinationality may be used in the presence of strategic uncertainty to gain advantage in an oligopoly game (see also Hughes and Oughton, 1992). In a somewhat more comprehensive formal treatment, Graham (1998) shows that, in an oligopolistic setting, possessing an advantage (in the form of being a lower-cost producer) over rivals is neither a necessary nor a sufficient incentive for a firm to become a TNC.

Removal of conflict in international oligopolies

It is undoubtedly the case that, compared to the 1960s and 1970s, oligopolistic interdependence is now increasingly between firms of different nationalities. Vernon (1974, cited in Frischtak and Newfarmer, 1994: 7) noted that 'concepts of oligopoly . . . behaviour, which heretofore have been treated within a single national market, must be applied in an international setting.' But as Frischtak and Newfarmer (1994: 7) observe, 'nearly two decades later, this insight is still understudied'. It is a testimony to the enduring character of Hymer's work that he coauthored the first and (to our knowledge) still the only empirical analysis of international oligopoly (Hymer and Rowthorn, 1970).

Oligopolists are likely to have a less clear understanding of the strategies and capabilities of rivals from other nationalities compared to their domestic rivals. Furthermore, as Kogut (1987, cited in Chesnais, 1995: 87) has observed, a mature oligopoly is itself an organisation regulated by fairly stable routines. These routines 'reflect national traits regarding anti-trust regulations, government interventions and the tolerance of competitive or co-operative behaviour' (ibid.). Such routines are likely to be absent or less well established in an international oligopoly. These factors suggest that implicit understanding and collusion are more difficult to arrive at in an international oligopoly, at least at the early stages of industry internationalisation. Consistent with this line of reasoning, in their analysis of rivalry between European and US companies in the 1960s, Hymer and Rowthorn (1970) argued that both European and US corporations were myopic in their assessments of competitors across the Atlantic and, as a result, tended to underestimate their own relative strength.

Hymer and Rowthorn viewed international competition largely in terms of the thrusts and counter-thrusts of US and European corporations who used 'direct foreign investment as one of their chief instruments' for competition over shares in the world market (Hymer and Rowthorn, 1970: 57). However in at least three important and inter-related respects, this scenario is of receding relevance. First, clearly, the key players in international oligopolies are no longer only American and European firms. Second, rivals from relatively new and emerging centres of competition, such as Japan and East Asia generally, have developed organisational competencies that have undermined existing, primarily transatlantic, oligopolistic structures (Chesnais, 1995).[8] Third, and more importantly, as such competencies have become appreciated and valued by the longer established oligopolists, they have sought to gain access to such competencies and even to internalise them. Consequently, TNCs have increasingly adopted new types of relationships and alliances with their rivals. DFI, the traditionally favoured form of international operation, is not necessarily suitable under such circumstances. DFI is an effective instrument for market-seeking investments but not for gaining new competencies.

The emergence of alliance relationships does not mean that the tension between collusion and rivalry, which characterises traditional oligopolies, has somehow disappeared. In fact, the reverse is the case: the tension is intensified as the interdependence now occurs in a more complex organisational context. Whereas in a traditional oligopoly it was market shares that were mainly at risk, in the context of new relationships and alliances what may be at stake is the firm's core competencies and the risk of their dissipation to a rival. As research by Hagedoorn (1993: 373) has shown, in many alliances 'joint activities may be a cover-up for an attempt to quickly absorb some innovative capabilities from others'. However, the option of avoiding alliance entanglements is restricted for two reasons. First, firms often lack the full range of capabilities for remaining competitive, and, second, market-based transactions for obtaining complementary skills and capabilities are often not feasible (Yamin, 1996). Consequently, for many TNCs the handling of inter-firm relationships in the form of various types of alliances has become a central strategic concern; the key task would seem to be the successful management of the complex mixture of competitive and cooperative dimensions inherent in alliances. As Hamel (1991) argues, alliances should be viewed as a framework for competition between the partners over the acquisition and internalisation of competencies. Thus, alliance management does indeed appear to be a form of 'removal of conflict' but in a somewhat different context compared to that envisaged by Hymer. The fact that alliances, particularly joint-venture alliances, are frequently terminated through acquisition (of the venture) by one of the parties (see for example Kogut, 1989) does lend credence to a removal-of-conflict interpretation of alliance dynamics.

Limitations of the removal-of-conflict explanation

As we have already noted, Hymer's removal-of-conflict explanation was premised on there being significant barriers to international operations. Hymer regarded international operations as the province of only large and powerful oligopolists. Such a view is no longer sustainable because, owing to ever increasing integration in the world economy, the costs of international operations have fallen dramatically. The number of TNCs is simply too large to be consistent with the view that only the largest firms can become transnationals (UNCTAD, 1997). The participation of small and medium-sized firms from developed economies and of firms from less developed countries casts doubts on the advantage explanation and also undermines the view that all TNCs necessarily operate in an oligopolistic environment.

From a theoretical standpoint, Hymer's exclusive reliance on oligopolistic interdependence, with the implication that in a more 'atomistic' structure inter-firm dependencies would be non-existent, is not justified. As Richardson (1960) has shown, in a large group or 'atomistic' setting an individual firm's investment plan would be indeterminate unless information about investment intentions of the rest of the group were somehow to be made available. As Richardson has argued, the often dense network of relations and co-operation between firms within and across industries is partly a consequence of *informational interdependence*. Interestingly, such networks can help explain the process of internationalisation of small firms from certain countries. For example, Chen and Chen (1998: 447) argue that Taiwanese firms become TNCs primarily through exploiting network linkages rather than firm-specific advantages. Furthermore, alliances between large oligopolistic firms are frequently part of a more complex network involving a great number of firms, many of whom are small firms providing technological specialisms lacked by the larger firms (Hagedoorn and Schakenraad, 1990, 1992). Even though large firms tend to have dominant nodal positions within such networks, it is unlikely that the emergence of the network itself can be explained simply in terms of oligopolistic interdependence.

Concluding comments

The conclusions of this chapter are somewhat similar to those in Yamin (1991), inasmuch as it has been shown that Hymer's removal-of-conflict explanation for international operations has withstood the test of time much better than his advantage explanation.

It is usual to categorise Hymer's contribution to the theory of DFI and the TNC as an 'industrial organisation' rather than a 'firm' explanation of these phenomena. This is not entirely accurate, particularly in relation to Hymer's advantage expla-nation. This chapter has hopefully demonstrated that the advantage explanation was largely cast within a particular view of the firm. Hymer's analytical portrayal of the firm was rather innovative at the time in that he viewed the firm as an instrument for internalising or superseding the market.

In retrospect, it can be seen, partly as a result of this view of the firm, that Hymer treated advantages in a rather narrow way as assets that are potentially tradable. We have argued that this is, at best, a weak basis for international operations. It is more accurate to categorise the removal-of-conflict framework as an 'industrial organisation' explanation. Hymer's principal insight that oligopo-lisitic interaction between firms can result in international operations and the TNC has received strong theoretical support. Nevertheless, even this aspect of Hymer's analysis requires updating in at least two respects. First, removal of conflict as a process occurs not only in battles over market share, which is how Hymer envisaged it, but also in the context of rather variegated and complex forms of organisational partnerships and alliances. Whereas battles over market share are essentially zero-sum games, competition within alliances has the potential to be a positive-sum game. Second, the oligopoly framework cannot explain either the full extent of participation in international operations or the full range of cross-border, inter-firm linkages observed in many industries.

Acknowledgements

I am grateful to Fred Burton, Mats Forsgren and to Christos Pitelis for comments on an earlier version of this paper.

Notes

1 As Hymer (1976: 1) noted, 'control is not an easy thing to define and the dividing line between some control and no control is arbitrary'.
2 Thus there are some similarities between Hymer's analysis and internalisation theory. There are also significant differences. In particular, Buckley and Casson (1976) stress the internalisation of intermediate markets (e.g. technology) whereas Hymer is mainly concerned with the internalisation of the final market (for the advantage).
3 See also Winter (1987), who provides an analytical distinction between an asset as a 'single item of property' and an asset as a 'useful thing or quality'. Significantly he points out 'it is decidedly problematic as to whether the realities denoted by knowledge, competence, skills, know-how or capability are the sort of thing that can be adequately discussed as an item of property' (p. 160).
4 Out of 26 transfer projects included in Teece's study, 12 were wholly owned subsidiaries (1977: 243). In these cases knowledge was transferred across organisational boundaries but within the same firm.
5 By 'transfer costs', we mean the opportunity cost of the time and effort spent by technical and managerial staff of the transferring and receiving organisations in explaining and understanding know-how and of utilising it in the production process of the receiving organisation.
6 Although Nelson and Winter consider 'perfect' replication to be a theoretical possibility, they nevertheless view the 'feasibility of close (let alone perfect) replication as being quite problematic' (1982: 118). Thus, replication is practically always partial. This is particularly likely when organisational replication takes place across borders. Note, however, that organisation replication may still be superior to an inter-firm transaction as a knowledge transfer mode.
7 It is relevant that where DFI takes place through acquisition, a number of difficulties are usually encountered in the incorporation of acquired companies into multinationals (Jemison and Sitkin, 1986; Rosenzweig and Singh, 1991). However, it is also relevant that when DFI takes place through mergers or acquisitions, its main purpose is not necessarily the transfer of technology: rather, the motivation is likely to be strategic asset-seeking (Caves, 1998; Jaideep and Kogut, 1997).
8 Such new competencies also imply an advantage explanation for international operations by newly emerging rivals. Thus new organisational skills probably compensated them for relative technological backwardness and enabled them to compete not only with domestic firms in host countries but also with the more established TNCs.

References

Buckley, P. (1990) 'Problems and Developments in the Core Theory of International Business', *Journal of International Business Studies*, 21, 4: 657–65.

Buckley, P. and M. Casson (1976) *The Future of the Multinational Enterprise*, London: Macmillan.

Cantwell, J. (1995) 'Multinational Corporations and Innovative Activities' in J. Molero (ed.) *Technological Innovation, Multinational Corporations and New International Competitiveness: The Case of Intermediate Countries*, Harwood Academic Publishers.

Casson, M. (1987) *The Firm and the Market: Studies in Multinational Enterprise and the Scope of the Firm*, Oxford: Blackwell.

Caves, R. (1998) 'Research on International Business: Problems and Prospects', *Journal of International Business Studies*, 29, 1: 5–19.

Chen, H. and T-J. Chen (1998) 'Network Linkages and Location Choice in Foreign Direct Investment', *Journal of International Business Studies*, 29, 3: 445–67.

Chesnais, F. (1995) 'World Oligopoly, Rivalry between "Global" Firms and Global Corporate Competitiveness' in J. Molero (ed.) *Technological Innovation, Multinational Corporations and New International Competitiveness: The Case of Intermediate Countries*. Harwood Academic Publishers.

Davies, H. (1977) 'Technology Transfer Through Commercial Transactions', *Journal of Industrial Economics*, XXVI, 2: 161–75.

Dixit, A. and A. Kyle, (1986) 'The Use of Protection and Subsidies for Entry Promotion and Deterrence', *American Economic Review*, 75.

Dunning, J. (1958) *American Investment in British Manufacturing Industry*, London: Allen & Unwin.

—— (1993) *Multinational Enterprise and the Global Economy*. Wokingham: Addison Wesley.

—— (1996) 'The Nature of Transnational Corporations and Their Activities' in J. Dunning (ed.) *Transnational Corporations and World Development*. London: International Thomson Business Press.

Dunning, J. and A. Rugman (1985) 'The influence of Hymer's Dissertation on the Theory of Foreign Direct Investment', *American Economic Review*, May.

Foss, N. (ed.) (1997) *Resources, Firms and Strategies: A Reader in the Resource-Based Perspective*, Oxford: Oxford University Press.

Frischtak, C. and S. Newfarmer (1994) 'Introduction: Market Structure and Industrial Performance' in C. Frischtak and S. Newfarmer (eds) *Transnational Corporations: Market Structure and Industrial Performance*, United Nations Library on Transnational Corporations vol. 15, London: Routledge.

Graham, M. (1998) 'Market structure and the Multinational Enterprise', *Journal of International Business Studies*, 29, 1: 67–83.

Hagedoorn, J. (1993) 'Understanding the Rationale of Strategic Technology Partnering: Inter-organisational Modes of Co-operation and Sectoral Differences', *Strategic Management Journal*, 14, 3: 371–85.

Hagedoorn, J. and J. Schakenraad (1990) 'Inter-firm Partnerships and Cooperative Strategies in Core Technologies' in C. Freeman and L. Soete (eds) *Explorations in the Economics of Technological Change*, London: Frances Pinter.

—— (1992) 'Leading Companies and Networks of Strategic Alliances in Information Technologies', *Research Policy*, 22: 163–90.

Hamel, G. (1991) 'Competition for Competence and Inter-Partner Learning Within International Strategic Alliances', *Strategic Management Journal*, 12: 83–103.

Hargreaves-Heap, S. and K. Hughes (1990) 'Strategic Uncertainty and Multinationality', *Economic Notes*, 3, 2: 417–28.

Horaguchi, H. and B. Toyne (1990) 'Setting the Record Straight: Hymer, Internalisation Theory and Transaction Cost Economics', *Journal of International Business Studies*, 21, 3: 487–94.

Hughes, K. and C. Oughton (1992) 'Foreign and Domestic Multinational Presence in the UK', *Applied Economics*, 24, July.

Hymer, S. (1968) 'The large Multinational "Corporation": An Analysis of Some Motives for International Integration of Business', *Revue Economique* 6, translated from the French by Nathalie Vacherot with an introduction by Mark Casson.

—— (1976) *The International Operations of National Firms: a Study of Foreign Direct Investment*, Cambridge, Mass.: MIT Press.

Hymer, S. and R. Rowthorn (1970) 'The Multinational Corporation and International Oligopoly', in C. Kindleberger (ed.) *The International Corporation*, Cambridge, Mass.: MIT Press.

Jaideep, A. and B. Kogut (1997) 'Technological Capabilities of Countries, Firm Rivalry and Foreign Direct Investment', *Journal of International Business Studies*, 28, 3: 445–65.

Jemison, D. and S. Sitkin (1986) 'Corporate Acquisitions: A Process Perspective', *Academy of Management Review*, 11: 145–63.

Kogut, B. (1989) 'The Stability of Joint Ventures: Reciprocity and Competitive Rivalry', *Journal of Industrial Economics*, 37: 183–98.

Kogut, B. and U. Zander (1993) 'Knowledge of the Firm and The Evolutionary Theory of the Multinational Corporation', *Journal of International Business Studies*, 24, 4, 625–45.

—— (1997) 'Knowledge of the Firm, Combinative Capabilities and the Replication of Technology', in N. Foss (ed.) *Resources, Firms and Strategies, A Reader in the Resource-Based Perspective*, Oxford: Oxford University Press.

Nelson, R. and S. Winter, (1982) *An Evolutionary Theory of Economic Change*, Cambridge, Mass.: Harvard University Press.

Olie, R. (1994) 'Shades of Culture and Institutions in International Mergers,' *Organisation Studies*, 15, 3.

Penrose, E. (1959) *The Theory of the Growth of the Firm*, Oxford: Oxford University Press.

Richardson, G. (1960) *Information and Investment: A Study in the Working of the Competitive Economy*, Oxford: Clarendon Press.

Rosenzweig, P. and Singh, J. (1991) 'Organisational Environments and the Multinational Enterprise', *Academy of Management Review*, 16, 2: 340–61.

Teece, D. (1977) 'Technology Transfer by Multinational Firms: The Resource Costs of Transferring Technological Know-How', *Economic Journal*, 87: 242–61.

Teece, D., G. Pisano and A. Shuen (1997) 'Dynamic Capabilities and Strategic Management' in N. Foss (ed.) *Resources, Firms and Strategies: A Reader in the Resource-Based Perspective*, Oxford: Oxford University Press.

United Nations Conference on Trade and Development (UNCTAD) (1997) *World Investment Report 1997: Transnational Corporations, Market Structure and Competition Policy*, Geneva: United Nations.

Winter, S. (1987) 'Knowledge and Competence as Strategic Assets' in D. Teece (ed.) *The Competitive Challenge: Strategies for Industrial Innovation and Renewal*, Cambridge, Mass.: Ballinger.

Yamin, M. (1991) 'A Reassessment of Hymer's Contribution to the Theory of the

Transnational Corporation' in C. Pitelis and R. Sugden (eds) *The Nature of the Transnational Firm*, London: Routledge.

—— (1996) 'Understanding "Strategic Alliances": The Limits of Transaction Cost Economics' in R. Coombs, A. Richards, P. Saviotti, and V. Walsh, (eds) *Technological Collaborations: The Dynamics of Cooperation in Industrial Innovation*. Cheltenham: Edward Elgar, 165–79.

4 Transaction costs theory and the multinational enterprise

Jean-François Hennart

This chapter critically reviews what many scholars (e.g. Caves, 1996, 1998) see as the dominant explanation for the multinational enterprise (MNE), the transaction costs approach.[1] An MNE is fundamentally an organization that extends employment contracts over national boundaries. In other words, the distinguishing characteristics of MNEs are their use of hierarchical methods of coordination (managerial directives) to organize cross-national interdependencies. Market prices are another method of organizing international interdependencies. To understand why MNEs exist, one must therefore explain why individuals located in separate countries are more efficiently coordinated when they are employees of an MNE than if they are independent entrepreneurs responding to market prices. This chapter argues that transaction costs theory provides the best and more parsimonious explanation of why this is the case, and hence the best reason for the existence and development of MNEs.

This chapter does not pretend to be an exhaustive survey of the literature on the transaction costs approach to international business. Rather it shows how transaction costs theory can provide a unifying paradigm to explain the most common forms taken by the expansion of firms across national boundaries. Owing to space limitations, not all applications of transaction costs theory to the MNE are covered, and the analysis focuses mostly on statics. After a brief outline of the transaction costs model, I show how it can account for the main motives behind the international expansion of firms. I then explain how some of the unconventional trade practices used by developing countries are second-best strategies used in response to government limitations on the expansion of MNEs. The third section shows how transaction costs theory can throw light on two of the main choices faced by MNEs entering foreign markets. The conclusion outlines the differences between the approach taken here and some of the other explanations of the MNE.

It is important at the outset to explain the differences between two distinct, yet related, phenomena. An MNE is a firm that has employees abroad. When it finances its activities abroad with funds obtained from its home country, it undertakes foreign direct investment (FDI). FDI is a country's export and import of long-term capital into investments controlled by its residents (as opposed to portfolio investments), as recorded in the capital account of its balance of payments. There is no one-to-one correlation between the expansion of firms across national boundaries (the growth of MNEs) and flows of FDI, since MNEs can (and do) obtain the funds necessary for their foreign expansion from the foreign country where they invest.[2] FDI is therefore a rather poor indicator of the growth of MNEs.

Transaction costs as a general theory of the MNE

In a chapter in *Multinational Enterprise in Historical Perspective*, D.K. Fieldhouse writes that

> Historical research has shown that the tidy logic of growth of firms theory, the main intellectual foundation for the concept of the MNC [multinational corporation], simply does not fit the unruly variety of corporate motivation. It is critical that most early theorizing was based on recent American experience, mainly in manufacturing and petroleum, and even this was not uniform. Still more variable were the historical reasons for US and European investment in overseas mining, plantations, and utilities. In none of these last did FDI commonly or necessarily flow from the growth patterns of metropolitan firms. In many of them capitalists established new corporate enterprises without a previous home base, specifically to produce a commodity which could only be obtained elsewhere, or to exploit an evident overseas need for public services, such as railways or telecommunications in Latin America. Motives for FDI were therefore infinitely more complex than any unitary theory of the MNC could possibly comprehend, and had no necessary connection with the internalization concept.
>
> (Fieldhouse, 1986: 25)

Are motives for the MNE so disparate that a general theory of the MNE cannot be constructed? This section demonstrates that transaction costs theory can in fact account for the wide variety of forms taken by the expansion of MNEs.

Structural and natural market imperfections

MNEs present a paradox. Operating overseas is usually more costly than operating at home, because a foreigner does not have the same contacts and knowledge of local customs and business practices as indigenous competitors, while being often subject to discrimination by host country governments and private institutions. Hence it is difficult to understand why firms based in one country would do business in another country. If a firm has some unique assets of value overseas, why not sell or rent these assets to local entrepreneurs, who could then combine them with local factors of production at lower costs than those experienced by foreign direct investors?

The answer to this paradox is that there might be circumstances under which using market exchange to coordinate the behavior of agents located in two separate countries is less efficient than organizing their interdependence within a multinational firm. When this is the case, a firm located in one country may find it profitable to incur the additional costs of operating in a foreign environment. This idea that MNEs owe their existence to "market imperfections" was first put forward by Hymer (1960, published 1976), Kindleberger (1969), and Caves (1971). The market imperfections they had in mind were, however, "structural" imperfections in markets for final products. Hymer, for example, considered two firms, each a final product monopolist in its own market, isolated from competition by high transportation costs and tariff and non-tariff barriers. A decline in these costs exposed them to each other's competition and reduced their profits. A combination of the two firms, through merger or acquisition, into an MNE would then maximize their joint income by forcing them to take into account the gains and the losses competition inflicts on them. The transformation of two domestic firms into one MNE thus internalized "pecuniary" externalities and produced a gain for the owners of these two firms, but not necessarily for society, since it redistributed income towards the MNE and away from its customers.

A similar case arose when the technology developed by firms based in one country was valuable abroad. That technology had often few substitutes and the number of potential licensees in any given foreign market was also often limited, thus creating a bilateral monopoly. The consolidation of licensor and licensee within an MNE (by acquisition or merger of the potential licensee or by vertical integration of the innovator into overseas manufacturing) reduced haggling and made it easier to enforce price discrimination schemes across countries (Hymer, 1976: 49–50). This analysis of the reasons behind the emergence of multi-national firms led Hymer to take a negative view of MNEs, which he considered "an instrument for restraining competition between firms of different nations" (Hymer, 1970: 443).

Hymer's world is one where market imperfections are structural, arising from structural deviations from perfect competition in the final product market due to exclusive and permanent control of proprietary technology, privileged access to inputs, scale economies, control of distribution systems, and product differentiation (Bain, 1956), but in their absence markets are perfectly efficient. By contrast, the insight of transaction costs theories of the MNE, simultaneously and independently developed in the 1970s by McManus (1972), Buckley and Casson (1976), Brown (1976), and Hennart (1977, 1982), is that "market imperfections" are inherent attributes of markets, and MNEs are institutions to bypass these imperfections. Markets experience "natural" imperfections, i.e. imperfections that are due to the fact that the implicit neoclassical assumptions of perfect knowledge and perfect enforcement are not realized (Dunning and Rugman, 1985; Teece 1981).

Market transaction costs

The dominant method of organization in markets is the price system. If knowledge were perfect and individuals perfectly honest, organizing interdependencies between individuals would be costless; in other words, transaction costs would be nil. The three tasks that must be performed by any system of organization – to inform individuals of the needs of others, to reward them for productive behavior, and to curb bargaining – would be costlessly performed by prices. Through prices everyone would be fully appraised of everyone else's needs, and incited to adapt to those needs so as to maximize social welfare. With a large number of buyers and sellers, prices would be exogenous, thus curbing bargaining. Prices would also reward agents in proportion to their output (measured at market prices): someone who takes the day off would see his income correspondingly reduced.

In practice, opportunism and bounded rationality make prices not fully efficient, and market transaction costs (the sum of information, enforcement, and bargaining costs) positive. This is because humans have "bounded rationality" and a tendency toward opportunism (Williamson, 1975). Bounded rationality means that humans do not have infinite intellectual abilities and are not perfectly knowledgeable. With bounded rationality, the value of the goods and services exchanged will never be perfectly measured; hence prices will provide flawed signals, and a price system will not maximize the social product. Agents will generate non-pecuniary externalities. Opportunism means that individuals cannot always be expected to take actions that increase the welfare of others at their own expense. Because of bounded rationality, transactors cannot always predict who will be opportunistic and who will not.[3] Positive measurement costs joined with opportunism will make it possible for individuals to cheat – i.e. given positive detection costs, they will be able to alter the terms of trade to their advantage within a given range without loss of revenue. Lastly, imperfect information will also segment the market, thus making prices endogenous, and bargaining profitable.

On the enforcement side, it is important to understand that the total costs of using prices to organize transactions are those of measuring outputs plus those of failing to do so, i.e. the level of cheating that can be expected from imperfect measurement. At some point the marginal benefit of spending an additional dollar to measure output will be less than the expected loss due to cheating, and further investment in measuring outputs will no longer make sense.

If it is very costly to measure the value of goods and services, and opportunities for bargaining and cheating are therefore high, it may pay to eliminate these opportunities by aligning the interests of the parties, i.e. by reducing the incentives they have to cheat. This can be achieved by breaking the connection between output and performance. The price system can be replaced by a mode of organization in which buyers and sellers no longer profit from their ability to cheat, but instead are rewarded for following the directives of a central party directing the exchange. These directives, which can better reflect the overall costs and benefits of the activity, will supersede flawed market prices. Such a system of organization is called hierarchy (Hennart, 1982, 1986c, 1993a, 1993b).

MNEs use hierarchy to eliminate market transaction costs. By transforming independent entrepreneurs into employees, they reduce their incentives to cheat. MNEs make it possible to organize some interactions which cannot be organized by prices, thus bringing gains of trade to the interacting parties and a net gain for society. Transaction cost scholars have shown, as we shall see below, that there are circumstances under which MNEs organize the international transfer of inputs more efficiently than markets. Hence while Hymer and Kindleberger see the MNE as a method of maximizing monopoly power, or, in other words, as a way of internalizing pecuniary externalities, for transaction costs theorists, MNEs arise to reduce transaction costs and internalize non-pecuniary externalities.

The distinction between pecuniary and non-pecuniary externalities is subtle but important. Pecuniary externalities arise from structural imperfections in markets for final products, while non-pecuniary externalities can be explained by natural market imperfections, i.e. imperfections in markets for intermediate products.

The benefits and costs of hierarchy

Some of the early attempts to explain MNEs have tended to suggest that the presence of transaction costs in international markets was a sufficient condition for the existence of MNEs. But if opportunism and bounded rationality reduce the efficiency of markets, they can also be expected to affect that of firms. Firms will experience positive organization costs that will have to be subtracted from the gains of exchange and coordination. Sometimes these costs will be higher than those experienced by markets. Even if they are lower, they still could be so high as to absorb all of the gains from exchange and no economic interaction will then take place, either within firms or in markets.

For example, during the first part of the nineteenth century, England had a technological advantage comparable to that enjoyed by US firms in the two decades following the Second World War. Property rights in knowledge were even weaker then than in the postwar period, so a theory of the MNE that solely focuses on the market transaction costs of knowledge transfer would predict that British firms would have chosen to set up captive manufacturing operations abroad as the most efficient way to capitalize on their knowledge. Yet while US firms have exploited since 1945 their technological advantage by vertically integrating into foreign manufacture, this was not how British know-how was transferred abroad in the first half of the nineteenth century. Rather, it was transferred through the migration of skilled artisans, who took that know-how with them and set up their own firms overseas. Why this difference in transfer modes? Because the costs of both market and interfirm exchange were so high in the nineteenth century as to make migration the only feasible alternative (Hennart, 1982: 128–30).

To be complete, a transaction costs theory of economic organization should therefore consider *simultaneously* the costs of conducting market exchange (market transaction costs) and those of effecting exchange within the firm (internal organization costs), and show how firms can, in some cases, reduce organization costs below those incurred in markets and below the potential gains of exchange. In other words, alongside a theory of why markets fail, we need a theory of why firms succeed.

Some scholars have argued that firms can be more efficient than markets because they replace failing market prices with internal ones (Buckley, 1983; Rugman, 1981). Although some firms do use prices for some types of internal coordination, this concept of "internal markets" fails to capture the fundamental reason why firms displace markets. Most employees are not guided and rewarded by market prices, but by directives voiced by their superiors, formalized through company rules, or internalized through indoctrination. Even in the relationship between head office and foreign subsidiaries, interdependencies and measurement problems limit the use of internal prices as control mechanisms (Robbins and Stobaugh, 1973: 511; Shapiro, 1984). If firms can be more efficient than markets when the latter fail, it is not because they replicate what markets do, but rather because they use a method of organization that is radically different from that used in markets (Hennart, 1982, 1986c).

As argued earlier, firms can succeed when markets fail because they use a system of organization, namely hierarchy, which has a very different incentive structure. Under hierarchy, parties to the exchange are no longer rewarded for their ability to change the market terms of trade in their favor but, instead, they are paid for carrying out the directives of a central party, the boss. Those directives can be explicit (in the form of direct orders or bureaucratic procedures) or implicit (when, through socialization, employees can be persuaded to do what their bosses want them to do even in the absence of managerial supervision). What makes hierarchy, in some circumstances, a more efficient method of organization than prices is the fact that it eliminates market transaction costs by breaking the connection between output and performance. This has, however, one unavoidable consequence: it tends to change the incentives of agents. Since they no longer are paid in proportion to the output they generate, but now in function of their obedience to managerial directives, they will tend to exert less spontaneous effort and initiative, a behavior we will call shirking. Now that rewards are no longer proportional to output, we cannot expect agents always to give their best, and management will have to expand resources to motivate employees. Employees will also have fewer incentives to carefully collect information than if they were working for themselves, since they do not directly benefit from it, but instead are supposed to pass it on to the boss. The firm will have to replace price constraints by behavior constraints. It will have to tell employees what to do, and to monitor their behavior. The costs of using hierarchy, "internal organization costs," are those of motivating employees to fully contribute to the firm's goals (so as to minimize shirking costs), and to collect information and transmit it faithfully to their superiors.

Hierarchy will therefore be a more efficient coordination method than prices when the costs of controlling shirking and of insuring effective information collection and transfer are lower than those of measuring goods and services and curbing cheating. Hence an MNE does not avoid the market when it takes on (internalizes) a transaction: it merely shifts the transaction from the market for goods and services to that for labor. The expansion of firms (the internalization of a market) will take place when transaction costs in the product market are higher than those experienced in the labor market.[4]

The preceding analysis offers some interesting implications for research. Keeping market transaction costs constant, whether a particular transaction will be internalized by the firm or not, will depend on the costs incurred by firms in monitoring employees. These costs are likely to vary across activities, across time periods, across countries, and across firms. Observing behavior is easy on machine-paced processes, because in that case an employee's behavior provides a good clue to his performance. Controlling shirking will be costly, on the other hand, for tasks that are not programmable but require judgment and on-the-spot decisions, and for those that require employees to be dispersed over space. As noted below, this explains why, for example, some activities are franchised while others are operated with employees, and why trademark owners usually operate themselves easily accessible units but franchise dispersed ones.

Another implication is that managing employees is also likely to be more costly, the greater the cultural differences between the MNE's home and target country.[5] Cultural differences between countries raise the cost of doing business there. One would expect that the cost of market transactions would grow less steeply with cultural distance than that of handling the transaction within the firm, because extending the firm abroad requires closer contacts with locals (employees, governments, and other stakeholders) than entering into market transactions with them (Johanson and Vahlne, 1977). If this is the case, the greater the cultural distance between the home base of the MNE and the target market, the less likely it is that the firm will internalize the transaction. As we shall see later, there is some evidence to support this point.

Why firms use both price and hierarchy

One criticism that has been levied against the previous analysis is that "the distinction made between markets and hierarchies is greatly overdrawn" since most real-world institutions do in fact use both methods of organization simultaneously (Perrow, 1988). While Perrow sees this as invalidating transaction costs theory, there is a simple answer to this apparent paradox. The answer (Hennart, 1993) lies in the distinction between methods or organization (prices and hierarchy) on one hand, and institutions (markets and firms) on the other. Institutions make use of the two methods of organization in various proportions, with markets using predominantly prices, but also some hierarchical behavior constraints, while firms use mostly hierarchical methods, albeit with some price constraints as well.

We have seen that firms replace price constraints by managerial directives, but that taking away price incentives reduces the motivation that employees have to contribute to the firm's goals. As individuals switch from being self-employed to being employees, their incentives to cheat decline with the decrease of the percentage of their output they get to keep, but so does their motivation to work. The firm must therefore increase the behavior constraints it will put on employees. Diminishing returns is a basic law in economics, and there are good reasons it should apply to methods of coordination. As firms increase their reliance on behavior constraints, the marginal returns to this method of organization will decline. As Ghoshal and Moran (1996) show, over-monitoring and micro-managing employees are likely to destroy morale and to kill initiative.[6] Hence, whenever it is important to elicit initiative and effort from employees, firms may find it advantageous to selectively reintroduce price constraints for some activities. They will pay employees through piecework, and they will set up some activities as profit centers and reward their managers for maximizing the profits of their subunits. In so doing they will end up using a mix of price and hierarchical (behavior) constraints. Hence what distinguishes the firm from the market is the mix or constraints used: firms are institutions that use primarily behavior constraints, while markets use mostly price constraints.[7] The additional assumption of diminishing returns to the exclusive use of a single method of organization (prices or hierarchy) allows transaction costs theory to account for the fact that most real-world institutions use a mixture of price and hierarchical constraints. Nevertheless, it is because firms use hierarchy, i.e. because they replace price by behavior constraints, that they can experience, in certain transactions, lower organization costs than markets. Going back to the exclusive use of prices within firms (setting up a full "internal market") would reintroduce the problems that the extension of the firm has sought to remedy.

The preceding analysis explains the existence in many MNEs of quasi-independent subsidiaries free to buy and sell at market prices to whatever internal or external customer they choose. While prices may be used in such MNEs to organize most interactions between parents and subsidiaries and between the subsidiaries themselves, some interactions, for example know-how, will remain organized through hierarchy. If all interactions were organized through market prices, subsidiaries would be independent firms (Hennart, 1993b).

Inversely, the increasing biases due to imperfect output measurement force firms to supplement price with behavior constraints. This is the case, for example, in the relationships between Japanese car assemblers and their suppliers, and those between franchisers and their franchisees. In this case, as we shall see below, the use of prices to organize the goodwill interactions between franchisors and franchisees would require a mechanism that would instantly price the impact of the behavior of each franchisee on the reputation of the brand, and would automatically credit or debit the account of the franchisees with the gains or losses their behavior inflicts on the overall reputation of the chain. Since such a price solution is presently technically infeasible, the impact of franchisee behavior on brand reputation is more efficiently controlled by a series of contractual rules (e.g. McDonald's QSC standards). The results are networks of franchisee firms linked to franchisors by franchising contracts, a mix of price and hierarchical constraints (Hennart, 1993a).

To sum up, MNEs are firms that expand across the boundaries of nation states. To explain why they do, one must explain why the method of organization that distinguishes them from markets, viz. hierarchy, can in some cases be a more efficient coordination mechanism than prices. This is the case whenever behavior constraints are more efficient than output constraints. This happens when the characteristics of outputs are poorly known and hard to measure. Inversely, behavior constraints are efficient when bosses have a good knowledge of the employee production function, and when observing behavior gives them good clues on performance. Because of diminishing returns to the exclusive use of a single method of organization, price or hierarchy, most real-world solutions are a mix of both, although the boundaries of firms are generally unambiguous. The following pages show that such a model can explain all the forms taken by the international expansion of firms.

Why do multinational firms expand abroad?

As we have seen, there are two basic (and non-mutually exclusive) reasons why firms may expand abroad. The first one, to which we now turn, is to internalize the pecuniary externalities firms inflict on one another when they compete on the market for final products. MNEs then arise to reduce competition. We will later discuss how MNEs internalize the second type of externalities, the non-pecuniary ones that result from "natural" market imperfections.

Structural market imperfections

Recall that pecuniary externalities are those that competitors impose on one another through the impact of their actions on the prices they face. One particular instance is competition. Consider a homogeneous good produced by single-plant monopolists located in a number of different countries. Competition between these producers will reduce their income. Competitors can, however, maximize their joint income if they agree to merge and concentrate production in the lowest cost plant. For Hymer, the MNE is the vehicle through which such collusion is organized.

This argument, nevertheless, only provides a partial explanation for the existence of MNEs since MNEs can also arise to internalize non-pecuniary externalities. Moreover, Hymer's argument is incomplete. Extension of the firm is not the only method available to reach collusion. Competitors can also coordinate their behavior through contract by taking part in a cartel (Casson, 1985). The main problem with a cartel is that of free-riding: all members would like to sell more in the high price market, but by doing so they lower prices. Consolidating all firms into an MNE eliminates incentives to cheat, but raises management costs and may be opposed by host governments. This suggests that, without legal restrictions on cartels, the propensity to internalize pecuniary externalities by cartel rather than through an MNE will be greater the easier it is to detect cheating and the lower the need to adapt to changing conditions. Hence cartels should be more prevalent in industries producing homogeneous products and characterized by slow growth and static technology (Casson, 1985).

Pecuniary externalities are also generated in the licensing process. Consider a patent owner licensing one producer in each country. Because of differences in the elasticity of demand, the optimal price for the product is likely to vary across markets. Maximization of rents (and hence of royalties received by the licensor) requires that licensees be prevented from invading each other's markets. In some cases, high transportation costs, tariffs, or government regulations segment markets. When barriers to trade are low, the licensor must explicitly forbid licensees from exporting products to other markets. In practice, such territorial restrictions are often illegal. A firm that integrates into foreign manufacture is, however, better able to prevent competition between plants producing the licensed product because it needs no explicit contract to eliminate competition between its subunits (Casson, 1979). Hence transaction costs theory explains when the internalization of pecuniary externalities will be achieved by the establishment of an MNE rather than by contractual means.

Natural market imperfections

Figure 4.1 sketches the decision-tree of a firm with proprietary intangible assets valued abroad. The firm becomes an MNE when it ends up having employees overseas. These employees can be in sales subsidiaries, when the firm manufactures at home but handles its exports with its own employees, or they can be in production subsidiaries when the firm manufactures overseas. According to our definition, the firm is not an MNE if it exports but uses independent distributors, or if it decides to transfer its intangibles by contract (license, franchise, management contract, etc.). Whether the firm is an MNE or not thus depends on whether it extends hierarchical control across national boundaries, through sales or production subsidiaries.

Figure 4.1 shows that the extension of an MNE overseas occurs as a result of a location and of a governance decision. The location decision is based on a comparison of delivered cost, itself a function of the relative production cost of a domestic and foreign location, of transportation costs, of tariff and non-tariff barriers to trade, and of political risk.[8] A second, largely independent decision, is whether hierarchy is more efficient than price to organize the interdependencies between agents located abroad and at home. The combination of location and governance decisions determines whether a firm will be multinational (Dunning, 1977, 1979, 1981).

A similar analysis can be used for a firm that requires inputs from abroad (Figure 4.2). The firm must choose between procuring its inputs from home or foreign locations (the location decision). It must also choose between integrating into the production of the inputs it needs or procuring them at arm's length from independent suppliers (the governance decision).

Figures 4.1 and 4.2 thus show that the expansion of firms abroad can take very diverse forms, from setting up sales subsidiaries to developing mines and plantations (all cases that correspond to the expansion of firms abroad are in italics). Yet, once a foreign location is optimal, whether international coordination will take place within the firm (whether an MNE will emerge) or through the market can be explained by the relative costs of using firm or market governance to organize that specific interdependency.

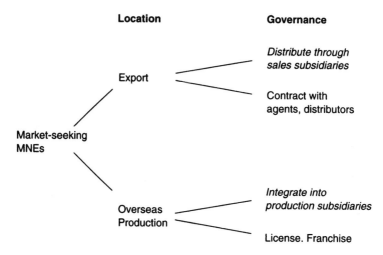

Figure 4.1 Decision-tree of a firm with proprietary intangible assets valued abroad

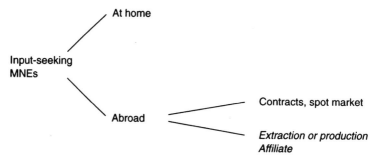

Figure 4.2 Decision-tree of a firm that requires inputs from abroad

International interdependencies can be of many types. Knowledge and reputation developed in one country can have productive uses in another. Products manufactured in one country may require complementary marketing services in another. Raw materials and components most efficiently produced abroad may be needed at home. Lastly, financial capital, abundant in one country, may be scarce in another. Table 4.1 presents the hypothesis that MNEs exist to organize all these international interdependencies. As we shall see in the following pages, all these motives for the existence of MNEs can be explained by the same set of theoretical tools.

Knowledge: licensing vs. foreign production

Most applications of transaction costs theory to the MNE have focused on the international exchange of one particular type of input – knowledge (Buckley and

Table 4.1 The transaction costs theory of the MNE

Type of MNE	Market internalized
Horizontal integration by R&D-intensive firms	Technological and managerial know-how
Horizontal integration by advertising-intensive firms	Reputation; managerial skills in quality control and marketing
Vertical integration into distribution	Distribution and marketing services
Vertical integration into raw materials and components	Raw materials and components
Freestanding firms	Capital

Casson, 1976; Cantwell, 1989; Casson, 1979; Caves, 1982; Hennart, 1977; Magee, 1977; Teece, 1981). Know-how developed in one country is often useful in others. When and why will the international transfer of such know-how be organized within a firm, and when will it be organized through arm's length or contractual exchange? Microeconomic theory tells us that markets are efficient when buyers and sellers have good knowledge of what is being sold. This suggests that knowledge itself will have a particular problem when it is the commodity being transacted. As Arrow (1962) first argued, the buyer of know-how does not, by definition, know its exact characteristics and is thus likely to underpay for it. If the seller were to provide that information, he would be revealing it to the buyer, and thus transferring it free of charge. The basic problem of the transfer of knowledge is therefore one of information asymmetry between buyer and seller. Information asymmetry will be lower the older the technology and the smaller the differences between the technological capabilities of the transactors.

The patent system offers one solution to this information asymmetry problem. By giving owners of knowledge a monopoly in its use, patents encourage them to disclose it, thus reducing information asymmetry between buyer and seller. However, the efficiency of a patent system crucially depends on (a) the ability of patents fully to describe the invention and (b) the power and the willingness of public authorities to establish and enforce monopoly rights in knowledge.[9] By taking a patent, inventors are disclosing their know-how to potential buyers (licensees), but also to potential imitators. It is therefore crucial that inventors be protected against infringement. Inventors who fear that their rights will not be protected will keep their inventions secret and will exploit them themselves, i.e. they will internalize the market for their knowledge by vertically integrating into the manufacture of products incorporating their know-how. On the other hand, when patent rights are well protected, knowledge holders will be able to sell or rent (license) the rights to their know-how to domestic and foreign manufacturers. The degree to which patents provide protection depends on technological factors (such as the extent to which knowledge can be clearly defined and described on paper and the difficulty of designing around the patent), and on government policies, such as the length of the patent grant, the efficiency of the court system, and the level of penalties for infringement. Arm's length transfer of knowledge through licensing will be more prevalent whenever patent rights are easy to establish and to defend, while transfer within the firm will be chosen for knowledge that is difficult to codify into patents and easy to copy (Caves *et al.*, 1982; Hennart, 1982). Since governments vary in the extent to which they provide patent protection, the efficiency of transferring knowledge through licensing will also depend on the country being entered.

All in all, the limited available research shows that patents are not a very effective method of knowledge appropriation because they do not provide patentors with solid rights of exclusive use and because the rights to transfer patents to others (licensing) are subject to governmental limits. The research and development (R&D) managers of US firms surveyed by Levin *et al.* (1987) reported that patents were generally a less effective method of knowledge appropriation than vertical integration into manufacture. On a scale of 1 to 7, with 7 being "very effective," they rated process patents to secure royalty income at 3.52, and product patents at 4.33. Other methods of appropriation that were associated with vertical integration, such as being the first to manufacture a product, or having a strong sales and service effort, were rated more highly. Being the first to sell a product rated 5.11 for processes and 5.41 for products. As we would expect, there were substantial differences across industries in the level of patent protection, with chemicals and drugs enjoying better protection than computers and communication equipment.

Given those differences in the protection given by patents, it is not surprising to see major differences across industries in the mix between international licensing and vertical integration into manufacturing as strategies to exploit knowledge abroad. Table 4.2, for example, shows the ratio of licensed production relative to total UK foreign production (the sum of sales by foreign licensees of UK firms and sales of foreign subsidiaries of UK concerns); this provides an index of the extent to which technology was transferred through contract. This ratio varies from a high of 71 percent in the shipbuilding industry to a low of 4 percent in food, drink, and tobacco.

International licensing is also often subject to limitations imposed by host governments. Host governments have disallowed the patenting of otherwise patentable knowledge, and they have outlawed patent clauses, such as grant-backs (which provide licensors with access to improvement made by licensees) and territorial restrictions (which make it possible to price-discriminate between markets). These government limitations further reduce the profitability of patenting and make it a second-best method of exploiting one's know-how (Contractor, 1984). One consequence is that licensing is primarily used to exploit "peripheral technology" in "peripheral markets." Because imperfect property rights in knowledge (imperfect patent protection and restrictions on licensing) prevent licensors from getting as high a return on their technology as vertical integration into manufacture, and expose them to potential technology leakages to

Table 4.2 Share of UK licensed sales in total foreign production (licensed sales
+ change that sales), 1983

Sector	Share %
Food, drink, tobacco	4.0
Chemicals and allied industries	25.8
Metal manufactures	12.3
Mechanical and instrument engineering	21.5
Electrical engineering	7.6
Shipbuilding	71.1
Motor vehicles	45.1
Textile, leather, clothing, footwear	5.0
Paper, printing and publishing	13.6
Rubber	34.8
Other manufacturing	21.2
All manufacturing	17.5

Source: Adapted from Buckley and Prescott (1989)

the other operations of licensees, firms prefer to exploit internally technology that they see as central to their future. Licensing is also used primarily in small, peripheral markets where the risks and the consequences of building up competitors are small and the limited market size does not warrant the high fixed costs of establishing production subsidiaries (Caves *et al.*, 1982).

There are few empirical tests of these propositions because of the difficulty of obtaining detailed information on large samples. Davidson and McFetridge 1984) tested the propositions that older technology was easier to license because it was better known, and the risk a firm runs in having its know-how build up competitors was lower if the technology it transferred was not central to its survival. Analyzing 1,382 cases of technology transfer undertaken by 32 US MNEs, they found, as expected, that the probability of licensing an innovation was greater the older the technology, the more peripheral it was to the innovator's business, the smaller the investment in R&D necessary to develop it, and the greater the innovator's experience in international licensing.

Another implication of transaction costs theory is that, keeping the transaction costs of licensing constant, the costs of transferring knowledge within the firm should be lower the smaller the cultural distance between the innovator's home country and the target country. This was also supported by Davidson and McFetridge (1985), who found that the probability that US firms would transfer an innovation internally (as opposed to licensing it) increased if the target country was geographically and culturally close to the United States. Buckley and Davies (1981) estimated the share of foreign subsidiary sales to total foreign sales of British firms (the sum of foreign subsidiary sales of British MNEs and sales by licensees of British firms). This measure of the extent to which British firms used hierarchical over market transfer of knowledge was higher in the former sterling area countries, which are culturally close to the UK, than in other countries.

While much of the literature has tended to focus on the problem of a firm seeking to exploit technology, the theory sketched above predicts that the presence of high transaction cost in the market for knowledge will also lead firms to expand abroad to acquire technology. The same transactional difficulties that make it difficult for a domestic firm to license some types of knowledge to foreign firms make it difficult for a foreign firm to license similar types of knowledge from domestic firms. The desire to acquire technology will therefore lead firms to expand abroad through acquisitions, joint ventures, and greenfield investments.

Reputation: franchising vs. foreign production

Trademarks are to reputation what patents are to knowledge: they are the legal instrument establishing property rights in reputation. Trademarks are valuable because they reduce customer search costs. Tourists and businesspeople are likely to patronize abroad businesses bearing trademarks of their own country. Hence a firm's home country trademarks are sometimes valuable abroad. The ability of a firm to exploit its reputation abroad depends on the extent to which its trademarks are protected from unauthorized imitation (counterfeiting). Counterfeiting will destroy the value of a trademark since counterfeiters have incentives to run down the reputation of the brand by selling lower-quality products if they sell to non-repeat customers. A firm that owns a trademark can exploit it by itself producing goods and services bearing its trademark, or by drawing franchising contracts to rent the use of its trademark to local entrepreneurs. The efficiency of franchising depends on the extent to which trademarks are protected from counterfeiting, since no one will rent what can be acquired for free.

Franchising is also subject to free-riding. A trademark becomes a public good to all those who are using it, in the sense that the quality of goods and services supplied by anyone using the trademark will affect all those who share the trademark.[10] Franchisees can maximize their income by reducing the quality of the goods sold under the trademark. The greater the proportion of non-repeat customers, and the higher the cost of detecting free-riding, the greater the payoff to franchisees who reduce quality, and the losses they will inflict on all the other users of the trademark. Consequently, franchisors write contracts that carefully stipulate minimum quality standards franchisees must follow and spend significant resources enforcing them.[11]

One way of reducing a franchisee's incentive to free-ride is to transform him into an employee. As an employee, the erstwhile franchisee is paid a straight salary, unrelated to the outlet's profits, and gains nothing from reducing quality. But breaking the link between output and reward has an unfortunate, but unavoidable side-effect: the former franchisee, now an employee, has little motivation to exert any effort which cannot be specified and measured by his employer.[12] Hence the choice between franchising independent owners and establishing company-owned outlets will depend on the comparison of two types of cost: that of monitoring employees to guarantee their level of effort vs. that of specifying

		Cost of monitoring employees	
		High	Low
Cost of specifying quality by contract	High	No transfers of reputation	Outlets operated by trademark owners
	Low	Franchised outlets	

Figure 4.3 Determinants of franchising

and enforcing a minimum level of quality by contract to prevent free-riding on quality (see Figure 4.3). Everything else being constant, franchising will be efficient when (a) it is relatively easy to write rules, which, if followed, will guarantee a minimum level of quality, and whose violation can be easily detected and proven to third parties and (b) it is relatively costly to ensure that employees will work hard and take initiatives. Trademark owners will operate outlets with their own employees in the reverse case. No international exchange of reputation will take place when it is difficult to monitor employees and contractually to stipulate quality.

These considerations explain why franchising is commonly used for the international exchange of goodwill in some industries, but not in others. In fast food, hotel, and car rental, drawing up and enforcing contractual quality standards is relatively easy, whereas the dispersion of outlets raises the cost of monitoring employees. Franchising is therefore common. The reverse seems to be true in banking, insurance, advertising, and management consulting. In these activities minimum quality levels are difficult to stipulate by contract in a manner that is enforceable in court, while the relatively small number of outlets necessary to reach customers makes monitoring employees relatively easy (Hennart, 1982: 89–93). In these industries goodwill is exploited in outlets staffed by employees of the trademark owner.

The relative levels of market transaction costs and internal organization costs also vary within a given firm. In the fast food industry, high-volume outlets in concentrated locations, which are easy to monitor, tend to be operated by the trademark owner, while small, dispersed outlets are franchised (Brickly and Dark, 1987; Hennart, 1982). Dunning and McQueen (1981) uncovered a similar pattern in the international hotel industry. Worldwide, more than half of the rooms in hotels operated by MNEs are run under franchise or management contracts, but the proportion is much greater (82 percent) in developing countries, where political risk and cultural distance raise the cost of managing hotels over that of franchising them to local operators.

Raw materials and components: spot purchases and long-term contracts vs. foreign production

One early and persistent reason why firms have expanded abroad has been to secure minerals and agricultural produce necessary for their downstream activities. The foreign investments of integrated oil companies into crude oil, those of steel firms in iron ore, and those of rubber manufacturers into natural rubber plantations are but a few examples (Wilkins, 1970, 1974). Transaction costs theory suggests that such "backward vertical integration" will be chosen whenever markets for raw materials and intermediate inputs are characterized by high transaction costs. These costs arise when (a) the number of parties to the exchange is small (small-number conditions) and/or (b) parties differ in the amount of information they have on the transaction (information asymmetry).

SMALL NUMBER CONDITIONS

Small-number conditions result from economies of scale, high transportation costs, government barriers, and physical asset specificity. Physical asset specificity arises when one or both parties to the transaction invest in equipment specially designed to carry out the transaction, and which has lower value in other uses (Williamson, 1985). When these conditions are present, spot markets are likely to fail, because a party making transaction-specific investments, and consequently for whom the costs of switching partners are high, will fear that the more flexible party will opportunistically renegotiate the terms of trade after investments have been made. One possible way for parties to protect themselves is to write a contract fixing the terms and conditions of the trade over a period of time corresponding to the life of the plant.

Contracts reduce enforcement costs by specifying *ex ante* the terms and conditions of the trade and the compensation to be paid in case of breach, relying on third parties (the courts or private arbitrators) to determine whether a violation has taken place, to decide on the compensation to be paid in each case, and to enforce payment of such compensation. Contracts suffer, however, from a number of limitations. They are more costly than spot markets, for while a large number of traders typically share the costs of running spot markets, the costs of writing contracts must be paid by the contracting parties themselves. The additional cost of writing a contract can be justified only if trades are long-lived. Contracts can be risky because they rely on enforcement by third parties (the courts or arbitrators). Breach, while obvious to those involved, may be difficult to prove to others. The aggrieved party has also limited control on the amount and form of the compensation he will receive for breach.

The most severe drawback of contracts is that they often fail under conditions of high uncertainty. As the degree of uncertainty increases, specifying *ex ante* all possible contingencies and the contractual changes to be made in each case becomes increasingly difficult. Yet leaving contracts incomplete allows parties to exploit each other. Hence contracts are efficient when uncertainty is low or when it can be indexed.

Here as elsewhere, an alternative to contracts is to have buyers and sellers of raw materials become employees of the same firm, i.e. vertical integration. Vertical integration transforms one of the parties into an employee of the other party. As an employee, the erstwhile trader is no longer rewarded for his opportunism, but instead for obeying the directives of his boss. Vertical integration makes it possible to reduce opportunism by aligning the incentives of both parties (Williamson, 1979).

This theoretical framework provides a convincing explanation of the pattern of vertical integration found in many domestic industries, for example that between coal mines and electric power plants (Joskow, 1985), between automobile assemblers and parts manufacturers (Monteverde and Teece, 1982; Walker and Weber, 1984), between aerospace firms and their component suppliers (Masten, 1984), and between wood processors and timber growers (Globerman and Schwindt, 1986). The same logic can be applied to foreign backward investments by MNEs, since they are vertical investments that cross borders.

The aluminum industry provides an interesting example (Stuckey, 1983). There are three stages in the production of aluminum: bauxite is mined, then shipped to alumina plants where it is refined into alumina, and alumina is then smelted into aluminum. In the late 1970s, close to 90 percent of transfers of bauxite, alumina, and primary aluminum was organized within MNEs. The reason is that markets for bauxite, and to a lesser extent for alumina, are narrow. Bauxite refining has high asset specificity because bauxites are heterogeneous and significant cost savings can be obtained when refineries are built to process a single type of bauxite. Once an alumina refinery is built, switching costs are high. Because bauxite is of low grade, transporting it long distances is costly. Lastly, high economies of scale in bauxite refining and smelting further reduce the number of potential buyers and sellers of bauxite and alumina. To organize what is often a bilateral relationship through spot markets would be hazardous, because, after investments have been made, the owner of the mine could exploit the owner of the alumina plant (or vice versa) by unilaterally changing the price of bauxite.

Using contracts also entails serious risks. Because both bauxite mining and refining require significant investments of long economic life,[13] contracts must cover very long periods – typically 20 to 25 years. Over such a long timespan they cannot effectively protect the parties against changes in the environment which impact their profit stream. The long-term contracts signed in the 1960s by Japanese bauxite purchasers specified prices that were denominated in dollars, with adjustments based on the quality of the bauxite actually shipped. Shortly after they were signed, the end of the Bretton Woods system of fixed exchange rates radically altered the profitability of the contracts by changing the local currency equivalent of the dollar prices, while the two oil shocks made the Japanese aluminum industry, which relied for its electricity on oilfired power plants, increasingly uncompetitive. This led to acrimonious bargaining, and to a shift from contracts to vertical integration (Stuckey, 1983).[14]

We have seen that the high degree of asset specificity in bauxites, and to a lesser degree in alumina and aluminum, has made vertical integration the overwhelming method to effect the transfer of these commodities. In contrast, coordination between stages in the case of alluvial tin is efficiently performed by spot markets. There is no asset specificity in the smelting of alluvial tin ores since these ores are very homogeneous (they are nearly pure tin). Tin ores are also of high value, so their transportation costs are low relative to their value, and they can be transported long distances. The result is an efficient market for tin ores, eliminating the need for vertical integration between mining and smelting.[15] Tin ores obtained from lode mining, however, tend to carry various impurities, and the smelters handling these ores must be specifically designed to treat those impurities. Consequently, the lode sector of the tin industry is characterized by greater vertical integration (Hennart, 1986, 1988).

The considerations outlined above explain the need for MNEs to own suppliers of other intermediate inputs, such as parts or subassemblies. In most cases MNEs will own their foreign suppliers when the components they manufacture are specific to the purchaser, while independent suppliers will be used for standard parts, which are sold in a relatively broad market.[16]

QUALITY CONTROL

Another reason for vertical backward investments is quality control. Quality control problems arise in situations of information asymmetry. If buyers cannot distinguish *ex ante* between good and bad quality, they will tend to reduce their offer price to reflect this risk. Sellers of high-quality products may not be able to persuade a buyer that the goods offered are of high quality, and will therefore avoid the market. Markets will fail in the sense that they will be used to sell goods of increasingly lower quality (Ackerlof, 1970). In that case, sellers and buyers have incentives to integrate.

The banana industry offers an interesting example of this motive for vertical integration. Bananas are certainly an unsophisticated product, so it is surprising that vertically integrated MNEs dominate their international trade.[17] But bananas are highly perishable, as they spoil 21 days after cutting. Their quality also depends on careful handling and proper ripening conditions. Improper handling and ripening are difficult to detect *ex ante*: damage incurred at the cutting and shipping stages will be revealed only once the banana reaches retailers. Hence it is difficult to achieve consistent high quality if grower, shipper, and distributor are separate concerns (Litvak and Maule, 1977; Read, 1986). Consistent quality is better assured by vertical integration because it reduces incentives to cheat at each stage (Casson, 1982). This explains why US banana distributors integrated early on into banana plantations (Wilkins, 1970).

Distribution and marketing services: independent distribution vs. company sales force

The international expansion of firms to take over the distribution of their products can be explained by the same general factors that lead to the integration of buyers and sellers of raw materials and components described above, i.e. the difficulty of coordinating the behavior of buyers and sellers of distribution services when markets for these services are narrow and when their quality is difficult to measure (Chandler, 1977; Hennart, 1982; Nicholas, 1983; Williamson, 1981).

SMALL NUMBER CONDITIONS

To distribute a product efficiently requires investments both in physical assets (warehouses, stocks, transportation networks, repair facilities, offices, or retail stores) and in knowledge. The distributor must learn how to demonstrate and service the product, how to price it, and how to adapt it to local tastes and conditions of use. These physical and intellectual investments vary in size and especially in specificity. In some cases, they are "general purpose" and can be used to sell the products of a number of manufacturers; in others, they are specific to a single supplier and have little or no value in other uses.

As in the case of backward vertical integration, there are two main, often reinforcing reasons why the market for distribution services is often narrow. First, distribution is often subject to high economies of scale or scope. A single distributor may be dealing with a single manufacturer; joining both in an MNE may solve the resulting bargaining stalemates. Second, effective distribution sometimes requires substantial manufacturer-specific investments. A distributor may be reluctant to make such investments, fearing that, after they are made, the manufacturer will opportunistically renegotiate the margins by threatening to sign a new contract with another distributor. This fear may cause the distributor to commit fewer resources to distribution than would be optimal (Nicholas, 1983).

Contracts may provide solutions. A manufacturer can persuade a distributor to make manufacturer-specific investments by offering exclusive distribution rights. Here again, the more uncertain the environment and the longer the time needed to recover its transaction-specific investments, the greater the chances that such a long-term contract will break down. In these cases, vertical integration of manufacturers into distribution may be the most efficient option. Integration into distribution will thus be observed in the distribution of products requiring specialized facilities or specific demonstration and repair.

This model is supported by some recent studies of the factors that determine whether firms will use independent agents or employees to handle their exports. Anderson and Coughlan (1987) found that the probability that US manufacturers of semiconductors would use their own employees to sell abroad increased with the level of product knowledge that they needed to sell the product effectively. Klein *et al.* (1990) analyzed the choice of Canadian exporters between independent distributors and a company sales force. They found that a company sales force was chosen when the effective distribution of the product required manufacturer-specific investments.

PERFORMANCE INSEPARABILITY

Another problem with independent distributors arises when consumers cannot separate the contribution that manufacturers and distributors make to the satisfaction they derive from the product-plus-service bundle (Chen and Hennart, 1998). For example, poor control by the retailer of the temperature in the freezers containing branded ice cream will affect its texture. A consumer will not be able to know whether the poor texture is due to poor manufacture or improper storage, thus allowing the manufacturer and the distributor to inflict uncompensated damages on each other (inversely, there is no easy mechanism to allocate rewards for investments made by either party to increase ice cream quality). The problem is similar to that experienced in franchising and arises when the distributor and the manufacturer can both affect the quality of the good and services as perceived by the consumer. One solution is for manufacturers contractually to negotiate the imposition of behavior constraints on retailers, of the type franchisors put on franchisees. Another is for manufacturers to integrate into distribution or for retailers to integrate into manufacturing. Vertical integration will be chosen if manufacturers cannot easily define and enforce contractual rules to prevent distributors from debasing quality but can cheaply and effectively monitor the behavior of distributors if they become employees (Caves and Murphy, 1976; Hennart, 1982).[18]

The observed pattern of vertical integration into distribution reflects a tradeoff between the need to have distributors make the requisite level of investments and keep quality at an agreed level, on one hand, and the cost of managing company-owned distribution facilities on the other. That cost rises if there are scope economies in distribution and if it is difficult to monitor the behavior of employees.

Inter-industry differences in the level of integration between manufacturers and distributors seem consistent with such a model. Here again, there is a striking parallel between domestic and international integration. Williamson (1981) has shown how the extent of domestic forward integration by US manufacturers varied at the turn of the century from none in the case of hardware, jewelry, liquor, and dry goods items, to full integration into both wholesaling and retailing in the case of new, complex, high-priced machines requiring specialized demonstration and repair. Vertical forward integration by MNEs abroad had then a similar pattern: no integration for dry goods, integration into wholesaling for products that required specialized handling, and integration into retailing in the case of new, sophisticated products which required demonstration, installation, and after-sales service and whose quality could be damaged by improper handling (Chandler, 1959, 1977; Hennart, 1982; Nicholas, 1983; Wilkins, 1970). In short, the observed pattern of vertical forward integration abroad, as well as that of backward vertical integration, is consistent with the view that MNEs expand abroad to bring in-house activities which are subject to high market transaction costs and relatively low internal organization costs.

Financial capital: loans vs. equity

Financial capital is, alongside know-how, reputation, and raw materials and components, a factor of production that can often be profitably transferred overseas since its return often differs across countries. As in the case of the other intermediate products considered above, financial capital can either be transferred across countries by contract (bonds and loans) between a lender and a borrower/ investor, or its international exchange can be organized by hierarchy. In the latter case, the market for financial capital is internalized, and the lender and the borrower are joined within an MNE.

Capital can be transferred on international markets through loans and corporate bonds. This mode of transfer gives the lender no right to the profits of the venture and no "general and discretionary right" to direct the behavior of the borrower. Lending involves making funds available to the borrower, to be paid back later with interest. There are many reasons why international lending is subject to high transaction costs. First, in contrast to many other transactions, the two parts of a lending transaction are not simultaneous. Money is lent today and repaid later. Unlike other physical assets, money is fungible, and can be used for purposes other than those approved by the lender. Finally, incentives in a loan transaction are often not symmetrical. Borrowers who invest in risky projects will capture, if they are successful, all of the returns of their investment net of interest payments and repayment of principal. If they fail, lenders will shoulder all the costs (Jensen and Meckling, 1976). While a borrower's loss of reputation is supposed to curb such opportunism, such reputation effects are weak in international lending, as it is often difficult for lenders to know whether the borrower's default was due to dishonesty, ineptitude, or just bad luck.

Default would not arise if lenders had perfect information on borrowers and projects and if the enforcement of loan contracts were costless. Given positive transaction costs, lenders will have to use a number of second-best strategies to protect themselves against default. One consists in concentrating on projects and borrowers known to them. Restricting the use of funds to purposes specifically authorized by them is another. However, this requires lenders to know what expenditures are needed to carry out the proposed business. A third strategy is to ask the borrower to pledge a collateral to be forfeited in case of default. Usually that collateral will consist of some of the assets financed through the loan (Hennart, 1994).

Attempts by lenders to protect themselves against default by using these three strategies will cause inefficiencies in the international market for financial capital. First, lenders will tend to screen out borrowers not personally known to them, those without long track records, and those undertaking projects with which they are not familiar. Second. lenders will try to avoid projects that do not yield good collateral. Good collateral are assets that are not specific to a particular user and have good resale value, for example general purpose trucks or airplanes. Because the value of collateral to a lender varies systematically across projects, so will the transaction costs of lending. Investments in mining or R&D offer poor collateral, because capital sunk into unsuccessful mines or R&D does not yield salable assets, and therefore will tend not to be financed by loans.

The market for financial capital is therefore likely to fail if prospective borrowers cannot show a good track record, if they are not known to lenders, or if they want to invest in projects that do not yield good collateral. One solution in that case may be to organize the market for financial capital within a firm, i.e. to have the lender become full or part owner of the borrower's business (or vice versa). This will reduce transaction costs for three main reasons. First, equity links provide lenders with much greater control than loan contracts, as equity owners have the right to review decisions *ex ante* and have easier access to internal documents.[19] By contrast, lenders are strictly limited in the quantity, quality, and timeliness of the information they can obtain on their borrowers. Equity control is also more flexible than loans, because it allows greater discretion to preserve the value of a going concern when problems occur (Williamson, 1988). Lastly, transforming borrowers into employees reduces their incentives to take excessive risks because their reward as employees is now more independent of the success of the project. This, of course, has also the unintended consequence of decreasing the borrower's incentive to exert effort.

The presence of transaction costs in the market for financial capital explains the respective roles played by lending (bank lending or corporate bonds) and by intra-firm transfers in the international movement of financial capital. Historically, banks have provided only short-term international lending, mostly on receivables (except during the 1970s and 1980s, when banks lent long term to newly developing countries, with disastrous consequences). In the nineteenth century. long-term international lending was through bonds, mostly issued by governments and railways, and through mortgages. In all these cases, the transaction costs of lending were relatively low. Governments have low default risk because of their ability to raise taxes to repay loans. Land is also a good collateral, especially in fast-growing economies, and in the nineteenth century considerable sums were lent by European investors to farmers in North America, Australia, and Argentina (Wilkins, 1989). The construction of railroads was also financed through bonds. In Europe and Russia governments guaranteed the bonds of railroad companies. Railroads were private in the US, but were given huge tracks of land, which they used as collateral.

Outside the transfers to developing countries made in the postwar period by bilateral or multilateral aid agencies, the bulk of long-term international financial transfers has been effected through MNEs. This transfer can take place in two ways. First, MNEs can emit shares in capital-rich countries and use the proceeds to finance projects in capital-poor ones, thus intermediating the international transfer of capital. The import of capital need not, however, be intermediated. For example, firms in capital-poor countries (or firms in capital-rich countries investing in capital-poor countries) may sell directly shares on the stock markets of capital-rich countries. The best example of this last type of transfer is that effected by the so-called "freestanding company" (Wilkins, 1988: Wilkins and Schroeter, 1998).

Freestanding companies were the dominant type of British MNEs until 1914, and were also important in The Netherlands, Belgium, and France (Wilkins and Schroter, 1998). While they were overshadowed by the more traditional type of MNEs after 1914, they continued to be formed after that time and some are still being established today (Hennart, 1998).

Freestanding firms do not fit at all the traditional model of MNEs developed in the literature and they seem to support Fieldhouse's contention that no single theoretical model can explain all the forms taken by MNEs. Freestanding firms were domiciled in the dominant equity markets of the time (in London, but also in Brussels, Paris, Amsterdam, Boston, etc.) and they raised equity there by selling shares directly to the public to finance investments that were located exclusively abroad. The traditional theory of the MNE argues that firms expand abroad to exploit the firm-specific advantages (such as proprietary technology) they have developed in their home market (Dunning, 1981). Besides a skeletal head office,[20] freestanding firms did not, however, conduct any business in their country of registration, as all of their actual operations (plants, mines, plantations) were abroad, typically in the least developed part of Europe (Spain, Italy, Russia), in the regions of recent settlement (Australia, Canada, the United States, Argentina), and in developing countries, both under colonial rule (India, Malaysia, the Dutch East Indies, Africa) and outside it (Persia, Siam, Latin America). While they were engaged in a wide variety of businesses, from services (hotels, utilities, docks, newspapers, banks) to manufacturing (breweries, jute mills, fish canning, flour milling), the majority of freestanding firms were in two sectors, namely agriculture (ranches and plantations – natural rubber, tea, sugarcane, cinchona) and mining and petroleum.[21]

Without any domestic business, it is hard to see how the *raison d'être* of freestanding firms could have been the exploitation of firm-specific advantages. The apparent paradox of freestanding firms is compounded by the fact that the technology they used abroad was generally unknown in their country of registration. A large number of British and Dutch freestanding firms were in tropical agriculture. While the British were active in tin mining at home, the mining techniques they used in the Far East came from California and New Zealand (Yip, 1969).

Here as elsewhere, the *raison d'être* of MNEs must not be sought in the internalization of firm-specific advantages, but in the internalization of markets, in this case, for financial capital. Freestanding firms allowed lenders, located in capital-rich countries, to exercise direct management control over the projects that made use of their funds. This made it possible to finance projects which, because of their characteristics (they were in areas poorly known by savers and had poor collateral) could not be financed through loans.

Freestanding firms usually started when affluent individuals recognized an investment opportunities and pooled their personal funds into "syndicates" to take advantage of them. After these syndicates had sufficiently developed the project, they obtained additional finance (and cashed in on their entrepreneurial skills) by floating shares on the principal stock market of the time. There is a wealth of evidence to support the view that the main reason for freestanding firms was the internalization of the market for financial capital.

First, case histories show how local firms registered in London or other capital-rich countries with an efficient stock market when they were unable to obtain sufficient local capital (Cushman, 1986; Drabble, 1973; Hennart, 1987, 1998). Second, freestanding companies had usually bigger capitalization than local firms. For example, in the Dutch East Indies, where Netherlands-registered freestanding companies worked side by side with Dutch-operated but locally registered firms, the Netherlands-registered companies had higher capital (Gales and Sluyterman, 1998). Third, as we have seen, freestanding firms were domiciled in capital-exporting countries with liquid capital markets, while their operations were concentrated in the rapidly developing but capital-poor countries of the time. Freestanding companies located their headquarters wherever they could efficiently access financial capital. While they were heavily concentrated in London prior to 1914, the imposition of capital export controls in the UK after the First World War led to a relative decline of London to the benefit of New York, where a number of freestanding firms were then formed to operate in Latin America (Hennart, 1998).

Fourth, the theory suggests that setting up a new venture as a freestanding firm would be efficient as long as equity capital could be raised more efficiently abroad than locally, and as long as the characteristics of the projects led to high transaction costs on the loan market. Freestanding firms created before 1914 survived longer in countries with underdeveloped capital markets. By the 1920s, UK-based freestanding firms had disappeared in the United States, whereas they survived in Malaysia and in Nigeria until the 1960s (Hennart, 1986b, 1987; Wilkins, 1988).[22]

Fifth, as predicted by our theory, the activities typically financed by freestanding firms, namely speculative agriculture and mining, were those that, yesterday as well as today, are difficult to finance through loans. Mining is risky, and much of the investment is in diggings and site-specific infrastructure, yielding poor collateral. As a result, new mining ventures cannot generally obtain debt financing, and have to be financed through equity.[23] Freestanding firms were also the dominant method used to finance, around the turn of the century, rubber and cinchona in South East Asia, and ranches in the United States and Argentina. All of these investments were substantial and then highly speculative, and used previously undeveloped land with little alternative uses, and hence little collateral value (Allen and Donnithorne, 1954; Jackson, 1968; Stillson, 1971).

To sum up, freestanding firms were the type of MNEs used to transfer financial capital internationally whenever lending would have been subject to high transaction costs and when the optimal scale of the investment was small. Freestanding firms were single-project firms (single mine, single plantation, single ranch, and so on), although they were often partly owned by trading companies, mining finance houses, or equipment sellers (Hennart, 1998). MNEs today perform the same function, since they also transfer financial capital across boundaries, but they tend to intermediate the transfer, in the sense that they raise money to make investments in a variety of projects that are not necessarily defined *ex ante*. In both cases, firms will expand abroad if hierarchy is a more efficient way than loans or bonds to link lenders and borrowers located in different countries.

Conclusion

The aim of this section has been to show that, contrary to what is sometimes asserted, transaction costs theory can account for all the major types of MNEs. As shown in Table 4.1, different types of MNE result from the internalization of various types of markets (naturally, in many cases the MNE will simultaneously be internalizing a number of markets). Hence transaction costs theory is a powerful tool to reveal the fundamental features of MNEs which are hidden behind the wide diversity of their forms.

New forms of investment and countertrade

One implication of the transaction costs argument that MNEs reduce the cost of organizing cross-border interdependencies is that attempts by governments to ban or limit their operations should, if binding, have generally negative consequences for the efficiency of the international organization of interdependencies involving knowledge, reputation, distribution services, raw materials and components, and capital. In this respect, transaction costs theory leads to conclusions and recommendations that are diametrically opposed to those made by the proponents of the "new forms of investment." Indeed, transaction costs scholars have shown that the development of nontraditional forms of trade, such as countertrade, can be seen as a second-best attempt by firms located in countries where governments discouraged the establishment of hierarchical links between home firms and foreign partners to recreate some of the incentives inherent in MNEs.

In the mid-1980s a number of scholars (Buckley, 1985; Oman, 1984) suggested that developing countries, rather than obtaining the inputs they needed from foreign firms as a bundle and giving the profits of the venture to the foreign investor (as happened with the expansion in their country of foreign-based MNEs), should instead purchase these inputs in unbundled forms through a wide range of contractual substitutes (such as licensing, franchising, turnkey and management contracts). These "new forms" of investment would have the advantage of leaving the profits in local hands, thus protecting developing countries from exploitation by foreign MNEs. Some of these scholars saw the trend toward these new forms as inevitable, and applauded their use as providing a solution to the conflicts between MNEs and host countries.

Transaction costs analysis suggests that preventing the transfer through MNEs of the inputs supplied by foreign investors (such as technology, management skills, and access to foreign markets) has negative efficiency consequences. MNEs align incentives between seller and buyer of inputs, and this property cannot always be fully emulated by contractual arrangements, no matter how sophisticated. Hence there are cases where the *mandated* replacement of MNEs by contracts will reduce the efficiency of transferring capabilities held by foreign firms to developing countries (Hennart, 1989a).

To better understand why, consider Figure 4.4. Efficient production overseas requires the combination of inputs held by A, a developing country firm, and B, a developed country firm. Sometimes the intermediate inputs supplied by A are sold in relatively efficient markets (for example, commodity chemicals), sometimes in inefficient ones (such is the case with tacit knowledge of local conditions). The same is true for developed country firm B. Sometimes its know-how is easy to license, and sometimes not. When the know-how held by B is easy to license, but the input contributed by A is difficult to measure, the arrangement that minimizes transaction costs consists in A taking a license from B, and holding title to the residual (cell 2). This is because A is both more incited and better able to cheat in the transfer of its input to B than B is in the licensing of its know-how to A. Giving a right to the residual to the party most likely to cheat reduces total transaction costs (Grossman and Hart, 1986). The "new forms" are in this case an efficient way to obtain foreign inputs. If, on the other hand, the inputs held by B are difficult to transact on markets, but A's inputs are sold on efficient markets, then efficiency demands that B keep full title to the profits, that it become a direct investor, buying A's input on the market (cell 3). Imposing the use of "new forms' is inefficient in this case, for it increases the level of total transaction costs incurred in combining inputs.

Davies (1977) provides some evidence to support this argument. He compared the technology transfer provisions of joint venture and licensing contracts between British and Indian firms (the Indian government prohibited then foreign firms from entering India with wholly owned subsidiaries). He found that the type and extent of knowledge transferred by joint venture agreements differed significantly from that in licensing contracts, with licensors providing only technical knowledge, while joint venturers were more likely to add tacit marketing and management advice. Because of the imperfections in the market for knowledge described above, some types of tacit know-how could only be transferred through

		Host country factors held by firm A	
		Marketable know-how	Non-marketable know-how
Home country factors held by Firm B	Marketable know-how	1) Indeterminate	2) B licenses A who sets up a wholly owned firm
	Non-marketable know-how	3) A licenses B who enters with a wholly owned affiliate	4) A and B joint venture

Figure 4.4 Institutional modes for market entry

MNEs. Restricting the entry of MNEs will therefore deprive the country of that know-how.

Countertrade

Consider the situation of a firm in a developing country whose government has banned the entry of foreign MNEs and which sees itself incapable of expanding abroad. It needs the tacit knowledge that is most efficiently transferred through hierarchy within MNEs. What can it do to recreate the incentives provided by hierarchy? One solution suggested by Williamson (1985) is to attempt to build reciprocity into its transactions. Reciprocity increases the enforceability of contracts by creating hostages that will be sacrificed in case of breach. This scenario provides the best explanation for the emergence of the most common forms of a particularly misunderstood type of trading arrangements known as "countertrade."

The term "countertrade" describes a variety of trade practices developed in the 1960s by Soviet-bloc countries to trade with Western firms, and which spread in the 1980s to developing countries. Between 1975 and 1984 the number of countries mandating countertrade rose from 15 to 88, and by the mid-1980s the consensus estimate was that trade under some sort of countertrade arrangement made up between 15 and 20 percent of world trade.

Countertrade has been generally described as a form of barter. As such, its increasing popularity among developing countries has been seen as a puzzling return to archaic practices (de Miramon, 1985). However, a careful look at the structure of three common forms of countertrade contracts (counterpurchase, buy-backs, and offsets) shows that they do not include barter clauses (i.e. the swapping of goods for other goods) but that they consist instead of two separate money-for-goods contracts, with imports made conditional on the exporter purchasing goods and services from the importer. Hence the essence of most countertrade contracts is not barter, but reciprocity (Hennart, 1989b).

Take the case of buy-back contracts. Buy-backs are long-term arrangements made up of two separate but linked contracts. The first contract is for the sale of a plant in exchange for hard currency. In the second contract the plant seller agrees to buy back part or all of the output of the plant in exchange for hard currency. How do we explain these clauses?

Buyers of plant and equipment, especially those located in developing countries, are often considerably less knowledgeable than sellers, and therefore exposed to their opportunism. The economic value of plants also usually depends on continued technical support from vendors. Once the plant is sold, the vendor is usually in a strong bargaining position *vis-à-vis* the plant buyer. Note that neither of these problems arises when plant sellers integrate vertically into foreign manufacture, since in this case they get their returns not from the sale of the plant but from the output generated by the plant. Consequently, they have no incentives to cheat plant buyers and strong incentives to provide them with technical assistance, since they now all belong to the same firm.

The turnkey contract is one solution to these problems that has been touted by the proponents of the "new forms." Under these contracts, full payment for the plant is contingent upon the satisfactory completion of trial runs. There is evidence, however, that such contracts do not protect uninformed buyers from opportunism by plant sellers (Abdhallah-Kodja, 1984).[24]

A buy-back contract under which the plant seller has to purchase some of the output of the plant is one way of reducing transaction costs in the sale of plants by establishing reciprocal commitments. A plant seller that has to take back some of the output of the plant has incentives to provide after-sales service at reasonable cost because interrupted supplies may have adverse consequences. Similarly, the price at which the plant seller agrees to take back the plant's output reveals whether the plant is outmoded or whether there is demand for the plant's output. Buy-backs are not perfect substitutes for vertical integration into manufacture by the plant seller, however, since they do not protect plant buyers against misrepresentations of operating costs.

Counterpurchase, the other major type of countertrade, can be explained in similar terms. Counterpurchase also involves two parallel goods-for-hard-currency contracts, but in this case the goods taken back are not those produced by the equipment sold, but typically those that lack a ready market. Through counterpurchase, a firm that has difficulty marketing its exports can use the threat of not buying to motivate their suppliers to market their products. This solution is likely to be sought if effective distribution of the product taken back requires manufacturer-specific investments. In that case, a simple distribution contract may not be enough to persuade the distributor to make such investments. One solution in this case is to have manufacturers and distributors hierarchically coordinated within an MNE. When this is not possible because of government restrictions, counterpurchase is the next best alternative.

In both cases, countertrade provides better protection against opportunism than simple contracts when markets for plants or marketing services are subject to high transaction costs, but that protection is not as good as that offered by hierarchical coordination. This suggests that countertrade contracts will mostly be used whenever there are barriers to having a foreign firm expand into local production or a domestic firm into foreign sales. Such is the case for firms located in countries that have banned or severely restricted both inward and outward foreign direct investment (Hennart, 1989b, 1990; Kogut, 1986; Mirus and Yeung, 1986; Murrell, 1982). This hypothesis was investigated by Hennart and Anderson (1993). They reasoned that if countertrade was a second-best alternative to MNEs, then a country's propensity to countertrade should be greater the higher the barriers it puts on entry by MNEs. Countertrade propensity should also be high when the host country might have wished to attract MNEs, but was prevented from doing so by its high level of political risk. The alternative hypothesis that a country's countertrade was driven by its inability to obtain foreign exchange to pay for its imports implied that its propensity to countertrade would be higher the more stringent its exchange control (the more overvalued its domestic currency) and the lower its international credit rating.[25] After controlling for a country's export volume, the results showed no statistically significant relationship between a country's countertrade activity and the stringency of its exchange controls. Furthermore, countries with good credit ratings tended in fact to do more countertrade than those with poor ratings. On the other hand, the higher a country's level of political risk and the limits it put on incoming foreign direct investment, the higher its level of countertrade. This supports the view that countertrade contracts are a second-best attempt to replicate the benefits of hierarchical organization when entry by MNEs is banned.[26]

Modes of market entry

Transaction costs theory can also throw light on two decisions that MNEs face when entering foreign markets: should they enter (a) with joint ventures or with wholly owned affiliates and (b) with acquisitions or with greenfield (*de novo*) investments?

Equity joint ventures

One international business institution that is supposedly gaining increasing importance is the equity joint venture (Dunning, 1997). There is no shortage of explanations why firms choose equity joint ventures, but most of the reasons given (pooling complementary inputs, pooling similar inputs) apply as well to other methods of combining the services of assets, such as contracts, greenfield investments, or mergers and acquisitions. Much of the literature thus fails to state the necessary and sufficient conditions under which equity joint ventures will be preferred to the above-named alternatives.

Equity joint ventures are shared equity arrangements.[27] The first step in the explanation of joint ventures is to explore the choice between equity and non-equity arrangements. While the literature has often lumped both types into theoretically vague categories such as "cooperative ventures" or "strategic alliances," it is important to distinguish between equity and non-equity ventures because they differ in their incentive structures, and hence in their suitability in organizing a particular type of transaction. Parties to non-equity arrangements (which, for the sake of simplicity, I shall call "contracts") are paid up front for their contribution and hence have the possibility to cheat if measurement costs are high. Equity arrangements, on the other hand, pay input suppliers from the profits of the venture to which they are contributing. Input sellers who deliver inferior inputs will shoulder part of the cost of their dishonesty, since supplying the venture with inferior inputs lowers the profits of the venture and imposes a loss on the input sellers/owners which is proportional to their equity stake. Equity arrangements are therefore more efficient than contracts when the market for the inputs to be obtained is subject to high transactions costs. As we have seen, some types of know-how, reputation, and distribution services fall into this category.

Equity joint ventures are a particular type of equity arrangement, in the sense that equity in the venture is shared between two or more input contributors/

owners. A simple explanation of this is that equity joint ventures arise when the markets for the intermediate inputs supplied by two or more parties are both subject to high transaction costs. Otherwise, as shown in Figure 4.4, the party with the more marketable input could gain by transferring this input by contract to the party with the less marketable input. Assume that the production of a particular good or service requires the combination of two types of knowledge, a and b, held by firms A and B, respectively. If a can be easily licensed, but not b, a and b will be combined by B, with A licensing a to B. If the reverse is true, B will license b to A. For a joint venture to be the chosen method to combine a and b, the market exchange of both a and b must be subject to high transaction costs (Hennart, 1988b).

Figure 4.4 shows the conditions that make equity joint ventures the optimal way to combine complementary inputs (link joint ventures). A similar logic can be used to explain cases where joint ventures will be used to pool similar inputs (scale joint ventures). Scale joint ventures will be optimal when (a) high transaction costs in the market for the inputs make vertical integration between one production stage and another desirable and (b) differences in minimum efficient scale (MES) between stages are such that sharing the equity of one of the two stages is desirable (Hennart, 1988b). In the aluminum industry, higher MES at the alumina than at the aluminum stage, joined to high transaction costs in the market for bauxite and alumina, have led aluminum companies to form joint ventures to operate captive, but efficiently sized, alumina refineries (Stuckey, 1983).

The presence of at least two simultaneously "hard to sell" inputs held by at least two separate parties is not sufficient, however, for joint ventures to emerge. Inputs that are difficult to exchange on the market could be combined if either firm bought out the other, or if they merged, or if either firm were able to replicate the other firm's assets by purchasing the necessary inputs on the market (the replication option). Further conditions for the existence of joint ventures must therefore be that (1) replicating the assets is more expensive than sharing them, and that (2) mergers and acquisitions of the firms owning the complementary assets are more costly than pooling the services of the assets in a joint venture. Condition (1) obtains when the desired assets have high fixed costs and low marginal costs. Besides the obvious case of governments restricting mergers and acquisitions, (2) will obtain when the assets that yield the desired services are a small and inseparable part of the total assets held by both potential partners or when a merger or a total acquisition would significantly increase management costs (Buckley and Casson, 1987; Hennart, 1988b; Kay et al., 1987).

While joint ventures constitute an efficient way to combine poorly marketable inputs held by two or more firms, they also have offsetting costs. The incentives that suppliers of inputs have to cheat are not totally eliminated, since each joint venture partner can only claim a fraction of the residual value of the business. Each partner may therefore still find it advantageous to maximize his gain at the expense of the venture by, for example, supplying fewer inputs to the venture than contractually agreed when it was formed. This contrasts with full equity control, where the parent, having full rights to the residual of the venture, is incited to maximize it. Another problem is that the joint venture partners may transfer to their wholly owned operations some of the inputs contributed to the venture by the other partners, and then use these inputs usurped from their partner to compete with them (Hamel, 1991). As a result, the efficiency of a joint venture hinges on the convergence of the goals of parties to the agreement, or, failing this, on the degree to which opportunism by the partners can be controlled by contractual means or by the appropriate design of the venture. Whenever partners have conflicting goals that cannot be reconciled by contracts, their actions will lower the profits available for sharing, and the joint venture mode of organization will prove to be very costly for one or both parties.

Joint ventures vs. wholly owned affiliates

This transaction costs model of the joint venture is consistent with the findings of the pioneering studies of Franko (1971) and Stopford and Wells (1972). These authors examined the choice made by US MNEs between wholly owned subsidiaries and joint ventures and concluded that MNEs resisted entering into joint ventures (a) when they already held or could acquire on the market all the assets necessary to operate abroad; and (b) when the market for the assets they were contributing to the venture was characterized by high transaction costs. Hence parents supplying their affiliates (or buying from them) intermediate products which had no market prices were likely to insist on full ownership. Similarly, parents who exploited types of knowledge and goodwill that were difficult to protect through contracts were less likely to form a joint venture (Stopford and Wells thought this was well proxied by the parent's R&D-to-sales and advertising-to-sales ratios). On the other hand, parents tended to choose joint ventures when they needed complementary resources that they could not easily acquire on the market. The need to joint venture was particularly strong (a) when the foreign affiliate represented a diversification move for the parent, and hence the parent needed industry-specific knowledge or distribution facilities; (b) when the MNE had little experience of the market entered, and hence needed country-specific knowledge; and (c) when it needed resources controlled by local firms. Similar findings are reported by Stopford and Haberich (1978) in the case of British MNEs, and by Yoshino (1976), Yoshihara (1984), and Tsurumi (1976) in the case of Japanese MNEs.

Econometric studies provide further support. Gatignon and Anderson (1988) found that the probability that US parents fully owned their overseas subsidiaries varied positively with the ratios of R&D expenditures to sales and advertising expenditures to sales of the industries of the parents, and with the firm's international experience (as proxied by the number of previous foreign investments). Joint ventures were more likely in countries with cultures radically different from the US, controlling for legal restrictions on incoming investment and political risk.[28] A study by Gomes-Casseres (1987), using the same database of pre-1975 affiliates of US MNEs, also showed that advertising intensity, international experience, a high percentage of intrasystem sales within the MNE, and familiarity with the host country all tended to lead to full ownership. Affiliates that were in an industry different from the parent's and which operated in resource-intensive industries, were more likely to be joint ventures. R&D intensity was insignificant, but an interaction term between diversification and R&D intensity had a significantly negative coefficient, indicating that when the subsidiary was outside the parent's core business, R&D intensity encouraged joint ventures, whereas when the subsidiary was active in the parent's main product line, R&D intensity led to full ownership of subsidiaries.

Hennart (1991) looked at the choice made by Japanese MNEs between partial and full ownership of their US subsidiaries. As in the case of US MNEs, Japanese investors were more likely to enter joint ventures when they had little experience in the US market or when their US subsidiary was either in a different industry from that of the parent or in a natural resource industry, indicating the need for country- and industry-specific knowledge and for access to natural resources. Unlike the other two studies, R&D and advertising intensities of the Japanese parents had, however, no impact on the choice between full and partial ownership of their subsidiaries. Hennart's explanation is that some R&D-intensive Japanese firms might have come to the United States to source knowledge via joint ventures, while others had entered to exploit it through wholly owned affiliates.

Hennart used the parent's R&D intensity, an improvement over Gomes-Casseres and Gatignon and Anderson's use of the R&D intensity of the industry of the parent. The correct operationalization of this variable should be the subjective evaluation by the parent of the risk of leakage of their knowledge if they chose joint ventures. This is what Bell (1996) used in his study of the determinants of the choice made by Dutch MNEs between full and partial ownership of their foreign affiliates. He found that parents who transferred crucial proprietary know-how to their foreign affiliates and who thought that know-how could easily leak out to third parties tended to choose wholly owned affiliates.

Hennart and Larimo (1998) looked at whether Japanese firms behaved differently from Finnish firms when choosing between wholly owned affiliates and joint ventures to enter the United States. They argued that because Japan is culturally further from the United States than Finland, the need to acquire the knowledge of how to operate in the United States would be higher, *ceteris paribus*, for Japanese than for Finnish firms. Joint ventures are a good choice to enter an unfamiliar country, since the management of the venture can be delegated to the local partner (Kogut and Singh, 1988). Hence Japanese investors should be more likely to opt for the joint venture. Controlling for all other factors that affect the choice between these two alternatives, Japanese investors were indeed more likely than their Finnish counterparts to choose joint ventures over wholly owned affiliates.

Joint ventures vs. acquisitions

As seen above, transaction costs theory suggests that joint ventures will be chosen over acquisitions in three cases:

1 in the presence of political, institutional, or cultural restrictions on acquisitions/merger;
2 whenever the foreign investor is worried about the impact of a full acquisition on the motivation of the top management team of the acquired firm; and
3 whenever the assets that provide the desired services are tied up with other, non-desired assets.

One implication of conditions (1) and (2) is that the ratio of mergers and acquisitions to joint ventures should be higher between firms domiciled in a given country than between firms domiciled in two different countries, since cultural and institutional barriers to acquisitions are higher for cross-national than for domestic mergers. Using European Community data on joint ventures and acquisitions/mergers between 1983 and 1992, Kay *et al.*, (1996) found that the ratio of acquisitions/mergers to joint ventures was highest between EU firms based in the same country, intermediate between EU firms based in different EU countries, and lowest between EU and non-EU firms.

Hennart and Reddy (1997) investigated condition (3). They looked at the choice made by Japanese investors in the United States between acquiring a US firm or joint venturing with one. They hypothesized that Japanese investors would be more likely to acquire American firms if they were "digestible," i.e. if they did not include unneeded assets. Digestible firms, they argued, were firms that were small, or, if large, that were divisionalized, so that Japanese investors could acquire only the relevant parts of the firm. The Japanese would, on the other hand, enter into a joint venture with large, non-divisionalized American firms, because through joint ventures they could access the services of desired assets without having to purchase undesired ones. As predicted, Hennart and Reddy found that the "digestibility" of the American partner had a statistically significant influence on the choice between joint ventures and acquisitions.

Acquisitions

Another major decision facing a firm entering a foreign market is whether to establish a new business from scratch (a greenfield entry) or whether to acquire an existing business (an acquisition). Transaction costs theory can throw light on this choice as well, although the theory here is somewhat less developed. Making an acquisition means purchasing a going business. Setting up a greenfield entry means purchasing local inputs in disembodied form and combining them with inputs held by the investor to form a productive unit. This suggests that the choice between greenfield entry and acquisitions should be determined, at least in part, by the characteristics of the contributions made by local and foreign factors of production, and how they interact.

Consider the following cases. In the 1960s American food companies thought that they knew better than their European counterparts how to advertise and distribute their products. At the same time, they did not know much about how to operate in Europe. Marketing know-how, tacit and not protected by patents, could not be profitably licensed. The most efficient way to leverage it abroad was to acquire European food companies with reputable trade names and quality products, and to provide these acquisitions with superior Yankee marketing know-how (Horst, 1974). Here acquisitions made sense since the American investors had little knowledge of European food tastes and production conditions, and US marketing know-how could efficiently be merged into an existing firm.

Japanese automobile assemblers, on the other hand, have entered the United States through greenfield investments. The Japanese automaker's competitive advantage has been superior quality, obtained through sophisticated plant design and labor management practices, such as work rotation, work teams, and quality circles (Florida and Kenney, 1991; Pucik and Hatvani, 1983). Because the successful implementation of many of these techniques requires a change in attitudes and values, they are very difficult to incorporate into an existing American firm (Brannen *et al.*, 1998). Instead it is much easier to inculcate them into a greenfield plant, since this makes it possible to select a location and a labor force that will facilitate the transfer.

The preceding analysis suggests that, *ceteris paribus*, acquisitions will be chosen over greenfield investments (1) the easier it is to merge the foreign investor's contribution with an existing firm and (2) the less knowledgeable investors are with the market entered. Diversified firms are firms where quasi-independent subsidiaries share general management or marketing know-how generated at headquarters. Hence we would expect that investors who are diversified, and/or who invest in industries unrelated to their domestic business, would tend to prefer acquisitions to greenfields. Acquisitions are also indicated when the foreign investor wants to combine and rationalize existing physical assets (economies of scale), or needs access to existing distribution channels (economies of scope) (Haspeslagh and Jemison, 1991). Greenfields will be chosen when the foreign investor wants to transfer socially embedded processes.[29]

The empirical literature provides some support. Caves and Mehra (1986), in the case of American firms, Zejan (1990) in the case of Swedish firms, and Barkema and Vermeulen (1998) in the case of Dutch ones, found a significant correlation between a parent's overall product diversification and its preference for acquisitions over greenfields. Hennart and Park (1993) looked at Japanese entries into the United States. Controlling for financial factors, such as the investor's leverage and the relative levels of stock prices and exchange rates, they found that R&D-intensive Japanese parents, whose advantage consisted in work practices that were socially embedded, favored greenfields over acquisitions. Acquisitions were chosen, on the other hand, by Japanese firms effecting a diversification. Financial factors were not significant. Andersson and Svensson (1994) analyzed the choice of Swedish MNEs between acquisitions and greenfields and confirmed Hennart and Park's findings that a parent's R&D intensity encouraged greenfield entry.

Conclusions

As Kay (1991: 143) has pointed out, "it is misleading to talk of 'the' transaction costs approach when there are in fact a number of variants of transaction costs reasoning." Transaction costs theory is an approach more than a set theory. The richness and the diversity of the literature this approach has stimulated is a sign of its fruitfulness. Given the subtle differences in the way various authors have used transaction costs theory to explain the MNE, it might be useful to highlight what is idiosyncratic in the version developed in this chapter.

First, I have argued that a full understanding of the expansion of MNEs requires a comparison of the costs of organizing interdependencies within firms and those of doing it in markets. A theory of why markets fail is not sufficient to explain the MNE; one must also have a theory of why firms succeed. The preceding pages argue that firms succeed not because they use "internal prices," but because they use a method of organization called hierarchy which extinguishes market transaction costs by changing the incentives of the parties. The unavoidable consequence of using hierarchy is the generation in firms of a different type of cost, which arises from the decrease in the motivation of employees who are no longer paid in strict proportion to their output measured at market prices. The choice of institutional form involves therefore a tradeoff between the cost of measuring intermediate outputs (market transaction costs) and that of motivating and directing employees who are no longer paid in strict proportion to their output (internal organization costs). Taking full equity is inherently costly, because it automatically dulls the incentives of agents. This simple model explains why firms will sometimes use non-equity forms (such as franchising) to exploit abroad their reputation, or will willingly choose to share the ownership of their foreign affiliates.

Second, the analysis of this chapter has focused on the organization of international interdependencies, not on the internalization of "firm-specific advantages." As the preceding pages show, there are many cases when firms expand abroad without any firm-specific advantages: for example when they make backward investments to procure raw materials and intermediate products. When US steel makers invest into the mining of Liberian iron ore, they do not do so to exploit abroad a monopolistic advantage in a superior proprietary technology. In fact, many steel firms have so little competence in the mining of iron ore that they have their captive mines managed by specialist firms (Cleveland Cliffs and Hanna Mining, for example). Similarly, many freestanding firms did not have any firm-specific advantages to exploit abroad because they had no domestic business. Focusing on the internalization of advantages also makes it difficult to explain why some firms invest abroad to acquire technology. There are many cases of Japanese foreign direct investors acquiring a share in American high-technology firms in exchange for fresh capital. In this case the Japanese investor does not have any technological advantages to exploit (Christelow, 1995).

The *raison d'être* of MNEs is more generally that they are more efficient than markets in organizing international interdependencies. In other words, MNEs exist because they internalize markets, including, but not exclusively, markets for advantages. Hence US steel makers invest abroad when organizing the coordination between mine and blast furnace through hierarchical processes which is less costly than procuring iron ore through long-term contracts. Focusing on the internalization of markets also offers a simple and straightforward explanation for technology-seeking investments: an equity link between a Japanese firm seeking access to technology and the high-technology American firm which possesses it is made necessary by the presence of high transaction costs in the market for knowledge, while high transaction costs in the international market for financial capital may explain why the American firm will need to offer an equity stake to its Japanese lender.

This brings us to our third point. The right question to ask to understand international business institutions is not so much what arrangements the MNE needs to use to safeguard its "monopolistic advantages," but rather, what is the most efficient way to combine the local and foreign inputs needed to operate in a foreign country? In all cases an MNE which operates abroad must obtain access to local inputs. It will keep full ownership of its foreign affiliate if it can access these inputs on the market. If this is not the case, and the necessary inputs are held by a local firm, the foreign investor will form a joint venture with that firm. But in all cases the most efficient solution will be the one that minimizes the costs of organizing the international interdependence between factors of production located in two separate countries.

Thinking in terms of interdependence also throws light on an apparent puzzle in the transaction costs theory of the MNE. The theory as it stands predicts that an inefficient market will be internalized, but it does not predict by whom. Recall our example of the banana industry. Transaction costs theory explains why plantations and distribution facilities ought to be integrated, but not why banana distributors have integrated into banana plantations rather than the reverse. As we have argued above, firms experience internal organization costs when they internalize a market. These costs arise because reducing cheating costs is achieved by reducing the motivation of employees. Whether the distributor will take over the banana plantation, or whether the reverse will take place, should depend on the costs experienced by firms of each country in motivating employees of the other country. Hence if the banana distributor is more skillful at monitoring banana plantation employees than the banana plantation is at monitoring employees of the distributor, the distributor will find it profitable to take over the banana plantation firm. In other words, the foreign direct investor will be the interacting party who has the better management skills, and therefore experiences lower cost in managing the other party's employees (Grossman and Hart, 1986). This explains why the pattern of vertical integration in the banana industry has been one of American shippers and wholesalers integrating into Central American plantations, and not one of Central American growers integrating into US distribution. It also explains why Middle East petroleum producers have been slow at integrating into European distribution in order to recreate the vertical links between crude oil production and refining that had been established by Western oil companies, but broken with the nationalization of their Middle East holdings.[30]

Acknowledgments

I wish to thank Jean Boddewyn, Peter Buckley, Mark Casson, Geoffrey Jones, Roger Sugden, Mira Wilkins, Bernard Yeung, and especially Kathleen Saul, for many valuable suggestions on an earlier version of this chapter.

Notes

1 Transaction costs theory differs in subtle ways from its close relative, internalization theory (Rugman, 1981). Internalization theory focuses on the internalization of advantages, while transaction costs theory considers the internalization of markets. The transaction costs theory version outlined here also presents a different explanation of why firms can be more efficient than markets and considers both home country and host country factors of production when considering the forms taken by expansion abroad. All these points are covered below.

2 In 1990, for example, more than 50 percent of the financing of the foreign affiliates of US firms was obtained locally (through reinvested profits or local borrowing) (Delapierre and Milelli, 1995: 18).

3 Contrary to what is sometimes asserted by its critics, transaction costs theory does not assume opportunism to be constant across space and time, and so what individuals rationally do to protect against opportunism will vary according to local conditions. One always locks one's car in New York except in special circumstances; one never locks one's car in Nova Scotia, except in special circumstances.

4 Note that, in contrast to principal-agent theory, transaction costs theory can accommodate any assumption about the risk preference of agents and principals, and is compatible with assumptions that both principals and agents are risk neutral.

5 This is true whether the firm operates the subsidiary through expatriates or through local personnel: the cross-cultural contact, with its potential for misunderstandings and deception (Root, 1987), must be made in all cases, whether between HQ and the subsidiary manager, between the subsidiary manager and his or her employees, or between the employees and local suppliers or customers.

6 The fact that there are decreasing returns to monitoring is perfectly compatible with transaction costs theory, contrary to what Ghoshal and Moran (1996) argue.

7 One can make the parallel assumption that the opportunities for fraud rise more than proportionally when one substitutes price for behavior constraints. Hence the presence of behavior constraints in market transactions (i.e. contracts).

8 Note that the imposition of tariffs *per se* is not a sufficient reason for foreign production, unless MNEs can minimize tariff payments by undervaluing intra-firm trade.

9 Tacit technology is difficult to define in a patent, and hence will be difficult to license (Hennart, 1982).

10 If its consumers are repeat customers, a franchisor who would reduce quality would bear the full monetary consequences of his action. However, the greater the percentage of repeat customers, the less valuable a franchised trademark, since repeat customers do not have high search costs and hence have less need for trademarked products. Hence we can expect the free-riding problem to be significant in the case of most franchised trademarks.

11 Franchisors also shirk when they fail to monitor the quality of the franchisees' output. One of the reasons for McDonald's success was its founder's policy of not granting

area franchises, but instead of franchising one outlet at a time. At the time, franchisors granted such area franchises in exchange for up-front cash payments, and then withdrew from the business (Love, 1987). One additional reason why franchisors may own outlets is that they can use such outlets to persuade potential franchisees that they will stay in the business.

12 In February 1996, for example, the average cash flow of an American franchised McDonalds unit was $15,340, or 13.7 percent of sales of $112,000. Company-owned stores had a lower cash flow of $12,690, equal to 10.4 percent of sales of $122,460. Hence franchised units were more efficiently run than company-owned ones (Gibson, 1996).

13 An efficiently sized bauxite mine costs half a billion dollars and a refinery between 500 million and a billion.

14 Similar problems arose in the iron ore industry following the slump in demand in the 1970s (Franz *et al.*, 1986).

15 There are some cases of vertical integration between mines and smelters in the lode sector, but they reflect political motives. For further details see Hennart (1986a, 1988a).

16 Fiscal considerations may also be relevant here. Vertical integration transforms arms length trades into internal ones. This makes it possible to alter the nominal price at which transactions take place without affecting revenues. By altering nominal prices, the MNE has the possibility of shifting accounting profits to low tax jurisdictions, to reduce *ad valorem* tariff duties, and to repatriate earnings disguised as expenditures. This possibility is limited by the presence of world prices for the goods shipped and by the sophistication of tax authorities.

17 In 1980, 60 percent of the banana export trade was handled by three vertically integrated MNEs (Casson, 1986: 51).

18 Inversely, retailers will vertically integrate into manufacturing if it is more difficult for them to control the quality of the manufacturers' goods than it is to control shirking by manufacturers if they are employees of retailers. Note that a third solution is to have retailers put their brand on the manufacturer's product (Chen and Hennart, 1998).

19 In large corporations this right is exercised through the board of directors.

20 "Just a brass nameplate in the City" is how Nicholas (1982) described it.

21 About three-fourths of the companies registered between 1862 and 1914 in Edinburgh to do business abroad were in mining and agriculture (Schmitz, 1993). Forty percent of the 2,544 British freestanding firms operating outside the US and Canada listed in a 1916 US Federal Trade Commission report (US FTC, 1916) were in mining, and another 28 percent were in agriculture. Sixty-nine percent of the Dutch freestanding companies identified by Sluyterman as active in 1913 were in tropical agriculture and in mining and petroleum extraction (Sluyterman, 1994).

22 As late as 1967 UK-registered freestanding firms were producing over 75 percent of Nigeria's tin output (Schatzl, 1971).

23 Today shares of small companies developing North and South American mines are sold directly to the public on the penny stock markets of Spokane, Denver, and Vancouver (Mikesell and Whitney, 1987), as they were in London in the heyday of the freestanding firm.

24 Here as well, there are performance inseparability problems, since failure of a turnkey plant may be due to defective technology or to mistakes made by local operators. Ascertaining who is responsible is often very difficult.

25 The traditional argument is that countertrade is barter. Barter makes it possible to bypass exchange control regulations by swapping exports for imports without having to use foreign exchange. A low credit rating makes it difficult to borrow foreign exchange, and thus encourages importers to resort to barter.

26 For similar findings at the firm level, see Marin and Schnitzer (1995).

27 Some authors restrict the term "equity joint ventures" to shared-equity greenfield ventures, and exclude partial acquisitions. I know of no theoretical reasons to exclude partial acquisitions, and, unless specifically noted, the term "joint venture" in the following paragraphs refers to both greenfield joint ventures and partial acquisitions.

28 Benito (1996) had similar results in the case of Norwegian firms investing abroad. Larimo (1993), on the other hand, did not find any impact of cultural distance on ownership preferences.

29 That acquired subsidiaries tend to be less integrated into the parent's network is suggested by the fact that Japanese manufacturing subsidiaries in the United States that had been acquired had, *ceteris paribus*, a statistically higher probability of being sold off between 1980 and 1991 than those that had been established as greenfields (Hennart *et al.*, 1998).

30 Alongside increasing managerial sophistication in some Arab countries (notably Kuwait), asymmetries between European countries and Middle East countries in restrictions on inward foreign direct investment are also a factor.

References

Abdallah-Khodja, K. (1984) "Algeria's Experience with New International Investment Relations," in C. Oman (ed.), *New Forms of International Investment in Developing Countries: The National Perspective*. Paris: OECD.

Ackerlof, G. (1970) "The Market for 'Lemons': Qualitative Uncertainty and the Market Mechanism," *Quarterly Journal of Economics* 74: 448–500.

Allen, G. C., and Donnithorne, A. G. (1957) *Western Enterprise in Indonesia and Malaya*. London: George Allen and Unwin.

Anderson, E. and A. Coughlan (1987) "International Market Entry through Expansion via Independent or Integrated Channels of Distribution," *Journal of Marketing* 51: 71–82.

Andersson, T. and R. Svensson (1994) "Entry Modes for Direct Investment Determined by the Composition of Firm-Specific Skills," *Scandinavian Journal of Economics* 96, 4: 551–60.

Arrow, K. (1962) "Economic Welfare and the Allocation of Resources for Invention," in K. Arrow (ed.) *The Rate and Direction of Inventive Activity*, Princeton, NJ: Princeton University Press, 609–25.

Bain, J. (1956) *Barriers to New Competition*, Cambridge, Mass.: Harvard University Press.

Barkema, H. and F. Vermeulen (1998) "International Expansion through Start-Up or Acquisition: A Learning Perspective," *Academy of Management Journal* 41: 7–26.

Bell. J. (1996) *Single or Joint Venturing? A Comprehensive Approach to Foreign Entry Mode Choice*, Aldershot: Avebury.

Benito, G.R.G. (1996) "Ownership Structures of Norwegian Foreign Subsidiaries in Manufacturing," *The International Trade Journal* 10: 157–98.

Brannen, M., J. Liker, and W.M. Fruin (1998) "Recontextualization and Factory-to-Factory Knowledge Transfer from Japan to the US: The Case of NSK," in J. Liker, M. Fruin, and P. Adler (eds) *Remade in America: Transplanting and Transforming Japanese Management Systems*, New York: Oxford University Press.

Brickly, J. and F. Dark (1987) "The Choice of Organizational Form: The Case of Franchising," *Journal of Financial Economics* 18: 401–20.

Brown, W.B. (1976) "Islands of Conscious Power: MNCs in the Theory of the Firm," *MSU Business Topics* 24: 37–45.

Buckley, P. (1983) "New Theories of International Business," in M. Casson (ed.) *The Growth of International Business*, London: Allen & Unwin.

—— (1985) "New Forms of International Industrial Cooperation," in P. Buckley and M. Casson (eds) *The Economic Theory of the Multinational Enterprise*, New York: St. Martin's Press.

Buckley, P. and M. Casson (1976) *The Future of Multinational Enterprise*, London: Macmillan.

—— (1981) "The Optimal Timing of a Foreign Direct Investment," *Economic Journal* 91: 75–87.

—— (1987) "A Theory of Cooperation in International Business," in F. Contractor, and P. Lorange (eds) *Cooperative Strategies in International Business*. Lexington, Mass.: Lexington Books.

Buckley, P. and H. Davies (1981) "Foreign Licensing in Overseas Operations: Theory and Evidence from the UK," in R. Hawkins and A.T. Prasad (eds) *Research in International Business and Finance*, Greenwich, Conn.: JAI Press.

Buckley, P. and K. Prescott (1989) "The Structure of British Industry's Sales in Foreign Markets," *Managerial and Decision Economics* 10: 189–208.

Cantwell, J. (1989a) "Theories of International Production." University of Reading Discussion Paper in International Investment and Business Studies.

—— (1989b) *Technological Innovations and Multinational Corporations*, Oxford: Basil Blackwell.

Casson, M. (1979) *Alternatives to the Multinational Enterprise*, London: Macmillan.

—— (1982) "Transaction Costs and the Theory of the MNE," in A. Rugman (ed.) *New Theories of the Multinational Enterprise*, New York: St. Martin's Press.

—— (1985) "Multinational Monopolies and International Cartels," in P.J. Buckley and M.C. Casson (eds) *The Economic Theory of the Multinational Enterprise: Selected Papers*, London: Macmillan, 60–97.

—— (1986) "Introduction," in Mark Casson & Associates, *Multinationals and World Trade* London: Allen & Unwin.

—— (1987) *The Firm and the Market*, Cambridge, Mass.: MIT Press.

Caves, R. (1971) "International Corporations: The Industrial Economics of Foreign Investment," *Economica* 38: 1–27.

—— (1982) *Multinational Enterprise and Economic Analysis*, New York: Cambridge University Press.

—— (1996) *Multinational Enterprise and Economic Analysis*. 2nd edn. New York: Cambridge University Press.

—— (1998) "Research in International Business: Problems and Prospects," *Journal of International Business Studies* 29: 5–19.

Caves, R. and S. Mehra, (1986) "Entry of Foreign Multinational into U.S. Manufacturing Industries," in M. Porter (ed.) *Competition in Global Industries*, Boston, Mass.: Harvard Business School Press.

Caves. R., and W. Murphy (1976) "Franchising: Firms, Markets, and Intangible Assets," *Southern Economic Journal* 42: 572–86.

Caves. R., H. Crookell, and P. Killing (1982) "The Imperfect Market for Technology Licenses," *Oxford Bulletin of Economics and Statistics*.

Chandler, A. (1959) "The Beginnings of 'Big Business' in America," *Business History Review*, Spring, 33, 1: 1–31.

—— (1977) *The Visible Hand*, Cambridge, Mass.: Belknap Press.

Chen, S. and J.-F. Hennart (1998) "When do Manufacturer Products carry Retailer Brands? A Transaction Costs Theory of Private Branding," unpublished manuscript.

Christelow, D. (1995) *When Giants Converge: The Role of U.S.–Japan Direct Investment*, Armonk and London: M.E. Sharpe.

Contractor, F. (1984) "Choosing between Foreign Direct Investment and Licensing: Theoretical Considerations and Empirical Tests," *Journal of International Business Studies* 15: 167–83.

Cushman, J.W. (1986) "The Khaw Group: Chinese Business in Early Twentieth Century Penang," *Journal of Southeast Asia Studies* 17: 58–79.

Davidson, W.H. and D. McFetridge (1984) "International Technology Transactions and the Theory of the Firm," *Journal of Industrial Economics* 32: 253–64.

—— (1985) "International Technology Transfer Mode," *Journal of International Business Studies*, Summer, 5–21.

Davies, H. (1977) "Technological Transfer through Commercial Transactions," *Journal of Industrial Economics* 26: 161–75.

Delapierre, M. and C. Milelli (1995) *Les Firmes Multinationales*, Paris: Vuibert.

Drabble, J.H. (1973) *Rubber in Malaya: the Genesis of the Industry*, Kuala Lumpur: Oxford University Press.

Drake, P.J. (1980) *Money, Finance, and Development*, New York: Wiley.

Dunning, J.H. (1977) "Trade, Location of Economic Activity, and the Multinational Enterprise: A Search for an Eclectic Approach," in B. Ohlin, P.O. Hesselborn, and P.M. Wijkman (eds) *The International Allocation of Economic Activity* New York: Holmes & Meier.

—— (1979) "Explaining Changing Patterns of International Production: In Defense of the Eclectic Theory," *Oxford Bulletin of Economics and Statistics*, November, 41: 269–95.

—— (1981) *International Production and the Multinational Enterprise*, London: George Allen & Unwin.

—— (1993) *Multinational Enterprises and the Global Economy*, New York and London: Addison-Wesley.

—— (1997) *Alliance Capitalism and Global Business*, London and New York: Routledge.

Dunning, J. and J. Cantwell (1984) "The 'New Forms' of International Involvement of British Firms in the Third World," Unpublished manuscript.

Dunning, J. and M. McQueen (1981) "The Eclectic Theory of International Production: A Case Study of the International Hotel Industry," *Managerial and Decision Economics*, 2: 197–210.

Dunning, J. and A. Rugman (1985) "The Influence of Hymer's Dissertation on the Theory of Foreign Direct Investment," *American Economic Review*, May, 228–32.

Fieldhouse, D.K. (1986) "The Multinational: A Critique of A Concept," in A. Teichova, M. Levy-Leboyer, and H. Nussbaum (eds) *Multinational Enterprise in Historical Perspective*, Cambridge: Cambridge University Press.

Franko, L. (1971) *Joint Venture Survival in Multinational Corporations*, New York: Praeger.

Franz, J., B. Stenberg and J. Strongman (1986) *Iron Ore: Global Prospects for the Industry, 1985–95*, Washington, DC: The World Bank.

Gales, B. and K. Sluyterman (1998) in M. Wilkins and H. Shroeter (eds) *Freestanding Companies in the World Economy*, London: Oxford University Press.

Gatignon, H. and E. Anderson (1988) "The Multinational Corporation Degree of Control over Subsidiaries: An Empirical Test of a Transaction Cost Explanation," *Journal of Law, Economics, and Organization* 4, 2: 305–36.

Ghoshal, S. and P. Moran (1996) "Bad for Practice: A critique of Transaction Costs Theory,' *Academy of Management Review* 21: 13–47.

Gibson, R. (1996) "McDonald's, U.S.-Franchisee Ventures are on the Rise," *Wall Street Journal*, June 26.

Globerman, S. and R. Schwindt (1986) "The Organization of Vertically Related Transactions in the Canadian Forest Products Industries," *Journal of Economic Behavior and Organization* 7: 199–212.

Gomes-Casseres, B. (1989) "Ownership Structures of Foreign Subsidiaries: Theory and Evidence," *Journal of Economic Behavior and Organization* 11: 1–25.

Greening, T. (1976) "Oil Wells, Pipelines, Refineries and Gas Stations: A Study of Vertical Integration," Ph.D. dissertation, Harvard University.

Grossman, S. and O. Hart (1986) "The Costs and Benefits of Ownership: A Theory of Vertical and Lateral Integration," *Journal of Political Economy* 691–719.

Hamel, G. (1991) "Competition for Competence and Inter-Partner Learning Within International Strategic Alliances," *Strategic Management Journal* 12: 83–104.

Haspeslagh, P. and D. Jemison (1991) *Managing Acquisitions*, New York: Free Press.

Hennart, J.-F. (1977) "A Theory of Foreign Direct Investment," Ph.D. dissertation, University of Maryland.

—— (1982) *A Theory of Multinational Enterprise*, Ann Arbor: University of Michigan Press.

—— (1986a) "The Tin Industry," in M. Casson and Associates, *Multinationals and World Trade*, London: George Allen & Unwin.

—— (1986b) "Internalization in Practice: Foreign Direct Investment in Malaysian Tin Mining," *Journal of International Business Studies* 17, 2: 131–43.

—— (1986c) "What is Internalization?," *Weltwirtschaftliches Archiv*, Winter, 791–804.

—— (1987) "Transaction Costs and Multinational Enterprise: The Case of Tin," *Business and Economic History* 16: 147–159.

—— (1988a) "Vertical Integration in the Aluminum and Tin Industries," *Journal of Economic Behavior and Organization* 9, 3: 281–300.

—— (1988b) "A Transaction Costs Theory of Equity Joint Ventures," *Strategic Management Journal* 9, 4: 361–74.

—— (1989a) "Can the *New Forms of Investment* Substitute for the *Old Forms*? A Transaction Costs Perspective," *Journal of International Business Studies* 20, 2: 211–33.

—— (1989b) "The Transaction Cost Rationale for Countertrade," *Journal of Law, Economics, and Organization* 5, 1: 127–53.

—— (1990) "Some Empirical Dimensions of Countertrade," *Journal of International Business Studies* 21: 243–70.

—— (1991) "The Transaction Costs Theory of Joint Ventures: An Empirical Study of Japanese Subsidiaries in the United States," *Management Science* 37, 4: 483–97.

—— (1993a) "Explaining the Swollen Middle: Why Most Transactions are a Mix of Market and Hierarchy," *Organization Science* 4, 4: 529–47.

—— (1993b) "Control in Multinational Firms: The Role of Price and Hierarchy," in S. Ghoshal and E. Westney (eds) *Organization Theory and the Multinational Corporation*, New York: St. Martin's Press.

—— (1994) "International Capital Transfers: A Transaction Cost Framework," *Business History* 36: 51–70.

—— (1998) "Transaction Costs Theory and the Freestanding Firm," in M. Wilkins and H. Schroeter (eds) *The Freestanding Firm in the World Economy*, London: Oxford University Press.

Hennart, J.-F. and E. Anderson (1993) "Countertrade and the Minimization of Transaction Costs: An Empirical Examination," *Journal of Law, Economics, and Organization* 9: 290–313.

Hennart, J.-F. and J. Larimo (1998) "The Impact of Culture on the Strategy of Multinational Enterprises: Does National Origin Affect Ownership Decisions by Foreign Direct Investors into the United States?," *Journal of International Business Studies* 29: 253–78.

Hennart, J.-F. and Y.-R. Park (1993) "Greenfield vs. Acquisition: The Strategy of Japanese Investors in the United States", *Management Science* 39, 9: 1054–70.

Hennart, J.-F. and S. Reddy (1997) "The Choice between Mergers/Acquisitions and Joint Ventures: the Case of Japanese Investors in the United States," *Strategic Management Journal* 18, 1: 1–12.

Hennart, J.-F., D.-J. Kim, and M. Zeng (1998) "The Impact of Joint Venture Status on the Longevity of Japanese Stakes in U.S. Manufacturing Affiliates," *Organization Science*, 9: 1–14.

Hill, C. and W.C. Kim (1988) "Searching For a Dynamic Theory of the Multinational Enterprise: A Transaction Cost Model," *Strategic Management Journal* 9: 93–104.

Horst, T. (1974) *At Home Abroad: A Study of the Domestic and Foreign Operations of the American Food Processing Industry*, Cambridge, Mass.: Ballinger.

Hymer, S. (1970) "The Efficiency (Contradictions) of Multinational Corporations," *American Economic Review*, May, 60(2): 441–48.

—— (1976) *The International Operations of National Firms*, Cambridge, Mass.: MIT Press.

Jackson, W.T. (1968) *The Enterprising Scot*, Edinburgh: Edinburgh University Press.

Jensen, M. and W. Meckling (1976) "Theory of the Firm: Managerial Behavior, Agency Costs, and Capital Structure," *Journal of Financial Economics*, 3: 305–60.

Johanson, J. and J.E. Vahlne (1977) "The Internalization Process of the Firm," *Journal of International Business Studies*, 8, Spring/Summer: 23–32.

Jones, G. (1996) *The Evolution of International Business*, London and New York: Routledge.

Joskow, P. (1985) "Vertical Integration and Long-term Contracts: The Case of Coal Burning Electric Generating Plants," *Journal of Law, Economics and Organization* 1.

Kay, N. (1983) "Multinational Enterprise: A Review Article," *Scottish Journal of Political Economy* 30: 304–12.

—— (1991) "Multinational Enterprise as Strategic Choice: Some Transaction Costs Perspectives," in C. Pitelis and R. Sugden (eds) *The Logic of the Transnational Firm*, London and New York: Routledge.

Kay, N., J.-A. Robe, and P. Zagnoli (1987) "An Approach to the Analysis of High Technology Joint Ventures," European University Institute working paper, Florence.

Kay, N., H. Ramsay, and J.-F. Hennart (1996) "Industrial Collaboration and the European Internal Market," *Journal of Common Market Studies*, 34: 465–75.

Kenney, Martin, and Florida, Richard (1993) *Beyond Mass Production*. New York: Oxford University Press.

Kindleberger, C.P. (1969) *American Business Abroad*, New Haven, Conn.: Yale University Press.

Klein, S., G. Frazier, and V. Roth (1990) "A Transaction Cost Analysis Model of

Channel Integration in International Markets," *Journal of Marketing Research* 23: 196–208.

Kogut, B. (1986) "On Designing Contracts to Guarantee Enforceability: Theory and Evidence from East–West Trade," *Journal of International Business Studies* 17: 47–62.

Kogut, B. and H. Singh (1988) "The Effect of National Culture on the Choice of Entry Mode," *Journal of International Business Studies* 19: 411–32.

Larimo, J. (1993) *Foreign Direct Investment Behaviour and Performance: An Analysis of Finnish Direct Manufacturing Investments in OECD Countries.* Acta Wasaensia no. 32, University of Vaasa.

Levin, R., A. Klevorick, R. Nelson, and S. Winter (1987) "Appropriating the Returns from Industrial Research and Development," *Brookings Papers on Economic Activity* 3: 783–820.

Litvak, I. and C. Maule (1977) "Transnational Corporations and Vertical Integration: The Banana Case," *Journal of World Trade Law* 11, 6: 537–49.

Love, J. (1987) *McDonald's: Behind the Arches*, New York: Bantam.

Mackenzie, C. (1954) *Realms of Silver: One Hundred Years of Banking in the East*, London: Routledge & Kegan Paul.

McManus, J. (1972) "The Theory of the Multinational Firm," in G. Paquet (ed.) *The Multinational Firm and the Nation State*, Don Mills, Ont.: Macmillan.

Magee, S. (1977) "Information and the Multinational Corporation: An Appropriability Theory of Direct Foreign Investment," in J.N. Bhagwhati (ed.), *The New International Economic Order*, Cambridge, Mass.: MIT Press.

Marin, D. and M. Schnitzer (1995) "Tying Trade Flows: A Theory of Countertrade with Evidence," *American Economic Review*, 85, 5: 1047–64.

Masten, S. (1984) "The Organization of Production Evidence from the Aerospace Industry," *Journal of Law and Economics* 27: 403.

Mikesell, R. and J. Whitney (1987) *The World Mining Industry*, Boston, Mass.: Allen & Unwin.

Miramon, J. de (1985) "Countertrade: An Illusory Solution," *OECD Observer*, 134, May: 24–29.

Mirus, R. and B. Yeung (1986) "Economic Incentives for Countertrade," *Journal of International Business Studies* 17, 13: 27–39.

Monteverde, K. and D. Teece (1982) "Supplier Switching Costs and Vertical Integration in the Automobile Industry," *Bell Journal of Economics* 13: 206–13.

Murrell, P. (1982) "Product Quality, Market Signaling, and the Development of East–West Trade," *Economic Inquiry*, 20, October: 589–603.

Nicholas, S.J. (1982) "British Multinational Investment Before 1939," *Journal of European Economic History* 11 (Winter): 605–30.

—— (1983) "Agency Contracts, Institutional Modes, and the Transition to Foreign Direct Investment by British Manufacturing Multinationals before 1935," *Journal of Economic History*, 48: 675–86.

Oman, C. (1984) *New Forms of International Investment in Developing Countries*, Paris: OECD.

Perrow, Charles (1988) *Complex Organization: A Critical Essay (3rd Ed)*, New York: Random House.

Pucik, V., and Hatvany, N. (1983) "Management Practices in Japan and their Impact on Business Strategy," in Robert Lamb (ed.), *Advances in Strategic Management*, 1, Greenwich, CT: JAI Press.

Read, R. (1986) "The Banana Industry: Oligopoly and Barriers to Entry," in M. Casson and Associates, *Multinationals and World Trade*, London: Allen & Unwin.

Robbins, S. and R. Stobaugh (1973) *Money in the Multinational Enterprise*, New York: Basic Books.

Root, F. (1987) *Entry Strategies for International Markets*, Lexington, Mass.: Lexington Books.

Rugman, A.M. (1981) *Inside the Multinationals*, New York: Columbia University Press.

Schatzl, L. (1971) *The Nigerian Tin Industry*. Ibadan.

Schmitz, C. (1993) "Patterns of Scottish Portfolio Foreign Investment 1860–1914," unpublished manuscript, University of St. Andrews.

Shapiro, A. (1984) "The Evaluation and Control of Foreign Affiliates," *Midland Corporate Finance Journal*, 25, Spring: 13–25,

Sluyterman, K. (1994) "Dutch Freestanding Companies between 1870 and 1940," unpublished manuscript.

Stopford, J. and K. Haberich (1978) "Ownership and Control of Foreign Operations," in Ghertman and Leontiades (eds) *European Research in International Business*, New York: North Holland.

Stopford, J. and L. Wells (1972) *Managing the Multinational Enterprise*, New York: Basic Books.

Stuckey, J. (1983) *Vertical Integration and Joint Ventures in the Aluminum Industry*, Cambridge, Mass.: Harvard University Press.

Swedenborg, B. (1979) *The Multinational Operations of Swedish Firms*, Stockholm: Industrial Institute for Economics and Social Research.

Teece, D. (1976) *Vertical Integration and Vertical Divestiture in the U.S. Oil Industry*, Stanford, Ca.: Institute for Energy Studies.

—— (1981) "The Multinational Enterprise: Market Failure and Market Power Considerations," *Sloan Management Review*, Spring, 22, 3: 3–17.

—— (1983) "Technological and Organizational Factors in the Theory of the Multinational Enterprise," in M. Casson (ed.) *The Growth of International Business*, London: George Allen & Unwin.

Tsurumi, Y. (1976) *The Japanese Are Coming*, Cambridge, Mass.: Ballinger.

US Federal Trade Commission (1916) *Report on Cooperation in American Export Trade*. Washington DC: Government Printing Office.

Van Helten, J.-J. and G. Jones (1989) "British Business in Malaysia and Singapore since the 1870s," in R.P.T. Davenport-Hines and G. Jones (eds), *British Business in Asia since 1860*, Cambridge: Cambridge University Press.

Walker, G. and D. Weber (1984) "A Transaction Cost Approach to Make-or-Buy Decisions," *Administrative Science Quarterly* 29: 373–91.

Wilkins, M. (1970) *The Emergence of Multinational Enterprise: American Business Abroad from the Colonial Era to 1914*, Cambridge, Mass.: Harvard University Press.

—— (1974) *The Maturing of Multinational Enterprise: American Business Abroad from 1914 to 1970*, Cambridge, Mass.: Harvard University Press.

—— (1988) "The Freestanding Company, 1817–1914," *Economic History Review* 61, 2: 259–82.

—— (1989) *The History of Foreign Investment in the United States to 1914*, Cambridge, Mass.: Harvard University Press.

Wilkins, Mira and Schroeter, Harm (1998) *The Free-Standing Company in the World Economy, 1830–1996*. London: Oxford University Press.

Williamson, O.E. (1975) *Markets and Hierarchies: Analysis and Antitrust Implications*, New York: Free Press.

—— (1979) "Transaction Cost Economics: The Governance of Contractual Relations," *Journal of Law and Economics*, 22, 2: 233–61.

—— (1981) "The Modern Corporation: Origins, Evolution, Attributes," *Journal of Economic Literature*, 19, 4: 1537–68.

—— (1985) *The Economic Institutions of Capitalism*, New York: Free Press.

—— (1988) "Corporate Finance and Corporate Governance," *Journal of Finance*, 63, 3: 567–98.

Yeung, B. and R. Mirus (1989) "On the Mode of International Expansion: The Role of Agency Costs in an Expanded Framework," unpublished manuscript.

Yip Yat Hoong (1969) *The Development of the Tin Mining Industry of Malaya*, Kuala Lumpur: University of Malaya Press.

Yoshihara, H. (1984) "Multinational Growth of Japanese Multinational Enterprises in the Postwar Period," in A. Acacia and T. Indue (eds) *Overseas Business Activities*, Tokyo: University of Tokyo Press.

Yoshino, M. (1976) *Japanese Multinational Enterprises*, Cambridge, Mass.: Harvard University Press.

Zejan, M. (1990) "New Ventures or Acquisitions: The Choice of Swedish Multinational Enterprises," *Journal of Industrial Economics*, 38: 349–55.

5 The eclectic paradigm of international production

A personal perspective

John H. Dunning

Some introductory remarks

In one respect at least, it is inappropriate that the present author should be contributing to a volume entitled *The Nature of the Transnational Firm*. This is because the eclectic paradigm of international production is not (and has never purported to be) an explanation of the transnational or multinational *firm*. Its focus of interest has always been directed to explaining the level and pattern of the foreign value-added activities of *firms*, and/or of countries.

There is of course, much common ground between the theory of international production. defined as the production financed by foreign direct investment, and explanations of the extension of the territorial boundaries of the firm; but the one major difference is that some variables which are *exogenous* to the latter set of explanations become *endogenous* when the subject of interest is groups of firms or countries.

It is perhaps worth observing that it has only been in the last 15 years or so that scholars have been preoccupied with explaining the existence and growth of the multinational enterprise, as opposed to the act of foreign direct investment. Stephen Hymer's thesis, for example, was entitled "The International Operations of *Firms*"; and might well have been subtitled "The Industrial Economics of Foreign Direct Investment." It is true that he viewed the act of foreign direct investment as a market-replacing activity, but, in seeking to explain the growth of US direct investment in Europe and Canada, he drew as much upon *industry-* as *firm*-specific concepts and variables. Eight years after he completed his thesis, in an article published in a French journal (Hymer, 1968), Hymer gave more explicit attention to the international firm *qua* firm; and it is quite clear that, in the intervening period, he had acquainted himself with the writings of Ronald Coase (1937) and Maurice Bye (1958).

The most influential theory of foreign direct investment, up to the early 1970s at least, was the product cycle theory, first put forward by Ray Vernon in a seminal article in 1966, although for a fuller exposition of the theory, the reader is invited to read the (somewhat neglected) monographs by Gary Hufbauer (1965) and Seev Hirsch (1967), both of whom were Vernon's students. Vernon, like myself, has always been interested in explaining foreign production as a form of international economic involvement, on a par with, but different from international trade. Though virtually all trade is conducted by firms, I am sure that no trade theorist would wish to argue that the penetration of foreign markets by domestic firms or of domestic markets by foreign firms could be explained by firms internalizing transnational markets. So, why, I wonder, when there is a shift in the location of production by international firms, should one have to play a new intellectual ball game?

I think one answer relates to the role of the firm in traditional trade theory. Quite simply, there wasn't one. To all intents and purposes, the firm was a black box. By the extremely restrictive assumptions underlying neo-classical trade theory, and as described in most international economics textbooks, markets – and markets alone – determine the structure of cross-border resource allocation. *Inter alia* this is because the transaction costs of using the market as an exchange and coordinating mechanism are assumed to be zero. Each firm produces only a single product (or more correctly engages in only one economic activity) from one particular location. It can possess no lasting competitive advantages over other firms producing in the same country. Trade under such circumstances is determined by factors exogenous to firms. Firms are simply production units, the function of which is to transform inputs into more valued outputs. Their actions are completely constrained by circumstances beyond their control. The fact that firms are able to penetrate foreign markets is entirely explained by their being able to secure location-bound resources on better terms than can firms located in the countries to which they export; it has nothing to do with any specific advantage which they *vis-à-vis* their competitors possess. It would serve no purpose for a firm to set up a branch facility in a foreign country because it would be in no better position to supply the market in that country than a local firm. Indeed, if it chose to produce the same goods, it would most likely be disadvantaged compared with firms from its home country.

But what happens when the assumption of the immobility of factors of production is broken down; or that technology is no longer presumed to be costless and instantaneously transferable across national boundaries? According to Vernon, foreign production is likely to replace exports whenever the cost of combining the intermediate products produced in the home market, but which are transferable across national boundaries at low or zero cost, can be used more efficiently (i.e. at lower cost) with the resources of a foreign country than with those of the home country. In such circumstances, foreign production represents a change in the location, but not the ownership nor the character of economic activity. The important assumption is that the intermediate products, to which the firm has privileged access (its so-called ownership advantages), and which made possible the exports in the first place, are the privileged property of the exporting firm; otherwise, a foreign firm might have acquired and made use of them at least as effectively as could the exporting firm. The question of the obstacles (or barriers) to such acquisition was not discussed by Vernon (who, in the early 1960s at least, was not aware of Hymer's thesis); indeed, at that time, Vernon appeared disinterested in organizational issues.

In the meantime, other studies almost entirely concentrated on the industrial organizational aspects of foreign direct investment. Here the question, explored by Horst (1972a, 1972b), Caves (1971, 1974a, 1974b), Baumann (1975), and other scholars (whose work is summarized by Clegg, 1987) was "How is it possible for the affiliates of foreign-owned *firms* to compete with indigenous firms on their own territory?" Again the emphasis was on *firms* and on industry-specific characteristics. It was, for example, observed that the subsidiaries of multinational firms tended to concentrate their activities in sectors with a number of distinctive characteristics; and that there were reasons to suppose that the ownership advantages of such firms reflected the structure of resource endowments and markets of their countries of origin. Thus, US-owned firms were more prone to possess advantages based on the supply of high-income goods and capital- or technology-intensive producer products, because these were intangible assets which the US economy was in a comparatively favored position to supply.

So, by the mid-1970s, there were two main approaches to understanding foreign production. The first essentially used the tools of locational economics, both to explain the origin and exploitation of competitive advantages of firms. The other drew upon the work of industrial organization economists, notably Bain (1956), in order to explain differences between the advantages possessed by indigenous and foreign firms (n.b. *firms*) in explaining why foreign-owned affiliates were concentrated in some industries but not in others. This approach was not interested in locational issues at all, nor with the origin of the advantages possessed by foreign firms. Moreover, these advantages were assumed to exist *prior* to the foreign investment being made, and to have nothing to do with the undertaking of foreign production *per se*. Richard Caves, however, did distinguish between advantages associated with being part of multi-plant complex; and he introduced surplus entrepreneurial capacity as a potential ownership advantage of a foreign investor, that clearly was only translated into an actual advantage if and when the foreign investment was made.

This, indeed, was the starting-point for scholars to switch their focus to the multinational firm as a market-replacing institution. It also coincided with more attention being paid to explaining the sequential growth of foreign production, in contrast to the initial act of investment, which was the predominant interest of economists in the Hymer–Kindleberger tradition.

There were other reasons, too, for this redirection of emphasis. Increasingly the uniqueness of foreign direct investment was identified, not only in terms of the resources it provided, but the way in which these resources were used. Researchers began to observe differences between the organization of activity among multinational firms, and between such firms and those of their non-multinational competitors. Partly it was felt that these differences reflected the fact that they were multi-plant firms, and that common ownership brought its own separate or distinctive characteristics,[1] and partly because that multinationality itself affected the response of firms to changes in their economic environment (Kogut, 1985). Questions of advantages which occurred to firms *as a result* of their foreign activities became of central interest, rather than those stemming from the possession of particular property rights which enabled them to penetrate foreign markets in the first place, or to optimize the geographical distribution of their production facilities. Multinationals might exist simply because the cost of engaging in cross-border transactions through the market was higher than where these transactions were organized within the same firm. The greater the cross-border market failure, which could be efficiently internalized by multinational hierarchies, then, *ceteris paribus*, the more likely foreign production would be to occur.

Throughout the last decade, the internalization theory has been the leading explanation of why a firm chooses to engage in foreign investment rather than organize its cross-border activities in a different way. It is difficult to quarrel with the theory if that is all it is seeking to explain.[2] But, when the theory also purports to explain the level, structure, and location of *all* international production, then, immediately, it opens itself to criticism unless, as Rugman would seem to claim in his various contributions (see, for example, Rugman, 1997), it takes on board all kinds of market imperfections; in which case the theory loses much of its incisiveness.

The origins of the eclectic paradigm

My own perception of the determinants of international production dates back to the time I wrote my first book, *American Investment in British Manufacturing Industry* (Dunning, 1958). Earlier research by Rostas (1948), Frankel (1955), and some UK study teams which visited the US in the early postwar period, had shown that the labor productivity in US manufacturing industry was, on average, 2.5 times higher than that in UK industry. The question which this fact posed in my mind was: "Was that difference in productivity due to the superior indigenous resources of the US economy (i.e. those traditionally explained by trade and location theories) or was it due to the better way US firms, *qua* firms, organized and managed the resources at their disposal?" My hypothesis was that if it was entirely due to the latter, then American-owned subsidiaries in the UK should perform at least as well as their parent companies, and fare considerably better than their UK-owned competitors. This I called the *ownership*-specific effect (n.b. not the firm-specific effect) as the productivity differences were assumed to rest on the country of ownership of the firm. If, however, US subsidiaries in the UK performed no better than their indigenous competitors, and hence much less well than their parent companies, I hypothesized that this would be due to the location-specific (and non-transferable) characteristics of the US economy. This I called the *location*-specific component of any productivity differential.

As might be expected, I discovered that US affiliates were not as productive as their parent companies, but more productive than their local competitors, which suggested that Anglo-American productivity differences, when measured at a *country* level, were partly explainable by location and partly by ownership-specific characteristics. However, my study omitted to ask a follow-up question, viz. to what extent was the origin of the ownership advantage of US firms itself home country specific?" Neither did it attempt to distinguish between the advantages that arose as a result of the direct investment in the UK and those that the US firm possessed *prior* to engaging in foreign production.[3]

I took up the theme of ownership and location advantages again in two papers written in the early 1970s. The first (Dunning, 1972) concerned the likely impact of Britain's entry into the European Economic Community (EC). In it, I suggested that while the removal of tariff barriers had consequences on the location of economic activity within the EC, it would also be likely to affect the competitive position of firms of different national origins differently, and, in consequence, the ownership of economic activity in the EC.[4]

The second paper (Dunning, 1973) was an attempt to review the various attempts which had been made to explain the activities of firms outside their national boundaries over the past decade. In that paper I tried to integrate the industrial organizational and locational approaches to understanding foreign production. I argued (like Hymer) that while the first was necessary to explain why foreign firms could compete successfully with domestic firms in supplying the latter's own markets, the second was relevant to explaining why these firms chose to supply their markets from a foreign, rather than a domestic, base.

In 1975 I was asked to present a paper at a Nobel Symposium on the International Location of Economic Activity which was held in Stockholm in June 1976. This symposium was organized by Bertil Ohlin and attended by leading international economists, economic geographers, and regional scientists. For the most part, the seminar was oriented towards an evaluation of country-specific factors influencing the changing distribution of international economic activity, but the starting-point of my paper was that a country's economic space could be considered in two ways. The first was the value of output produced within its national boundaries independently of the ownership of that production. The second was the output produced by its own firms, including that part produced outside its national boundaries. This further distinguished between the competitive advantage of countries and firms which I have been at pains to stress in several of my writings.[5]

In explaining the activity of firms outside their national boundaries, I extended the ownership and locational advantages identified in my earlier research to include another set of choices available to firms, which related to the way the firms organized the use of their ownership and locational advantages. In other words, I acknowledged that to explain international production, one had also to explain why firms opted to use their ownership advantages for further value-added activities, rather than sell these advantages (or their rights) to foreign firms. I further accepted that the way in which a firm responded to exogenous locational costs and benefits might also affect its long-run competitive position. I finally distinguished between those ownership advantages that arose as a direct result of a firm engaging in international production and those that it might possess prior to its becoming a multinational. These former advantages, in particular, I argued, could not be separately sold to independent foreign firms to exploit. They could be realized only through vertical or horizontal integration, or putting it another way, by the common ownership of related activities along a particular value-added chain or across two or more value-added chains.

I would be the first to admit that, in my work on internalization advantages, I was considerably influenced by my colleagues Peter Buckley and Mark Casson of the University of Reading, who were in the process of writing *The Future of the Multinational Enterprise*, although my first exposure to the concept of internalization, as applied to the multinational firm, came in 1972 when I read an article by J.C. McManus in Guy Paquet's edited volume on *The Multinational Firm and the Nation State*. A year later, on a visit to Uppsala in Sweden, I had conversations with Nils Lundgren, a Swedish economist who was thinking along the same lines in his attempt to explain the growth of Swedish foreign direct investment.[6] Nevertheless, I regarded this new insight as a useful addition to my own approach to explaining the determinants of the foreign production, and not a replacement of it, a view I still hold today.

Over the past two decades, I have benefited enormously from the comments of friends and colleagues on the eclectic theory (or paradigm, as I now prefer to call it) of international production.[7] I accept that in my earlier work I did tend to look at internalization advantages more as those that arose from the way ownership advantages were exploited rather than as a market replacement activity which conferred its own hierarchical advantages. While, as set out in my book *Multinational Enterprises and the Global Economy* (Dunning, 1993a), I still prefer to think of ownership advantages as any kind of income-generating assets that make it possible for firms to engage in foreign production, I readily acknowledge that these may arise as a direct consequence of market-replacing activities. But, even here, I believe that a firm's ability to benefit from such activities must be related to the assets which it possesses *prior* to the act of internalization.

The economies of common governance arise because a firm integrates its existing activities with new activities. For example, a firm that is currently producing in country A, and believes it will benefit from diversifying its risks if it produces in country B, will gain from such diversification, only if it produces in both country A and country B! A firm that benefits from the cross-border economies of scope or scale will only do so if the new investment is *in addition* to its existing investment. A firm that makes a foreign acquisition to obtain new and up-to-date technology, presumably does so because it believes it can use that technology along with its existing assets to strengthen its competitive position.[8] This may seem an obvious point, but to me at any rate, the distinction between benefits that accrue from the gains to be had from internalizing the market of an existing asset and those that arise from coordinating existing assets with new assets, *vis-à-vis* some alternative use which might be made of those assets, is an important one.

To some extent, I believe these are semantic points. Much more important is the debate as to whether the extent to which ownership advantages in the eclectic paradigm are assumed to be exogenous or endogenous variables. If the former, then, of course, the main question of interest surrounds their use, or, in some cases, their mode of acquisition. Or is it that only those ownership advantages that directly arise from market-replacing activities are endogenous? I must say, I find (some of) the internalization literature very ambiguous on this point.

But, again, much depends upon the perspective and the timeframe taken. From the viewpoint of explaining why some countries are net outward direct investors[9] and others are not, other factors exogenous to firms but endogenous to countries must be accommodated. Also, in explaining the changing competitive position of firms, it is perfectly clear that this may have as much to do with the creation of new ownership-specific advantages as it has to do with the changing characteristics of markets or hierarchies.

I shall return to this latter point later, but it does seem that at least some internalization economists acknowledge that a firm's propensity to engage in foreign investment may change as factors other than market-replacing or locational advantages change. Once that is admitted, it is surely not unreasonable to hypothesize that today's level and structure of international production may be influenced by the past ownership advantages, or changes in these advantages, of the firms undertaking the production.

Let me now reiterate the main ingredients of the eclectic paradigm.[10] The subject to be explained is the extent and pattern of international production. The paradigm avers that at any given moment of time this will be determined by the configuration of three sets of forces:

1 the (net) competitive advantages which firms of one nationality have over those of another nationality in supplying any particular market or set of markets. These advantages may arise either from the firm's privileged possession of a set of income-generating assets,[11] or by their ability to coordinate existing assets with other assets across national boundaries in a way that benefits them relative to their competitors, or potential competitors, who are not able or willing to undertake such production.
2 the extent to which firms perceive it to be profitable to internalize the markets for the assets; and by so doing add value to their output
3 the extent to which firms choose to locate these value-adding activities outside their national boundaries.

The eclectic paradigm further argues that the significance of each of these advantages and the configuration between them will vary among industries (or types of value-added activities), regions, or countries (the geographical dimension) and among firms. Thus there are likely to be country-specific differences in the ownership advantages of (say) Korean firms compared with (say) Canadian firms. The extent of market failure influencing whether or not the market for technology is internalized is likely to be different in (say) the wood and pulp industry than in (say) the semi-conductor industry; while the relationship to the comparative locational advantages of Thailand and Taiwan as a manufacturing base for motor vehicles may be differently regarded by (say) the Toyota than (say) the Honda Corporation.

The eclectic paradigm is more to be regarded as framework for analyzing the determinants of international production than as a predictive theory of the multinational firm. I have frequently argued that no single theory can be expected to satisfactorily encompass all kinds of foreign production, simply because the motivations for, and expectations from, such production vary such a great deal. The variables necessary to explain import-substituting investment are likely to be different from those that explain resource-oriented investment; and both are likely to be different from those that explain rationalized or strategic asset-seeking investment. In formulating operational hypotheses about the relationship between individual OLI variables and the level and pattern of international production, it is important to specify the context in which this relationship is being examined.

Some criticisms of the paradigm

Let me now turn to the criticisms of the eclectic paradigm, some of which have been dealt with by other contributors to this volume.

A shopping list of variables?

First it is claimed that the variables identified by the paradigm are so numerous that its predictive value is almost zero. There is a modest (but only a modest) amount of truth in this contention. In our defense, however, we would make three important points. The first is that each and every OLI variable identified in the eclectic paradigm is founded on economic theory. For example, all the L variables – be they labor costs, tariff barriers, or the presence of competitors – rest on the tenets of location theory, and also the assumption that firms will seek to locate their value-added activities at the most profitable points in space.[12] Similarly, the internalization variables all relate to the production and transaction costs and benefits of different modalities of coordinating multiple economic activities. Here, we draw upon Coasian, Williamsonian, and Penrosian theories of the firm (or the growth of the firm), and, like these scholars, we argue that the higher the net production and transaction costs (or the lower the net benefits) of using the cross-border markets, relative to those of internal administrative fiat as a mechanism for coordinating resource usage, the greater will be the incentive for firms to engage in international production.

Second, as we have already written, the purpose of the paradigm is not to offer a full explanation of all kinds of international production but rather to point to a methodology and to a generic set of variables which contain the ingredients necessary for any satisfactory explanation of particular types of foreign value-added activity.

The third point is that much of this kind of criticism can be directed toward other general theories of international production – and, indeed, to general theories of international trade as well. The kinds of market failure relevant to explaining resource-based investment are totally different from those explaining rationalized investment. Partial theories do not suffer from this same deficiency;

however, unlike the general theories, they can only explain some kinds of foreign direct investment. The product cycle theory has little relevance to resource-based foreign investment. Knickerbocker's follow-my-leader or oligopolistic interaction approach (Knickerbocker, 1973) is entirely dependent on a particular type of market structure. Kojima's normative macro-economic theory (Kojima, 1978, 1982) cannot easily encompass intra-industry investment. Aliber's theory (1970, 1971) is only relevant for explaining multinational activity in different currency areas. The risk diversification thesis (see for example Rugman, 1980) cannot readily explain much of strategic asset-seeking foreign investment. And so on!

Interdependence of OLI variables?

It is suggested that it is misleading to give the impression that the triumvirate of variables which make up the eclectic paradigm are independent of one another. For example, a firm's response to its exogenous locational variables might itself influence its ownership advantages, including its ability and willingness to internalize markets. A particular R&D strategy, intended to strengthen a firm's competitive position. may require modification to the siting of its existing innovatory facilities; while a change in a firm's organizational structure may directly affect its ability to penetrate the markets of its competitors. Over time the separate identity of the variables becomes even more difficult to justify.

Nevertheless, conceptually, I believe there is something to be said for separating those reasons for international production which are primarily due to the net competitive advantages of firms of a particular ownership – including their ability to choose the right location and mode of organization to exploit or augment these advantages – from those to do with the immobile resources and markets of the countries in which they operate. The policy implications of a decline in inward direct investment, which results from a reduction in the attractiveness of a country's location-bound resources, are very different from those that reflect the strengthening competitive position of its indigenous, relative to foreign-owned, firms. An increase in outward direct investment due to the integration of markets allowing the better exploitation of the economies of common governance (e.g. as is encouraging more Pan European direct investment) flags a very different message to the governments of home countries than investment driven out by unattractive conditions in the domestic market (e.g. as was the case in India for most of the 1970s and early 1980s, South Africa and the Philippines in the mid-1980s and Sweden in the mid- and late 1980s).

In my more recent writings (Dunning 1993a, 1995), I have fully acknowledged the ways in which the OLI variables determining the foreign production of firms and countries may be linked to one another. Thus, as is set out more formally in the next sub-section, inward direct investment based upon the O advantages of the investing firms in time t may well affect the L advantages of the host country in time t + 1; while the response of firms, by use of either a "voice" or an "exit" strategy, to market failure (Hirschman, 1970) may well influence the shape of their future O advantages. Indeed, I would go further and suggest it is the successful coordination of the O advantages of foreign and domestic firms with their own L advantages, and how each affects and is affected by the modality of resource deployment, that determines the extent to which a particular country is able to upgrade its wealth-creating capacities over a period of time.[13]

No role for strategy: A static approach?

It is argued that the eclectic paradigm takes no account of differences in the strategic response of firms to any given configuration of OLI variables. This criticism may be coupled with another that suggests the paradigm is couched in static (or comparatively static) terms and offers little guidance as to the *path* or *process* of the internalization of firms (or of countries). In my book *The Globalization of Business* (Dunning, 1993b), I took on board this criticism (which incidentally may be applied to the internalization theory of the multinational enterprise). My reasoning is as follows. At a given moment of time, the pattern of international production represents a point on a set of trajectories toward (or, for that matter, away from) the internationalization of production by firms. That trajectory itself is set by the continuous and iterative interaction between the OLI configuration over a succession of time periods and the strategy of firms in response to these configurations, that, in turn, will influence the OLI configuration in subsequent time periods. Let OLI_{t0} be the OLI configuration in time $_{t0}$, OLI_{t1} the OLI configuration in time $_{t1}$, S_{t-n} the past (i.e. pre t_0) strategies of firms still being worked out, and $\Delta S_{t0} \rightarrow _{t1}$ be any change in the strategic response of firms to that configuration between time t_0 and t_1. Then *ceteris paribus*

$$OLI_{t1} = f(OLI_{t0} \, S_{t-n} \, \Delta S_{t0} \rightarrow _{t1}) \tag{1}$$

If we extend the analysis to a second time period t_2, then

$$OLI_{t2} = f(OLI_{t1} \, S_{t-n} \, \Delta S_{t1} \rightarrow _{t2}) \tag{2}$$

This analysis further suggests that S_{t-n} and $S_{t0} \rightarrow _{t2}$ determine the path of the movement from OLI_{t0} to OLI_{t2}.

Strategic response is, of course, just one of the many *endogenous* variables which might affect the OLI configuration of firms (mainly by its impact on 0 and I advantages). Others include technological or organizational innovations, changes in the composition of senior management or labor productivity, new marketing techniques, mergers, acquisitions, and so on. No less significant are *exogenous* changes, such as changes in population, raw material prices, exchange rates, government policies toward outward or inward direct investment and so on. If we take all endogenous variables other than strategy to be *EN* and all exogenous variables to be EX, and we assume that changes in *EN* and EX do not affect the firms' strategies, then we can rewrite equation (1) as

$$\text{OLI}_{tl} = f(\text{OLI}_{t0}\, S_{t-n}\, \Delta S_{t0} \to_{tl} \Delta \text{EN}_{t0} \to_{tl} \Delta \text{EX}_{t0} \to_{tl}) \tag{3}$$

Equation 2 can be similarly reconstructed and it is easy to incorporate any change in strategy which embraces the response to Δ EN and Δ EX if it occurs before $_{tl}$ is reached by adding * to $\Delta S_{t0} \to_{tl}$ in the equation.

Of course, it may be argued that this drives a coach and horses through the generality of eclectic paradigm; as the nature of the interaction between the value of most exogenous and endogenous variables likely to affect international production and the strategy of firms are difficult to predict. Yet, from the time of Vernon (1966) onwards, economists and business analysts have been trying to do just that. Vernon, for example, suggests that both the strategy of firms and the locational advantages of at least some value-added activities associated with the production of a product change as that product moves through its cycle. As the product becomes more widely demanded, as foreign governments are tempted to impose import restrictions to encourage local production, and as the fear of competitors (or the threat of entry by new competitors) usurping one's own foreign markets becomes more pronounced, then the ownership (or potential ownership) advantages of firms and the attractions of a foreign location become altered in a way that leads to more foreign direct investment. Thus a firm's O and L position affecting investment in time t + 1 (e.g. the mature stage of the product cycle) is affected both by its OL configuration in the early (i.e. the innovating) stage of the cycle, and by the changes in the exogenous variables, e.g. demand by the foreign customers, and endogenous variables, e.g. the presence (or absence) of economies of plant size, and any changes in the strategy of firms consequential upon these eventualities.

Later scholars more explicitly introduced a time- and strategy-related dimension into their analysis. Again, reinterpreting Knickerbocker's analysis in terms of the OLI paradigm, we may say that firms are prompted to go overseas, in part at least, because they consider their O advantages are (or could become) threatened, if they do not follow their competitors' lead or because their advantages would be less without their presence.[14] In other words, the strategy followed by firms in response to a given OLI configuration in time $_{t0}$ is governed by their desire to protect or influence that configuration in $_{tl}$. (This incidentally does not necessarily mean that all firms will engage in more foreign direct investment.)

Most studies on the internationalization process, which have traditionally been the province of marketing or organizational scholars, implicitly or explicitly assume not only that I or L advantages change as a firm enlarges its foreign markets or gains experience of these markets, but also that the action taken will be influenced by the response to the OLI configuration and the likely action of other firms and governments on that configuration, both in the presence and absence of their own investments.

The investment development path (IDP)

It is then possible to formalize the introduction of strategy and changes in endogenous and exogenous variables into the OLI paradigm; and in some cases at least, to offer broad predictions of the outcome of such changes over time. This, indeed, is precisely what the concept of the investment development cycle or path seeks to do (Dunning, 1981, 1988, 1993a; Dunning and Narula, 1996). The basic hypothesis is that as a country develops, the configuration of the OLI advantages facing foreign-owned firms that might invest in that country and of its own firms that might invest overseas, undergoes change, and that it is possible to identify both the conditions making for the change and their effect on the trajectory of development. The concept also suggests the ways in which the interaction between foreign and domestic firms might itself influence the country's investment path; but only recently has this aspect been incorporated into the literature cycle.[15]

The IDP identifies several stages of development a country might pass through. The first stage is one of pre-industrialization, in which a country is presumed to have no inward or outward investment, in the first case because it has insufficient locational attractions and in the second because its own firms possess no ownership advantages. Depending on its resources, government policy, the organization of activity, and the strategy of firms, the OLI configuration changes so as first to attract inward investment in resource-based sectors, in the traditional and labor-intensive manufacturing sectors, in trade and distribution, in transport and communications, construction, and perhaps some tourism.

Depending very much on the extent to which the country is able to create a satisfactory legal system, commercial infrastructure, and business culture, and to provide both domestic and foreign firms with the transport and communications facilities and human resources they need; and depending on its infrastructure and government policy pursued toward inward direct investment (cf. Japan, which largely disallowed such investment in the 1960s, with Germany which adopted an open-door policy toward it), its locational attractions will increase; and because foreign firms are likely to have more experience in manufacturing the goods and services now likely to be demanded (and have probably penetrated the local market by imports in any case) inward investment will continue to grow. Gradually it, and any investment by indigenous firms, will affect both supply and demand conditions for the products supplied by foreign firms and their desire to internalize their markets for the competitive advantages. To begin with, L&O advantages are likely to complement each other. Thus, as supply capabilities improve, they give rise to agglomerative or cluster-type economies and increases in labor productivity, while the introduction of new machinery and production methods is likely to lead to lower real labor costs and scale economies. The latter are also made possible by growing markets.

The improvement in the locational advantages of countries may also help indigenous firms to develop their own competitive advantages. The growth of Japanese outward investment and, more recently, that of several developing countries is entirely consistent with a reconfiguration of the OLI advantages of indigenous firms brought about by the development process. Once again, changes in the value of both exogenous and endogenous variables affect each of these components. In this early stage, the role of government is especially important. In various of his writings (see, for example, Ozawa 1989, 1992, 1996), Terutomo Ozawa has demonstrated the critical role of the Japanese government in influencing the ability of Japanese firms both to generate competitive advantages relative to their competitors, and to locate their value-added activities outside of Japan. It has also affected the strategy of the Japanese companies themselves.

As countries move along their development path, the OLI configuration facing outward and inward investors continues to change. Some foreign (and domestic) firms, which earlier found a country attractive to invest in because of its low labor costs or plentiful natural resources, no longer do so. In other cases, locational advantages have become more attractive as a technological infrastructure and pool of skilled labor is built up. This, in turn, makes it possible for domestic firms to develop their own O advantages and begin exporting capital.

Next, as countries reach some degree of economic maturity, the OLI configuration facing their own firms may be such that their propensity to engage in outward direct investment exceeds that of foreign-based firms to engage in inward investment. Again, whether or not this happens rests on the strategy of both firms and governments to generate the competitive (and especially innovatory) advantages of their own firms and to make their own locations attractive to both domestic and foreign investors.

The literature is replete with examples of the kind of variable likely to influence the OLI configuration over time and the determinants of the value of these variables. Predictions for individual countries are difficult because they require forecasting the behavior of governments. Different countries at the same stage of their development paths seem to display different propensities to engage in outward and inward investment. Others may display similar propensities for different reasons. Thus, in the late 1980s, both Sweden and Japan were significant net outward investors, but whereas the Japanese push outwards represented a positive restructuring to make way for the upgrading of its domestic industry, in the Swedish case, it was more symptomatic of the falling competitiveness of the domestic economy. By the mid-1990s, however, Swedish inbound investment was rising quite rapidly, in part, because of Swedish accession to the European Union in 1995 (Zander and Zander, 1996).

The final stage of the IDP occurs when there is a fluctuating balance between outward and inward direct investment. This arises when there is some degree of convergence between the level of development and the economic structure of countries, and also where firms engage in FDI, not primarily to exploit their existing competitive advantages in a foreign location, but rather to augment these advantages by acquiring complementary assets or new markets. In the mid-1990s, this stage has been reached by the more advanced industrial economies, whose wealth creation and productivity growth are increasingly based on their ability to harness and effectively to utilize all forms of knowledge or intellectual capital. At this stage, too, the role of government is often of critical importance in influencing the quality of L specific advantages; and in setting the competitive environment for their own firms to effectively exploit the opportunities offered by the global economy (Dunning and Narula, 1996).

I have illustrated at some length from the IDP, because it does introduce (albeit at a macro level) a dynamic element into the theory of international production. Moreover, it confirms that the equation(s) set out above do seem to make sense. The configuration of OLI variables affecting the (say) Japanese firms in the world economy in 1997 is a function of the OLI configuration facing them in (say) the mid-1980s and the changes in the endogenous and exogenous variables which have affected their behavior in the intermediate period. Of these, there is strong evidence that the way in which these two sets of variables interact is, itself, is an important factor determining the movement towards a new OLI configuration. We also believe that the concept outlined is very relevant in explaining the growth of outward investment from Third World countries, especially from Korea, Singapore, Taiwan, and Mexico.

The Kojima criticism of the eclectic paradigm

We next turn to Kiyoshi Kojima's criticism of the eclectic paradigm (Kojima, 1982). To Kojima, my approach, and that of the Reading economists as a group, is purely a micro-economic phenomenon. Indeed, he seems to assume that the internalization and eclectic paradigms are trying to explain the same phenomenon. They are not. As far as I am aware, no one from the internalization school has sought to explain the changing propensity of *countries* to invest or be invested in over time.[16]

Nevertheless, Kojima is right in supposing our macro-economic perspective is different from his. Let me give an analogy: suppose the subject for explanation is the trade in goods. Kojima would be interested in answering the question "Why does one country export certain types of goods and import other kinds of goods?," whereas I would be concerned with explaining whether a particular country was a net importer or exporter of particular types of goods or of all goods. And, I admit that, at a macro level, the latter is a somewhat meaningless question, as in the last resort, and over a sufficiently long period of time, the balance of payments must balance. But, this is not the case with the stocks and flows of international investment; and hence the concept of the IDP does have some meaning.

Moreover, investment owned and controlled by multinationals is a different phenomenon from portfolio investment. So, indeed, is trade conducted *within* multinationals different from trade between independent parties. In other words, organizational issues do inject the need for a set of analytical tools different from those offered by traditional trade theory.

This is where I think Kojima's criticism of the eclectic paradigm (and of internalization theory) falls down. He insists upon applying a strictly neo-classical framework of thought to explain a phenomenon that is outside that framework of thought. Moreover, like neo-classical theory, his approach to international direct investment is more normative than mine. However, in various of my writings (see, for example, chapter 10 of Dunning 1988, and chapter 13 of Dunning 1993a), I have attempted to give some normative content to the eclectic paradigm by suggesting the conditions for optimizing the benefits which host countries might secure from inbound FDI.

Acquiring a competitive advantage through foreign direct investment

Let me first readily accept that strategic asset-acquiring foreign direct investment has become one of the most important forms of cross-border economic activity over the last decade, as, indeed, has the growth of inter-firm strategic alliances. Both forms of trans-border economic involvement reflect the perceived need by corporations domiciled in one country not only to capture the technological and marketing synergies offered by firms in other countries, but also to harness or tap into the created assets – and particularly the intellectual assets of foreign competitors, suppliers, and customers.

Recent technological advances, more intensive inter-firm competition, the opening up of new markets, and the increasing mobility of some kinds of firm-specific assets have, then, led foreign production not only as a means of exploiting the existing O specific advantages of the investing firms, but also as a vehicle for augmenting these advantages. Nowhere is this more clearly demonstrated than in the sourcing of technological assets. Several recently published studies[17] have shown that multinational enterprises from all countries, but particularly those from Japan and Europe, are increasingly reaching beyond their national borders to create or gain access to resources and capabilities that complement their existing core competencies. These same studies have also suggested that the locational requirements of strategic asset-seeking foreign investment are different from that of natural resource-seeking, market-seeking or efficiency-seeking foreign investment, inasmuch as the former is attracted less by the need to reduce production costs, overcome trade barriers, and exploit economies of scale, but more by the presence of high-quality physical and human infrastructure and a favorable political and commercial ethos towards A&Ms and cooperative alliances.

Extending the eclectic paradigm to embrace non-equity alliance formation

This brings us neatly to an extension to the eclectic paradigm which I first set out in an article published in the *Journal of International Business Studies* in 1995 (Dunning, 1995).[18] The title of the article was "Reappraising the Eclectic Paradigm in an Age of Alliance Capitalism," and its main theme was that as cooperation and competition are increasingly becoming complementary modalities for resource creation and allocation in market-based economies, so the concept of the individual firm as an independent source of intellectual capital is no longer sustainable. Rather, it is better viewed as an organizer of a collection of created assets, some of which it generates internally and others which It obtains from other firms, yet over which it exercises some kind of influence or control.

Accepting this view, then, the O advantages of MNEs will depend not only upon those internally generated, but also upon their competence to seek out, harness, and influence the innovation, price, and quality of assets of other institutions with which they have an ongoing cooperative relationship. Such a relationship may take various forms, such as a strategic technological or marketing alliance between two or more competitors; a sub-contracting agreement between a firm and one (or more) of its suppliers; or a licensing or franchising agreement between a firm and one (or more) of its customers.

Similarly, in its choice of a foreign site for its value-added activities, an MNE will be influenced not only by how location-bound resources and/or markets affect its direct costs, but also by how they affect its ability to acquire and exploit the O specific assets of related firms with which it has some kind of alliance. The costs and benefits of accessing these latter assets by some form of cooperative agreement, rather than by a direct acquisition or merger, will determine the modality by which the O advantages of firms of one country are coordinated with those of another and also with the L advantages of that country; hence, the I component of the eclectic paradigm, as initially applied to the markets versus hierarchies choice, needs to be widened to embrace more "voice"-oriented strategies of firms, directed to capturing the benefits of quasi-integration offered by trans-border coalitions and cooperative relationships.

In short, the content and significance of the OLI configuration affecting the determinants of international production need to be reconsidered in the light of the emergence of alliance capitalism and contemporary technological developments, all of which are pointing to the need of firms to embrace a plurality of intra- and inter-firm cooperative relationships if they are to be successful competitors in the global marketplace. A fuller analysis of the kind of modifications which need to be made to the eclectic paradigm is set out in Dunning (1995) (reprinted in Dunning, 1997).

Conclusions

Let me conclude by re-emphasizing six points. The first is that, although I have sometimes illustrated the eclectic paradigm by references to the individual firm, my main focus of interest is in explaining the international production of all firms from a particular country or group of countries. Because of this, I contend that it is not correct directly to compare the merits and demerits of the eclectic paradigm with that of internalization theory.

Second, I accept that some ownership-specific advantages are directly the result of firms internalizing the market for its intermediate products across national borders. However, since this very act of internalization puts the internalizing firms at an advantage relative to non-internalizing firms, I think it appropriate to refer to this benefit as an ownership-specific advantage and to internalization as the modality by which this advantage is realized.

Third, I acknowledge that the eclectic paradigm, as originally conceived, is uncomfortable in dealing with the dynamics of international production. However, I would argue that it can help to explain why an industry or country's international investment profile may be different in two points of time. To link these two points one needs to introduce changes in the exogenous or endogenous variables, including strategy and how these, in turn, affect the OLI configuration. I have illustrated from the IDP how this may be done at a macro level (which essentially evens out differences in strategic behavior). At an industry or micro level, only a detailed examination of the profile of individual firms can resolve this problem. The reclassification of firms into strategic groups (McGee and Thomas, 1986) is helping to show us that the type of strategic behavior is not an idiosyncratic variable but can be related to certain characteristics of firms (or groups of firms).

Fourth, I have endeavored to explain differences between my approach and that of Kiyoshi Kojima, and I hope I have made it clear that this is primarily a difference in emphasis and perspective rather than of reasoning between us.

Fifth, I have emphasized that as strategic asset-acquiring FDI and non-equity alliances have become more important forms of international economic involvement, so the OLI configuration of the eclectic paradigm requires some reappraisal. At the same time, I contend that the paradigm remains not only a powerful analytical tool for examining the causes and effects of MNE activity, but that, when set within a clearly specified context of industry, firm specific variables can offer a series of operationally testable hypotheses.[19]

Finally, I wish to stress that the eclectic paradigm is not an explanation of international production on the same level as (for example) the product cycle or appropriability theories. Its main advantage is that it offers a general framework for theorizing about all kinds of international economic involvement, including trade in goods and intermediate products. Its main drawback, which applies no less to any generalized theory of trade, is that, because the motives in foreign production are so different, no one model can hope to explain equally well each and every kind of multinational activity.

This is why in the mid-1980s we began to refer to the eclectic *paradigm* rather than eclectic *theory* of international production. At the same time, each of the specific theories is consistent with the tenets of the paradigm, and to this extent, both the paradigms and the theories are necessary for a complete and operational explanation of all forms of foreign production by firms and countries.[20]

Notes

1 As explored by Caves (1980) by use of the "separability" theory explaining why firms should wish to control separate, but related, value-added activities.
2 But see chapter 7 by E. Graham in this volume.
3 It is these latter which are solely the result of the internalization of markets, which the internalization economists assert may be the only advantages which a foreign investor may have over a local firm. I agree, but, de facto, advantages of the first kind are likely to be no less important in explaining the initial act of foreign investment.

4 Which indeed is exactly what has transpired. For an examination of the impact of European economic integration on transatlantic production see Dunning (1993b).

5 See especially chapter 4 of Dunning (1993a).

6 The only English source of Lundgren's thoughts on this matter is his comment on my paper for the 1976 Nobel Symposium in Ohlin *et al.* Birgitta Swedenborg took up and extended the theme in her excellent study on Swedish MNEs (Swedenborg, 1979).

7 For an explanation of the difference between a paradigm and a theory see e.g. Dunning (1988, chapters 1 and 2, and 1993a, chapter 4).

8 If there is no synergy between a firm's existing assets and those it acquires, it is difficult to see how this can be thought of as a direct investment; although I readily admit there are such investments which are classified in this way.

9 A net outward direct investor is one where the value of the stock of outward direct investment (or the flow of outward investment over a given period of time) exceeds the value of the stock of inward direct investment (or the flow of inward investment over a given period of time).

10 For a fuller exposition see Dunning (1988a, 1993a, 1995).

11 It is worth noting that such advantages may stem from the forces of monopoly or of (dynamic) competition. Most references to the competitive advantages of firms embrace both types of advantages, and it is in this sense we use ownership advantages as well.

12 Profitable, that is, from the viewpoint of the investing companies. We also use the word "profitable" in a generic sense to embrace the long-term commercial goals of these companies.

13 Witness, for example, the case of Singapore and the way in which the Singaporean government has used the O advantages of foreign investors in conjunction with those of its own firms and with the L attractions of its own immobile resources and capabilities, to advance its postwar economic prosperity (Haley *et al.*, 1996).

14 For example, by their competitors capturing markets which might otherwise be theirs.

15 See Tolentino (1990) and various contributions to Dunning and Narula (1996).

16 But, see chapter 5 of Buckley and Casson (1985). Also, as early as 1975 Peter Buckley and I introduced the notion of the investment development cycle at a conference of the UK Chapter of the Academy of International Business, in Manchester.

17 See, for example, Dalton and Serapio (1995), Almeida (1996), Dunning (1996), Kogut (1996), and Kuemmerle (1997).

18 Reprinted in Dunning (1997).

19 For a recent attempt to do this using the principles of internalization theory, see Buckley and Casson (1997). By adding O specific variables to the analysis, and giving more attention to the implications of strategic asset acquiring FDI and alliance capital, the models they prepare could well be used to test the tenets of the eclectic paradigm.

20 For a recent discussion on the interaction between the eclectic paradigm and various operational theories of international business activity, see Dunning (2000).

References

Aliber, R.Z. (1970) "A theory of foreign direct investment," in C.P. Kindleberger (ed.) *The International Corporation*, Cambridge, Mass.: MIT Press.

—— (1971) "The multinational enterprise in a multiple currency world," in J.H. Dunning (ed.) *The Multinational Enterprise*, London: Allen & Unwin.

Almeida, P. (1996) "Knowledge sourcing by foreign multinationals: Patent citation analysis in the US semi-conductor industry," *Strategic Management Journal* 17, Winter special issue, 155–65.

Bain, J. (1956) *Barriers to New Competition*, Cambridge, Mass.: MIT Press.

Baumann, H. (1975), "Merger theory, property, rights and the pattern of US direct investment in Canada," *Weltwirtschaftliches Archiv* III, 4, 676–98.

Buckley, P.J. and M.C. Casson (1976) *The Future of the Multinational Enterprise*, London: Macmillan.

—— (1985) *The Economic Theory of the Multinational Enterprise*, London: Macmillan.

—— (1997) *Internalization Theory: An Extension*. Paper presented to AIB (UK Chapter) Conference at Leeds, England, April.

Bye. M. (1958) "Self financed multiterritorial units and their time horizon," *International Economic Papers* 8: 147–78.

Casson, M.C. (ed.) (1990) *The Multinational Enterprise*, London: Edward Arnold.

Caves, R.E. (1974a) "Causes of direct investment: Foreign firms' shares in Canadian and United Kingdom manufacturing industries," *Review of Economics and Statistics* 56: 272–93.

—— (1974b) "Multinational firms, competition and productivity in host country markets," *Economica* 41: 176–93.

—— (1980) "Investment and location policies of multinational companies," *Schweiz, Zeitschrift für Volkwirtschaft und Statisik* 116: 321–27.

Clegg, L.J. (1987) *Multinational Enterprises and World Competition*, London: Macmillan.

Coase, R.H. (1937) "The nature of the firm," *Economica* (new series) 4: 386–405.

Dalton D.H. and M.G. Serapio (1995) *Globalizing Industrial Research and Development*, Washington, DC: US Department of Commerce, Office of Technology Policy, Asia Pacific Technology and Programs, October.

Dunning, J.H. (1958) *American Investment in British Manufacturing Industry*, London: Allen & Unwin.

—— *The Location of International Firms in an Enlarged EEC. An Exploratory Paper*, Manchester: Manchester Statistical Society.

—— (1973) "The determinants of international production," *Oxford Economic Papers* 25: 289–336.

—— (1981) *International Production and the Multinational Enterprise*, London: Allen & Unwin.

—— (1988) *Explaining International Production*, London: Unwin Hyman.

—— (1993a) *Multinational Enterprises and the Global Economy*, Wokingham, England and Reading, Mass.: Addison Wesley.

—— (1993b) *The Globalization of Business*, London and New York: Routledge.

—— (1995) "Reappraising the eclectic paradigm in the age of alliance capitalism," *Journal of International Business Studies* 26 (3): 461–93.

—— (1996) "The geographical sources of competitiveness of firms: The results of a new survey," *Transnational Corporations* 5 (3), December.

—— (1997) *Alliance Capitalism and Global Business*, London and New York: Routledge.

—— "The Eclectic Paradigm as an envelope for economic and business theories of MNE activity," *International Business Review* 9 (1), forthcoming.

Dunning, J.H. and R. Narula (eds) (1996) *Foreign Direct Investment and Governments*, London and New York: Routledge.

Frankel, M. (1955) "Anglo-American productivity differences – their magnitude and some causes," *American Economic Review* 45, May: 94–112.

Haley, C.V., L. Lan and M.-H. Toh (1996) "Singapore incorporated: Reinterpreting Singapore's business environment through a corporate metaphor," *Management Decision* 34 (9): 17–28.

Hirsch, S. (1967) *The Location of Industry and International Competitiveness*, Oxford: Oxford University Press.

Hirschman, A. (1970) *Exit, Voice and Loyalty: International Differences in Work-Related Values*, Cambridge, Mass.: Harvard University Press.

Horst, T. (1972a) "Firm and industry determinants of the decision to invest abroad: An empirical study," *Review of Economics and Statistics* 54: 258–66.

—— (1972b) "The industrial composition of US exports and subsidiary sales to the Canadian market," *American Economic Review* 62: 37–45.

Hufbauer, G.C. (1965) *Synthetic Materials and the Theory of International Trade*, London: Duckworth.

Hymer, S. [1960] (1976) *The International Operations of National Firms: A Study of Direct Investment*, Cambridge, Mass.: MIT Press.

—— (1968) "La grande firme multinationale," *Revue Economique* 19: 949–3.

Kindleberger, C.P. (1969) *American Business Abroad*, New Haven, Conn.: Yale University Press.

Knickerbocker, F.T. (1973) *Oligopolistic Reaction and the Multinational Enterprise*, Cambridge, Mass.: Harvard University Press.

Kogut, B. (1983) "Foreign direct investment as a sequential process," in C.P. Kindleberger and D. Audretsch (eds) *The Multinational Corporation in the 1980s*, Cambridge, Mass.: MIT Press.

—— (1985) "Designing global strategies: Profiting from operational flexibility," *Sloan Management Review*, Fall: 27–37.

—— (1996) "Platform investments and volatile exchange rates: Direct investment in the US by Japanese electronic companies," *Review of Economics and Statistics* 78 (2), May: 221–31.

Kojima, K. (1978) *Direct Foreign Investment: A Japanese Model of Multinational Business Operations*, London: Croom Helm.

—— (1982) "Macro economic versus international business approaches to foreign direct investment," *Hitosubashi Journal of Economics* 23: 1–19.

Kuemmerle, W. (1997) "Building effective capabilities abroad," *Harvard Business Review*, March/April: 61–70.

McGee, J. and H. Thomas (1986) "Strategic groups: Theory, research and taxonomy," *Strategic Management Journal* 7: 141–60.

McManus. J.C. (1972) "The theory of the multinational firm," in G. Paquet (ed.) *The Multinational Firm and the Nation State*, Toronto: Collier-Macmillan.

Ozawa, T. (1989) "Japan's strategic investment policy towards developing countries: From the ad hoc to a new comprehensive approach," mimeo.

—— (1992) "Foreign direct investment and economic development," *Transnational Corporations* 1 (1): 27–54.

—— (1996) "Japan: The macro-IDP, meso-IDPs and the technology development path (TDP)," in J. H. Dunning and R. Narula (eds) *Foreign Direct Investment and Governments*, London and New York: Routledge.

Rostas, L. (1948) *Comparative Productivity in British and American Industry*, Cambridge: Cambridge University Press.

Rugman, A.M. (1980) "Internalization theory and corporate international finance," *California Management Review* XIII: 73–79.

—— (1997) *The Scientific Papers of Alan Rugman*, vol. 1. London: Edward Elgar.

Swedenborg, B. (1979) *The Multinational Operations of Swedish Firms: An Analysis of Determinants and Effects*, Stockholm: Almquist & Wiksell.

Tolentino, P.E. (1990) *The Internationalization of Philippine Firms*, London: Routledge.

Vernon, R. (1966) "International investment and international trade in the product cycle," *Quarterly Journal of Economics* 80: 90–207.

—— (1974) "The location of economic activity," in J.H. Dunning (ed.) *Economic Analysis and the Multinational Enterprise*, London: Allen & Unwin.

—— (1979) "The product cycle hypothesis in a new international environment," *Oxford Bulletin of Economics and Statistics* 41: 255-67.

—— (1983) "Organizational and institutional responses to international risk," in R.J. Herring (ed.) *Managing International Risk*, Cambridge: Cambridge University Press.

Zander, I. and U. Zander (1996) "Sweden: A latecomer to industrialization," in J.H. Dunning and R. Narula (eds) *Foreign Direct Investment and Governments*, London and New York: Routledge.

6 The resource-based approach to multinational enterprise

Neil Kay

Introduction

This chapter looks at the possible relevance of resource-based approaches to the analysis of multinational enterprise. We shall consider what such approaches may contribute to questions concerning the nature of multinational enterprise,[1] and in particular why a firm might choose this method of expansion over alternatives. It will be suggested that the resource-based perspective has been unjustly neglected in the study of multinational enterprise, and that recognition of the potential contribution it can make in this context could be of considerable benefit to research into multinational enterprise.

There have been a number of works employing what could be described as resource-based approaches in the strategic management literature, and these have been surveyed by Mahoney and Pandian (1992) and Peteraf (1993). These approaches tend to take *The Theory of the Growth of the Firm* (Penrose, 1959) as their starting point and we shall be looking at her approach in the next section. However, before doing so we can note some interesting aspects of the impact of the resource-based approach in recent years, and the recognition of Penrose's contribution in particular. First, Penrose's work has had a considerable impact on the managerial literature, less so on the economic literature, even though Penrose's work is explicitly an economics-based approach to resource allocation in the firm. Indeed, it is not difficult to find economic textbooks on the theory of the firm and the organisation of industry that make no mention of her work. Second, while there is now recognition of the contribution this approach can make in the managerial literature, the recognition tends to be concentrated in the strategic management literature with little note being made of it in the international business literature. For example, while the Social Science Citations Index records some hundreds of citations to Penrose (1959) in managerial journals such as *Strategic Management Journal* for the period 1981–97, over the same period the book has only a handful of citations in journals concerned with international business. This neglect appears particularly strange when it is noted that much of Penrose's work following the publication of *The Theory of the Growth of the Firm* was concerned with multinational enterprise.

It will be argued below that some of the reasons for the biases in the way that Penrose's framework has been recognised tell us some things about the potential contribution this approach may be able to make to the study of multinational enterprise. In the section that follows we shall look at her approach and how it can be adapted to the study of multinational enterprise. We shall also consider possible reasons for the relative neglect of Penrose's work in the international business field. The subsequent section develops a simple resource-based approach to the analysis of multinational enterprise that builds on Galbraith and Kay (1986) and Kay (1997). We shall then examine the potential complementarity of resource-based and transaction-based perspectives on multinational enterprise. We finish with a short concluding section.

Penrose, the resource-based approach, and multinational enterprise

What might be described as the resource-based approach (Penrose, 1959) and transaction cost economics (Williamson, 1975, 1985, 1996) are concerned with how the boundaries of the firm may be affected by the relationship of resources (or assets) to alternative uses. However, in the resource-based approach the boundaries of the firm expand because resources are *not* specialised to particular uses, while in transaction cost economics the boundaries expand because resources *are* specialised to particular uses.[2] Clearly, these are very different perspectives on the nature of the firm that are difficult or impossible to reconcile. We shall discuss the relationship between the two perspectives further below, but first we shall consider the foundations of the resource-based approach.

The Penrosian view of the growth of the firm could be summarised briefly as follows. The firm is a collection of resources, and its expansion is dictated by the interplay between internal resources and external opportunities. The emphasis is on the role played by productive resources, especially management. The nature and availability of internal managerial resources limit the direction and extent of expansion that a firm can undertake at any one point in time. However, as Penrose points out,

> if the argument is accepted that a firm will expand only in accordance with plans for expansion and that the extent of these plans will be limited by the size of the experienced managerial group, then it is evident that as plans are completed and put into operation, managerial services absorbed in the planning processes will be gradually released and become available for further planning.
>
> (Penrose, 1959: 49)

Firms will typically find it cheaper and less risky to concentrate on their existing products, *ceteris paribus*, but may expand into new areas in pursuit of growth (pp. 82–84). These directions are influenced not only by external opportunities but also by the nature of the internal resources available to pursue these expansion opportunities, especially pools of unused managerial resources available to help plan expansion: 'The selection of the relevant product-markets is necessarily determined by the 'inherited' resources of the firm – the productive services it already has' (p. 82).

Perhaps the best illustration of the expansion process envisaged by Penrose is provided by her study of the Hercules Powder Company (Penrose, 1960). This piece was originally intended to be part of the 1959 work and illustrate its arguments, but was dropped in order to keep down the size of the book. Hercules Powder was one of three firms formed in 1913 as a consequence of an antitrust-instigated break up of E.I. Dupont de Nemours. Over the next 40-odd years, Hercules grew steadily and by 1956 it had 11,365 employees. It was technically a multinational enterprise, though only 3 of its 25 plants were located overseas. What marked the expansion process detailed by Penrose was the diversification process with a gradual accretion of new markets and technologies by Hercules from relatively specialised technological origins. Starting with explosives and its technological skills in organic chemicals, Hercules diversified into a wide range of technologies and markets, including protective coatings, plastics, agricultural chemicals, papermaking chemicals and petrochemicals. Hercules usually had some relevant technological or market experience that gave it a base from which to enter the new activity, though the links were stronger in some areas than others.

It is perhaps unfortunate that no room for it could be found in *The Theory of the Growth of the Firm* since the paper provides an excellent illustration of how Penrose's approach can be applied to issues relating to corporate strategy. Indeed, the analysis and supporting diagram tracing the expansion of Hercules into related markets and technologies parallel Rumelt's (1974) analysis and supporting diagram of a similar expansion process for carborundum. The two pieces of analysis are highly complementary and help to confirm Penrose's acknowledged status as the founder of the resource-based approach to corporate strategy.[3]

However, this paper effectively represents the end-point of Penrose's development and application of the framework associated with her name. Even though she turned to issues related to the development of multinational enterprise, she made little subsequent reference to how her approach could be applied to the problems she examined. In part this may be a reflection of the industry she now chose to specialise in, viz. the international petroleum industry.[4] If one wanted to find an industry in which Penrose's view of the growth of the firm was perhaps least obviously applicable, it would be difficult to find a better example than the international petroleum industry. First, as Penrose discusses (1968: 46–47), *vertical expansion* in the international petroleum oil industry was generally regarded as revolving around flows of crude oil and related desires to ensure access to supplies and outlets, and to maintain continuity of throughput. None of these inducements for vertical integration has any obvious connection to pools of unused managerial resources.

Second, *horizontal expansion* in a highly vertically integrated system may be dominated by a number of constraints other than available managerial resources. For example, expanding one part of the system in isolation as productive resources were released (say in refining) would run the risk of unbalanced growth if the other parts of the system did not expand at the same rate. Furthermore there might be no guarantee that the other parts would release resources at that same rate. Moreover, expansion in some stages was highly uncertain and contingent on factors only partially under the control of the firm, such as success or failure in exploration and in political relations with producer nations. Also, if any firm wished to expand by acquiring existing capacity at any stage, it would find that much of the capacity of the industry was already locked up within the vertically integrated majors; Penrose (1968: 88) noted that at the time of writing just seven companies owned more than 75 per cent of non-US crude oil production, nearly 60 per cent of the refining capacity of Europe (the largest refining centre), and probably an even higher percentage of the marketing stage. In short, having idle managerial resources in one particular stage of production might not be the most obvious or important factor influencing the expansion of the firm which might in practice be dominated by other influences.

Third, and most critically, *diversification* was only a minor interest of oil companies' activities and mentioned only in passing by Penrose (1968: 146–47). The corporate strategies of most of the large firms in the industry were still largely focused around the industry's major products.[5] Penrose estimated that only about 8–13 per cent of oil company new investment (including R&D) fell into the category of diversification (p. 147), and indeed many of these investments were subsequently to be judged failures, though it could not be expected that this would be known at the time Penrose wrote. Further, many oil company diversification moves in this period fell into the category of conglomerate expansion[6] and did not obviously draw on the particular bundles of managerial expertise associated with operations in the petroleum industry. By way of contrast, no single group of industries constituted more than 16 per cent of sales in the Hercules Powder Company case at the time Penrose was writing.

In short, the Penrosian picture of the growth of the firm is one that, superficially at least, is less obviously applicable to the international petroleum industry than to many others. This does not mean that the Penrosian perspective is inappropriate; as we shall see, Ollinger (1994) shows how it may be relevant in this context also. However, explanations for integration that do not explicitly draw on a resource-based perspective are more common in the petroleum industry. This is reflected in her subsequent analysis of the industry. While her analysis of the economics and politics of the international petroleum industry is of the highest quality,[7] there is little in it that makes direct connections with *The Theory of the Growth of the Firm*. For example, there are only two minor footnotes referring to *The Theory of the Growth of the Firm* in her 1968 economic study of the oil multinationals (pp. 27, 40): one refers to the profit motive and one to the difficulty of identifying the boundaries of the firm. Neither footnote indicates if and how the earlier work could be of relevance to the analysis of multinational enterprise. It has to be said that if you do not make explicit how your own approach can be of relevance to a new area of analysis, then it is not surprising if others overlook your potential contribution.

However, Penrose had earlier (1956) published a paper which did apply her resource-based approach to the case of multinational enterprise. But while the perspective is consistent with her resource-based approach, ironically the emphasis is still on domestic expansion; first on the part of the firm in its home-based activities, and second from the perspective of the overseas subsidiary which, Penrose argues, can with some exceptions be treated as a separate firm (pp. 226–27): 'once established a subsidiary has a life of its own, and its growth will continue in response to the development of its own internal resources and the opportunities presented in its new environment' (pp. 225–26). The links between parent and overseas subsidiary are recognised but treated almost as an afterthought: 'It should not be forgotten that a very considerable input of the managerial and technical resources of the investing firm may be required to ascertain what foreign opportunities exist and how they may best be taken advantage of' (p. 228). However, once the foreign subsidiary has been established, Penrose argues it will tend to develop largely independently of the parent: 'a foreign subsidiary, once it is established, is, with important exceptions, more appropriately treated as a separate firm' (pp. 226–27). The most important exception is finance; Penrose argues that the managerial resources necessary for expansion will now tend to be largely contained within the local subsidiary (p. 226).

Clearly, the extent to which the overseas subsidiary could be treated as a separate firm is debatable and it would not be difficult to find examples where the overseas subsidiary is kept on a tight rein with limited local discretion and managerial capacity. However, perhaps more important is the focus on *domestic* diversification (both by the parent and the foreign subsidiary) and the relative neglect of parent–subsidiary relations (Penrose's arguments were strongly influenced by her observations of the behaviour of one particular Australian subsidiary of a foreign multinational). This raises a central question: what advantages may be obtained from first creating, then maintaining the multinational firm? If the home and overseas subsidiaries can be treated as effectively separate firms once the latter have been established (as Penrose suggests), then an internal capital market would seem a very weak reason for sustaining such a structure. After all, if the firm had decided to invest in domestic opportunities for expansion instead of going abroad, it could reasonably expect to obtain similar internal capital market advantages, but without the disadvantages of expansion into markets with which it is unfamiliar and has no presence. This is not a very convincing platform from which to analyse the evolution of the multinational enterprise.

It was Wolf (1977) who first really built on Penrose's work to formulate a resource-based perspective on multinational enterprise. He pointed out that a firm could expand in a number of different directions, including within its domestic industry, domestic industrial diversification, or geographic diversification abroad (including exporting and multinational expansion). As Penrose noted, the impetus for growth could come from internal or external stimuli or growth. Some influences that will push the firm in the direction of diversification (e.g. market saturation) will tend to favour domestic diversification, others geographic diversification (including multinational expansion). Wolf concluded that exporting, foreign investment and domestic diversification all offered alternative ways of exploiting under-utilised resources that could have been a product of firm size and technical expertise. As he argues, the major contribution of his paper is that it does not consider domestic diversification and international expansion as isolated phenomena but instead treats them as having a common foundation.[8]

Caves (1982: 12–15) later provided an excellent outline of the dynamics of multinational expansion which helps to show how a resource-based perspective can be applied in this context, though his interpretation is framed more in terms of transaction costs than in terms of the resource-based approach. He points out that firms may wish to explore ways of exploiting their intangible assets (such as technological or marketing ability), but as Penrose pointed out, managerial limits to expansion constrain the number of opportunities a firm can pursue at any one time. Caves argues that firms will tend to explore domestic expansion first, since there are fixed costs of entering new foreign markets in terms of learning how things are done abroad. Information costs encourage the firm to do more of the same and avoid the information and search costs associated with going abroad. The reason that foreign expansion is eventually considered is because returns to continued domestic expansion will eventually decline as markets saturate and diversification opportunities dry up; the firm may eventually find foreign investments becoming attractive expansion opportunities, even allowing for the additional information costs associated with foreign expansion. However, all other things being equal, the firm will still prefer to expand into new areas that allow it to economise on these additional information costs, the first preference being to expand into foreign markets where the firm faces the least disadvantage in terms of language and culture.

Caves presents his argument as a transaction cost explanation of the dynamics of MNE expansion. However, it reads better as a resource-based account of how the multinational enterprise might evolve; the transaction cost perspective is generally concerned with alternative *modes* of organisation, while Caves is concerned here is with alternative *directions* for expansion. We shall develop this point below, but for the moment we shall simply note that Caves's approach is consistent with the Penrosian notion that each individual firm is a pool of resources, and that this particular pool of resources may be better suited to some directions of expansion than others. All things being equal, we would expect the firm to prefer expansion opportunities that make more use of its productive resources compared to expansion opportunities that make lighter use. As Caves points out (1982: 14–15), empirical research tends to support these arguments in the case of the international firm. Firms tend to become major players in their domestic markets before they go abroad (Horst, 1972), and also there tends to be a preference for entering foreign markets that are as similar as possible to domestic markets (e.g. US firms into Canada).[9]

Some of these points are echoed by Buckley (1990) in his discussion of a paper[10] by Hymer (1968). In Hymer's interpretation, firms will tend to pursue horizontal expansion until market concentration forces other expansion choices on the agenda, including diversification. Consistent with Wolf's analysis, the diversification decision encompasses new industries (product diversification) and overseas diversification (internationalisation).

In the next section we shall pursue these lines of argument to indicate how they may help provide a basis for a resource-based perspective on the evolution of multinational enterprise.

Multinational enterprise as a bundle of resources

We can build on the ideas set out at the end of the last section to develop a simple, resource-based approach to the development of multinational enterprise. We shall assume that the different businesses in our example are identical in terms of cost, demand, and growth potential if they are to be operated as independent businesses. This allows us to suppress business-level influences and to concentrate on the possible impact of alternative resource linkages associated with alternative expansion plans. We shall also distinguish between *directions* and *modes*. A strategic move by a firm typically involves both a direction (e.g. foreign market entry) and a mode by which this move will be carried out (e.g. licensing, joint venture, wholly owned subsidiary). Unfortunately, much analysis in the literature is incomplete because it is sometimes assumed that it is sufficient to analyse a move from the point of view of choice of *either* mode *or* choice of direction. The analysis here builds on Galbraith and Kay (1986) and Kay (1997).

With these points in mind, suppose we have a manufacturer of men's wallets considering various growth possibilities. The firm makes and sells its wallets in a single national market and the various expansion opportunities are identical in terms of the revenue opportunities they would generate. The first possibility is shown in Figure 6.1 and is a simple specialisation option. The firm could continue to make wallets for the domestic market and expand its product range through product differentiation. It could continue to use the same production facilities, exploit common R&D activity, use the same distribution channels, and sell to the same customer base within the same national market.

Figure 6.1 indicates how this option could exploit resource or asset sharing right across the board. In turn, sharing of both tangible and intangible assets can generate cost reductions through providing opportunities for increased specialisation and fuller exploitation of indivisibilities in the respective cases; the gains in the specialisation option are essentially those associated with economies of scale and learning curve opportunities. The categories are mostly self-explanatory and tend to correspond to actual and observable functions and resources of firms, with the exception of the C-links (C1 to C5 inclusive). This firm has accumulated a pool of expertise and knowledge relating to how to operate in this national context. It has familiarity and experience of the country's legal, political, and

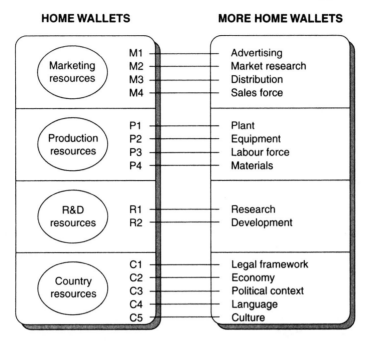

Figure 6.1 Option 1: specialisation

cultural systems, as well as its language and the structures and processes of the national economy. Unlike the other categories of resources, such expertise tends not to be associated with a particular function or activity but to be diffused through the firm; for example, the co-ordination of all activities of the firm may benefit by having a single shared language throughout the firm. While the gains from shared country characteristics may be less visible and obvious than the gains from, say, sharing machinery, they are none the less real gains that the firm may exploit from domestic expansion.

Figure 6.2 shows the specialisation option and consolidates the gains from links within each category. The lower-case 's' (as in 'Ms') stands for specialisation and indicates that the link represents the potential for resource sharing in the case of expansion involving continued product specialisation. However, Figure 6.2 also shows three alternative strategies: diversification, exporting, and multinational expansion, all starting from the original base of 'home wallets'. Again, for simplicity we assume that the new area of activity has similar demand-side revenue characteristics to the starting base in each case, allowing us to concentrate on the implications of potential resource sharing in each option.

If the firm were to diversify into purses (option 2) it could expect to exploit country linkages from domestic expansion (the C-link) and some resource sharing in marketing (Md), production (Pd) and R&D (Rd). Some resources in each of these latter categories may be shared between the product markets, while others

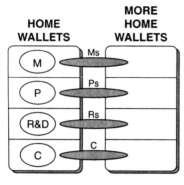

Option 1: Specialisation

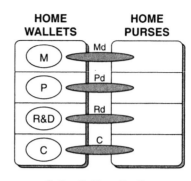

Option 2: Diversification

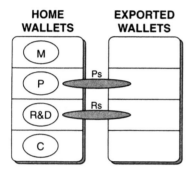

Option 3: Exporting

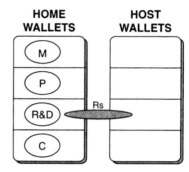

Option 4: Multinational Enterprise

Figure 6.2 Some options for expansion

may be specific to one product market; for example, there may be partial sharing of distribution channels, with some outlets shared and others carrying only wallets or purses. There may be some sharing of production techniques, equipment, and labour force across product markets, while some may be specialised to either wallets or purses. Similarly, some R&D activity may be applicable to both areas (say, research into materials and fastenings), while others may be specific to one of the product markets (especially at the development stage). The partial sharing of resources is indicated by the 'd' (for diversification) in Figure 6.2.

Option 3 is the exporting option. Here we assume to begin with that transport costs are negligible and that the firm is exporting wallets to a new foreign market where the country characteristics (including language) are completely different from that associated with its home base. Consequently there is no country level expertise transferable to the new market, and the firm also has to set up a completely new distribution system, with a new sales force, new market research, and new advertising campaigns appropriate to the new market. However, the firm is able to consolidate its production in its home base and so exploit resource-sharing economies in production, and of course the relevant R&D activity can be spread across both markets. Consequently, the firm exploits Ps and Rs links in the exporting option.

Finally, the firm is considering the alternative of moving into the same foreign market, but through setting up a manufacturing facility in the foreign market to service local demand. The M, R&D and C considerations are the same as in the exporting case, the difference being now that the firm sacrifices P linkages by having to duplicate production facilities in the two countries.

This highly stylised starting point gives us a base from which to begin to analyse the evolution of multinational enterprise from a resource-based perspective. First, the firm would normally have a rank order preference of specialisation – exporting – multinational expansion when the options are analysed in terms of potential resource linkages. Domestically based specialisation offers richer linkages than exporting, which in turn may be expected to generate more extensive linkages than multinational expansion. Clearly, some things may happen to disturb this rank ordering (and we shall discuss some of them below), but it gives us a first approach to the kinds of gains that be might be expected from the three options. Second, option 2 (diversification) offers potential linkages in more categories than either exporting or the multinational option, but the links are more diffuse in the diversification case with exporting offering stronger linkages in production and R&D (Ps and Rs compared to Pd and Rd), and the multinational offering stronger links in R&D (Rs compared to Rd). Even with this simplified starting point we cannot say a priori that domestic diversification would be preferable to either of the two foreign expansion options in terms of potential economies; this will depend on whether the more extensive linkages associated with diversification would generate more gains than the limited but concentrated economies from foreign expansion. However, what we can say is that if there were diversification opportunities that offered high levels of resource sharing in terms of marketing and technological characteristics, then this option would normally be preferred to foreign expansion. It would only be when the firm had to turn to diversification opportunities involving significant shifts *away* from the firm's marketing and technological bases that the linkages from diversification would be weakened sufficiently to be beaten by the concentrated (but limited) linkages offered by foreign expansion. In this perspective, the firm is likely to prefer to explore opportunities for domestic diversification before making a serious effort to pursue overseas expansion.

This description of how the firm is likely to expand is broadly consistent with the dynamics of multinational expansion described above by Caves. Seen from a resource-based perspective, the firm in our example will have a first preference for specialisation as a growth option and we would expect it to pursue this until and unless there is some blockage or deterrent to pursuing this option.[11] It should be noted that these rank orderings only matter if there is some constraint on expansion, such as Penrose's (1959) limit of available managerial resources; the existence of such a constraint means the firm cannot pursue all potentially attractive investment opportunities, but has to prioritise them. Next, domestic expansion will normally be preferred to foreign expansion, and if the firm cannot pursue specialisation it will prefer to move into areas as closely related as possible to its existing market and technological bases. It will pursue the diversification route until and unless the linkages available from diversification are weaker than the concentrated production and R&D economies associated with the exporting option. Finally, the multinational route for expansion appears here as the least preferred option considered in resource-sharing terms, and would normally only be considered when there were blockages or impediments to the other options for expansion, including exporting.

This perspective has a number of implications and, in particular, can be related to various findings in the empirical literature:

1 Size of firm and multinationalism

A number of empirical studies have found that larger firms are more likely to become multinationals (Dunning, 1993: 151–52), though it is generally accepted that size may be acting as a composite variable for other influences (p. 151). In the resource-based perspective outlined here, not only might size itself be important, but it might also be acting as a proxy for diversification. The growth process outlined above puts a particular interpretation on the relationship between size, diversification, and multinationals. In this perspective, firms become multinationals not because they need to be large and diversified to consider this option, but because having become large and diversified, the more obvious and richer-linked domestic expansion opportunities have already been exploited. Thus, the empirical findings on size of firm are consistent with the picture of the firm expanding until it begins to run out of richly linked domestic opportunities, and only then turning to foreign expansion such as multinationalism.

A fuller analysis in this context would explore the relation between supply-side and demand-side aspects in the expansion process. In particular, domestic expansion may become less attractive because there are declining opportunities to exploit supply-side economies, or because the demand side itself weakens in terms of revenue potential from expansion, or both. Whatever the cause of the diminishing attraction of domestic expansion in practice, the result is to increase the relative attractiveness of foreign expansion (including multinationalism) in terms of growth opportunity.

2 R&D intensity and multinationalism

In our stylised resource-based example above, the only linkage the firm can exploit from multinational expansion is R&D. Providing there is no customisation of the product to foreign market specifications, R&D costs in the multinational case can be spread over double the turnover compared to its domestic base alone. However, this is the only linkage recognised in our example. Unless the firm can exploit economies from R&D, *any* domestic expansion would beat multinationalism considered on resource-based terms, since even conglomerate expansion into unrelated product markets would exploit C-linkages from domestic expansion.

In our simple example, R&D activity appears as a necessary but not sufficient reason for foreign expansion. Some impediments to exporting must also exist, since this option could not only exploit R-linkages but add P-linkages as well. These impediments could include transport costs, or trade barriers such as tariffs and quotas. There must also be impediments to further specialisation (market saturation or antitrust threats may be impediments here) and diversification (exhausting diversification opportunities are obvious possible impediments in this context). In the absence of such impediments, domestic expansion would allow the firm to exploit richer linkages compared to the multinational alternative.

Therefore, the exploitation of R&D linkages is not a sufficient justification for the firm to go multinational; there must also be further impediments in the way of the other possible options for growth. What we can say, however, is that the stronger the R-linkages (Rs) the firm can exploit from multinational expansion, the sooner the firm is likely to turn to this growth option, all other things being equal. If the firm's business has only modest R&D content, then the weak economies from the Rs linkage are unlikely to be worth the sacrifice of the C-linkages (and possibly other linkages) the firm could exploit from domestic expansion. On the other hand, if the firm is a high R&D spender, it increases the chances of multinational expansion beating residual diversification opportunities. In short, the more research-intensive the firm, the more likely that economies from multinational Rs links in Figure 6.2 will have a chance of providing more gains than the economies from the diversification option. We would expect the propensity of a firm to go multinational to be directly linked to its research intensity.

Again, this expectation tends to be consistent with the empirical evidence (Dunning, 1993: 149–50). A number of studies have suggested that multinationals tend to be research-intensive compared to non-multinationals. According to the approach developed here, the proper interpretation of this is not that firms go multinational in order to exploit economies in R&D; even a simple resource-based perspective suggests that there may be better ways of doing this that allow the exploitation of other linkages as well. Instead, the appropriate interpretation is that the firm would have no justification for going multinational in the absence of significant R-linkages. If significant R-linkages can be exploited, then in some circumstances impediments to the pursuit of the other options in Figure 6.2 may eventually lead to the multinational option.

3 Concentration and multinationalism

We would expect industrial concentration and multinationalism to be linked, since a firm in such markets is more likely to be encouraged to explore growth opportunities outside its main base due to market saturation or anti-trust pressures. However, for our firm in Figure 6. 2, industrial concentration itself would not be sufficient to stimulate multinational expansion – it would still need to beat the diversification and specialisation options. The effect of industrial concentration in this context is similar to the effect of research intensity on multinationalism;

their presence is not sufficient to stimulate multinationalism, but their absence is likely to mean that the firm will prefer other growth opportunities. If a firm is operating in a market with a low degree of concentration, it is likely still to have specialisation growth opportunities open to it before it considers more weakly linked options. Conversely, a high degree of concentration may trigger a search for alternatives, including multinational expansion.

Again, the evidence broadly supports this, with Dunning (1993: 429) commenting that 'the average concentration ratios of the sectors that account for the greater part of MINE activity are considerably higher than for the rest of industry'.[12]

4 Domestic clustering of resources

One of the implications of the resource-based perspective developed above is that the firm will only turn to multinationalism *after* priority has been given to more richly linked options involving clustering of assets in the domestic base, and once impediments have been put in the way of continued expansion of this nature. We would expect that these preferences and processes would lead to the firm preferring to cluster its resources in its home base.[13] This is indeed what tends to happen in most cases; for example, Dunning (1993: 47) measures the percentage of assets accounted for by foreign affiliates of some of the largest companies in the world, and the figures show that for the world's 13 largest non-petroleum companies for which figures were available (ranked by net sales), not one had a majority of assets accounted for by foreign affiliates in 1989. Even European multinationals (such as ICI, Hoechst, Renault, Peugeot, and Fiat) tended to concentrate the majority of their assets in their national bases despite their smaller home markets.

5 Marketing-based multinationals

In our example in Figure 6.2 we have assumed that technical know-how is the only intangible asset that multinationals can exploit. However, marketing know-how may also be at least partially transferable in some cases. In the unusual case of global brands with relatively homogeneous advertising world-wide, the firm may be able to exploit a great deal of marketing resource sharing cross-frontier. At the other end of the spectrum, a technically identical product may be sold with very different advertising and to very different consumers in different countries. In such cases there may be little or no sharing of marketing expertise cross-frontier. There may even be considerable differences in the extent to which marketing competencies transfer globally within the same sector. For example, Cadbury Schweppes operates in two related sectors: soft drinks (which is characterised by a number of strong global brands) and chocolates (which tends to characterised by highly differentiated national preferences) (Kay, 1997: 116–18).

As with technical know-how, even where marketing know-how is important, this is not in itself sufficient to stimulate expansion using the multinational option. However, it may help reinforce R-linkages in cases where marketing activity does have some transfer value cross-frontier. Consequently the resource-based perspective developed here suggests that firms in which marketing activity (and marketing resources) are important are more likely to follow the multinational route. This is broadly consistent with the empirical evidence, which has generally found (with some qualifications) that multinational activity tends to be positively related to advertising intensity (usually measured as advertising expenditure as a percentage of sales; see Dunning, 1993: 162).

6 Psychic distance

In options 3 and 4 there are no C-linkages between business units when the firm goes into a foreign market. This may not be a reasonable assumption in many cases. For example, if a Canadian firm goes into the New Zealand market or a Mexican firm into the Venezuelan market, there are likely to be at least partial elements of our C-link in Figure 6.2 which may be exploited between the markets in which the firm is operating in the respective cases. These elements could include language, society and culture, political systems, and legal traditions.

The concept of psychic distance associated with the Scandinavian literature in international business is of relevance in this context. Psychic distance is defined as 'factors preventing or disturbing the flows of information between firms and market. Examples of such factors are differences in language, culture, political systems, level of education, level of industrial development, etc.' (Johanson and Wiedersheim-Paul, 1993: 18). Psychic distance may be generally interpreted as the inverse of the C-link; to the extent there is an absence of C-linkages between the firm's activities in different countries, we would expect psychic distance to increase. In our resource-based approach, we would expect the firm to give priority to expanding into markets with the richer set of linkages, *ceteris paribus*. In this context, that would mean markets that allow greater use of C-links, i.e. markets with the lowest psychic distance from the firm's home base. This tends to be consistent with the predictions and the empirical evidence of the Scandinavian literature.[14] Firms tend to prefer to move first into markets with lower psychic distance relative to their home market (and higher implied C-linkages); they tend to move into psychically distant (and more weakly C-linked) markets only later in the internationalisation process. One interesting aspect of this is that it suggests that there may be fruitful connections that may be made between the Scandinavian approach and the resource-based perspective.

In the next section we shall consider how resource-based approaches may relate to the role of transaction or co-ordination costs in the analysis of multi-national enterprise.

Resources and transactions

The discussion so far has focused on resources rather than transactions. Our firm is considering expanding in three different *directions* – specialisation, diversification, and into a foreign market. In the case of the foreign market, the firm can service it by concentrating its production resources at home (exporting) or by setting up a separate subsidiary to produce in the foreign market (multinational expansion). However, so far we have assumed that the firm is only considering go-it-alone in terms of pursuing these alternative directions for expansion. This simplifying assumption has been helpful in analysing the actual behaviour discussed in the previous section. In practice, however, the firm may also have opportunities to co-operate with other firms in its expansion plans. This raises the issue of *modes* of organisation, or the method chosen by the firm to pursue a particular direction for expansion.

Directions and modes are complementary decisions. It would be unwise for any firm to decide on the one before it has settled on the other, just as it would be unwise for any traveller to commit themselves to any destination before they have decided how they are going to get there. However, when we look at questions of *modes* of expansion, the emphasis shifts away from resources and towards transaction or coordination costs. This is not to say that the nature of resources is unimportant in this context; resource characteristics and relations can, and do, play a fundamental role in influencing the costs of alternative modes for organising economic transactions. What is different about the question of choice of modes is the emphasis. In looking at the question of *directions* for expansion, we were holding mode constant and looked at the efficiency implications of alternative patterns of resource linkage. In looking at *modes* of expansion, it is more useful to hold the resource connections constant and consider the efficiency implications of alternative ways of making these connections. Examples of the latter include questions of whether a firm should transfer technology through a wholly owned subsidiary or by licensing a local firm.

There are numerous modes through which resources can be shared (in the case of horizontal moves) or transferred (in the case of vertical moves). In the context of international business, go-it-alone solutions include exporting and the multi-national, while co-operative solutions with other firms include joint venture, licensing, subcontracting, and franchising. In principle, we have a ready-made tool kit for analysing choice of mode in the industrial organisation literature, namely transaction cost economics (Coase, 1937: Williamson, 1975, 1985, 1996). This framework expresses choice of mode in comparative institutional terms and considers the efficiency implications of alternative market and organisational arrangements. However, a difficulty with this approach is that Williamson argues that asset specificity (assets specialised by use or user) tend to be a prerequisite for the existence of transactional problems and the substitution of market exchange with hierarchical or firm organisation. Since related diversification is by definition based on assets or resources that are *not* specialised by end use, this means that it is difficult for transaction cost economics to account for the growth of diversified firms (Kay, 1992, 1997). Consequently, much of the theoretical and empirical analysis in transaction cost economics has been limited to the special case of the vertically integrated firm.

This emphasis on vertical relations is carried over into the analysis of multinational enterprise in transaction cost economics. The topic is relatively neglected in the framework, and when it is discussed it tends to be treated as an extension of the standard asset specificity interpretation of firm organisation:

> A more harmonious and efficient exchange relation . . . predictably results from the substitution of an internal governance relation for bilateral trading under those recurrent trading circumstances where assets, of which complex technology transfer is an example, have a highly specific character.
>
> (Williamson, 1985: 294)

Here Williamson is arguing that specificity of assets encourages the growth of multinational enterprise as an alternative to market options such as licensing. However, Contractor's (1981) study provides evidence that asset specificity may actually help *sustain* market relationships such as licensing arrangements by ensuring the licensee is kept dependent on the licensor.[15] Also, the transaction cost economics emphasis on vertical relations and specialised assets is difficult to reconcile with the fact that the bulk of multinational expansion involves the horizontal transfer of intangible assets such as technical and marketing know-how into new applications in foreign locations (Kay, 1997).

The international business literature takes a rather different approach to the question of transactions costs and the boundaries of the firm. Cantwell and Hennart (this volume) provide excellent surveys of transaction costs in the international business context. In general, analyses of transaction costs in the international business (IB) literature[16] appear much more broadly (and soundly) based than in the industrial organisation (IO) literature.[17] For example, appropriabiity problems in the case of intellectual property are generally recognised as a major transaction cost issue in the IB literature, while transaction cost economics in the IO literature tends to be largely concerned with issues associated with asset specificity.

At this point it might seem reasonable to conclude that we have an obvious division of labour. If the preceding discussion were accepted, resource-based approaches would seem appropriate for the study of directions of expansion while transaction cost approaches as developed in the IB literature might be more appropriate for the study of modes of expansion.[18] This is arguable up to a point; the problem is that neither approach is sufficient by itself for dealing with the expansion decisions of the firm. There is a real danger that analysing a move solely as a decision as to which direction to take or which mode to adopt will lead to problems. It is essential to bear in mind that each expansion move has a dual nature in that a firm is making a choice of both a direction and a mode. If you heard that your aunt was cycling to Minsk, it would naturally raise at least two questions: Why Minsk? Why a bicycle? If all you know is that she has a brother in Minsk, this might help explain why she wants to go there, but does not explain why she wants to cycle. Alternatively, if all you know is that she loves to cycle, this might help explain her choice of transport, but not why she wants to go to Minsk. However, this particular move requires both direction *and* mode to be explained. Similarly, if a firm makes a particular move, we have to be able to justify why this direction *and* this mode were chosen over alternatives. Failure to do both may lead to analysis that is at best incomplete, and at worst misleading.

The last point may seem obvious, but it has been honoured more in the breach than in the observance in many areas of analysis of firm behaviour, including the study of multinational enterprise. This can lead to the problem of limited comparators (Kay, 1997). This is the tendency to provide an explanation for a phenomenon that appears satisfactory when only limited alternatives are considered, but breaks down when the agenda is widened to include all relevant alternatives to the move in question.

One example of limited comparators discussed in Kay (1992, 1997: 58–61) is Williamson's explanation for the conglomerate. Williamson argues that failures in the external capital market may lead to the internalisation and divisionalisation advantages provided by the conglomerate being a more efficient solution than one in which all the divisions remained independent and traded as separate firms. There is nothing wrong with this explanation of the conglomerate considered as a *mode* but it is simply not adequate as an explanation for the conglomerate as a *direction*. Since specialised and related diversification strategies can exploit the same gains from internalisation and divisionalisation that the conglomerate exploits, *and* add further gains from economies of scale and scope that are closed to the conglomerate, there would appear to be nothing that the conglomerate can do that more specialised strategies cannot do better. This is a problem of limited comparators that comes from looking at the conglomerate in terms only of alternative modes and not of alternative strategies.

A second problem of limited comparators can also be frequently found in the international literature in the context of various modes of co-operative strategies such as joint ventures, licensing, strategic alliances, and mergers. A frequent approach to this problem is to identify various 'objectives', 'goals', or 'motives' or 'reasons' for the mode under discussion. Some of the checklists produced in this fashion can be quite elaborate and extensive. However, there are often problems associated with these approaches. First, the checklists produced for the different modes typically produce almost identical items, such as 'sharing R&D', 'production economies' and 'market access'. Second, the apparent variety of reasons for co-operative strategies can generally be reduced to a couple of simple generic items: sharing some resource or increasing market control; supply-side economies and monopolistic distortions respectively. The problem with some parts of this literature is that they can analyse these moves as *directions* while omitting to justify them as *modes* in the respective cases. Since these moves are in fact different ways of doing the same thing, this is a serious defect since supposed investigation of the 'motives' underlying each mode turn out to be spurious. There is no surprise that the checklists of the reasons for different forms of co-operative activity turn out to be so similar; we should only start to ask questions if they did not. But the similarity does not tell us anything very interesting about these modes that we should not know already.

Finally, the problem of limited comparators also applies to analysis of multinational enterprise. Explaining why the multinational *mode* is chosen over alternatives (say, because of transaction costs) does not explain why the multinational *direction* is chosen. One thing that the resource-based analysis of the multinational helps to highlight is the thinness of resource linkages exploited by this direction of expansion. The most obvious question to be suggested by Figure 6.2 is why any firm would wish to consider such a weakly linked option when domestic expansion can normally provide richer linkages. The multinational trick of exploiting intangible assets appears less impressive when it is recognised that domestic expansion can normally perform this trick, and a lot more besides. The explanation for multinational expansion in the resource-based perspective developed here is that it has run out of domestic alternatives. In this view, the expansion of the multinational is not so much a sign of global strength, more an indicator of domestic weakness. These issues are likely to remain obscured if the focus on the multinational is restricted to its role as a mode of organisation. In particular, it is difficult to explain the behaviour patterns we looked at in the last section if analysis of the multinational is restricted in this fashion.

There is one last point that can be made here concerning the dual nature of expansion moves, in that it is generally possible to obtain two correct but different answers to the same question. For example, one answer to the question 'Why do international airlines form strategic alliances?' could be, 'Because it facilitates resource sharing in areas such as routing and ticketing', while another could be, 'Because national governments and anti-trust authorities are likely to impede merger alternatives'. The first answer looks at the logic underlying the direction of the move; the second concentrates on the logic of the mode of co-ordination chosen. Both may be correct, but both are certainly incomplete. Thus, when Penrose looked at 'the economic advantages alleged to flow from extensive (vertical) integration' in the international petroleum industry (1968: 46), the answers she gave related to the advantages of vertical integration as a *mode* of organisation compared to the alternative of trading in the spot market for crude oil. It should be possible to acknowledge that this may help explain why the vertical integration mode was adopted, while noting that this still leaves open the question of why the firm has chosen to give priority to certain directions for expansion over others – what could be described as the true Penrosian question.

In fact, Ollinger (1994) provides just such an analysis. His study of the growth of firms in the US oil industry showed firms tending to pursue richly linked horizontal and domestic expansion opportunities before extending into more weakly linked markets and technologies (such as international, energy, and petrochemical markets), then finally into unrelated markets such as insurance, real estate, and office equipment. While, as we noted above, it is true that the oil industry may be less obviously associated with Penrosian growth processes, it is equally true that these processes can be uncovered if the right questions are asked, which in this context means asking questions about directions rather than modes.

As well as focusing on directions rather than modes, another reason for the difference between Ollinger and Penrose's analyses of the oil industry is the timespan involved in the respective cases. Ollinger's analysis covered six decades of oil industry evolution, while Penrose's coverage of the same industry was typically concerned with much shorter implied timeframes (as might be expected, given the greater neoclassical emphasis in her later work). Thus, Ollinger shows how Penrosian analysis can be applied to the growth of firms in the oil industry, something that Penrose herself omitted to do.

Finally, Ollinger's study also serves to highlight possible directions for developing resource-based perspectives. The resource-based approach outlined in the previous section provides a basis for analysing the process of growth in comparative static terms. Like transaction cost economics, it compares alternative institutional forms in terms of potential efficiency implications, and does so by assuming that resources (including technology) do not change over the period of the analysis. Consequently, the dynamics of resource transformation over time and technological evolution tend to be overlooked in this perspective.

Up to a point this is not a problem. Contrary to some interpretations, there is no automatic merit in introducing a dynamic perspective if a simpler static approach will suffice. If a resource-based perspective can tie together a number of empirical findings (as shown above) without the added complication of dynamic analysis, then well and good. However, there must be at least a suspicion that the resource-based perspective would be enriched by incorporating dynamic elements, and extending the analysis to match the timeframes dealt with by Ollinger. This argument is reinforced by Porter's recent work (1990), which demonstrates that the development of corporate strategies and competitive advantage for internationally successful firms can only be properly understood in many cases by looking at the evolution of the firms and their associated industries over several decades.

Conclusions

This chapter has been concerned with the potential value of a resource-based perspective on multinational enterprise. It was suggested that the theory of the growth of the firm as developed by Penrose provides an excellent perspective from which to analyse multinational enterprise. Penrose herself did not fully outline the possible relevance of her approach in this context, and the framework's potential has not been recognised to the same extent that it has in some other areas concerned with the growth of firms.

The potential relevance of a resource-based approach was illustrated above (see section 'Multinational enterprise as a bundle of resources') and it was argued that the approach is well suited to help analyse the alternative directions of expansion that firms may pursue, both domestic and foreign. It was argued that it was essential to distinguish between *directions* and *modes* of expansion, and that while resource-based perspectives might help in the analysis of directions, analysis of transaction or co-ordination costs must be employed to analyse modes properly.[19] It was emphasised that every strategic move involved both a direction and a mode, and failure to realise this could lead to the problem of limited comparators with incomplete or misleading analysis. Perhaps one of the strongest conclusions this leads to is that the inclusion of a resource-based perspective is essential if the analysis of multinational enterprise is to have adequate foundations.[20]

Notes

1 By multinational enterprise we follow the usual definition of this being a firm with operations in more than one country.

2 In transaction cost economics, asset specificity (assets specialised by use or user) influences choice of mode of economic organisation. If there is a high degree of asset specificity, then the possibility of opportunistic behaviour on the part of the other party to a transaction may lead to a firm protecting its investment by throwing corporate boundaries around the transaction and internalising the trade. See Williamson (1975, 1985, 1996) for further discussion.

3 The relatively few citations to this work in the Social Science Citations Index confirm that this paper has been widely overlooked and unjustly neglected.

4 It appears Penrose's choice of this industry as a special subject for study was influenced by her particular circumstances. She had gone with her husband to teach at the University of Baghdad (1957–59). As she herself notes, 'if one is interested in the growth of firms, especially in their expansion abroad by direct investment, and one is in Baghdad, what can one do but look at the international oil industry?' (Penrose, 1971: vii).

5 See Kay (1982: 100), drawing on work by Rumelt (1974).

6 Examples included ventures into department stores and fish farming.

7 For example, she pinpoints (Penrose, 1968: 199) the fallacies in the arguments put forward some years before by the Anglo-Persian Oil Company that a 60-year concession 'was a necessary condition for the sinking of further large capital sums in the installations in Persia'. As she points out, the discounted present value of anything 60 years hence has little relevance for current investment decisions, *especially* if the risk is high. This is a shrewd observation that one would expect of an economist of Penrose's calibre and is typical of the able and confident manner in which she handles her material. However, it has to be said that there is little of what could now be described as Penrosian about such analysis, but is instead what one would expect a well-trained and competent neo-classical economist to produce.

8 Wolf's contribution has not received the recognition it deserves, with Kashlak and Joshi (1994) being a rare exception. Kashlak and Joshi build on Wolf's argument that product and geographical diversification should be regarded as alternative methods of expansion, but that IB (international business) researchers still tend to focus on geographic diversification, while strategic management (SM) researchers still tend to focus on product diversification.

9 The empirical research on this is reviewed by Caves (1982: 62–65).

10 Originally written in French and recently rediscovered by Mark Casson.

11 In emphasising the resource-based perspective, we are ignoring the effect of risk and uncertainty; for example the firm may try to avoid further specialisation so as to not be overly dependent on a particular market and/or technological base. See Kay (1997) for further discussion of this issue.

12 See Kay (1997: 172–73) for further discussion of other studies of the effect of industrial concentration on the decision to go multinational.
13 This is also consistent with arguments put forward in Porter (1990).
14 See, for example, a number of papers in Buckley and Ghauri (1993), especially the contribution by Johanson and Wiedersheim-Paul.
15 See Kay (1993: 255–56) for further discussion of this point.
16 See for example, Buckley and Casson (1976).
17 The standard framework here is provided by Williamson (1975, 1985, 1996).
18 See also Cantwell's comparison between resource-based approaches and transaction cost economics from the point of view of ownership advantages.
19 In Kay (1997) it was suggested that since 'transaction cost economics' is now generally associated with Williamson's particular interpretation of transaction costs, it might be better to use the more neutral term 'co-ordination costs' to refer to costs of organisation associated with alternative modes.
20 No mention has been made here of Dunning's eclectic theory or paradigm (see Dunning, this volume), partly because he himself points out that the theory was not developed as a theory of the multinational firm as such. However, his framework implicitly recognises the importance of both co-ordination costs and resources, with 'ownership advantages' in the eclectic paradigm depending on the resources possessed by the firm.

References

Buckley P.J. (1990) 'Problems and developments in the core theory of international business', *Journal of International Business Studies* 21: 657–65.

Buckley, P.J. and M. Casson (1976) *The Future of the Multinational Enterprise*, London: Holmes & Meier.

Buckley, P.J. and P.N. Ghauri (eds) (1993) *The Internationalization of the Firm*, London: Academic Press.

Caves, R.E. (1982) *Multinational Enterprise and Economic Analysis*, Cambridge: Cambridge University Press.

Coase, R.H. (1937) 'The nature of the firm', *Economica* 4: 386–405.

Contractor, F. (1981) 'The role of licensing in international strategy', *Columbia Journal of World Business* 16: 73–83.

Dunning, J.H. (1993) *Multinational Enterprises and the Global Economy*, Wokingham: Addison-Wesley.

Galbraith, C.S and N.M. Kay (1986) 'Towards a theory of multinational enterprise', *Journal of Economic Behavior and Organization* 7: 3–19.

Horst, T. (1972) 'Firm and industry determinants of the decision to invest abroad: An empirical study', *Review of Economics and Statistics* 54: 258–66.

Hymer, S.H. (1968) 'The large multinational "corporation": An analysis of some motives for the international integration of business', *Revue Économique* 19: 949–73. Trans. by N. Vecherot, intro. by Mark Casson (1989) mimeo, University of Reading.

Johanson, J. and F. Wiedersheim-Paul (1993) 'The internationalization of the firm – four Swedish cases', in P.J. Buckley and P.N. Ghauri (eds) *The Internationalization of the Firm*, London: Academic Press, 16–31.

Kashlak, R.J. and M.P. Joshi (1994) 'Core business regulation and dual diversification patterns in the telecommunications industry', *Strategic Management Journal* 15: 603–11.

Kay, N.M. (1982) *The Evolving Firm: Strategy and Structure in Industrial Organisation*, London: Macmillan.

—— (1992) 'Markets, false hierarchies and the evolution of the modern corporation', *Journal of Economic Behavior and Organization*, 17: 315–33.

—— (1993) 'Markets, false hierarchies and the role of asset specificity', in C.N. Pitelis (ed.) *Transaction Costs, Markets and Hierarchies*, Oxford: Blackwell.

——(1997) *Pattern in Corporate Evolution*, Oxford: Oxford University Press.

Mahoney, J.T. and J.R. Pandian (1992) 'The resource-based view within the conversation of strategic management', *Strategic Management Journal* 13: 363–80.

Ollinger, M. (1994) 'The limits to growth of the multidivisional firm: A case study of the U.S. oil industry from 1930–90', *Strategic Management Journal* 15: 503–20.

Penrose, E.T. (1956) 'Foreign investment and the growth of the firm', *Economic Journal* 66: 220–35.

—— (1959) *The Theory of the Growth of the Firm*, Oxford: Basil Blackwell.

—— (1960) 'The theory of the growth of the firm. A case study: The Hercules Powder Company', *Business History Review* 34: 1–23.

—— (1968) *The Large International Firm in Developing Countries: The International Petroleum Industry*, London: Allen & Unwin.

—— (1971) *The Growth of Firms, Middle East Oil and Other Essays*, London: Frank Cass.

Peteraf, M.A. (1993) 'The cornerstones of competitive advantage: A resource-based view', *Strategic Management Journal* 14: 179–91.

Porter, M.E. (1990) *The Competitive Advantage of Nations*, London: Macmillan.

Rumelt, R.P. (1974) *Strategy, Structure and Economic Performance*, Boston: Harvard Business School.

Williamson, O.E. (1975) *Markets and Hierarchies: Analysis and Antitrust Implications*, New York: Free Press.

—— (1985) *The Economic Institutions of Capitalism*, New York: Free Press.

—— (1996) *The Mechanisms of Governance*, New York: Oxford University Press.

Wolf, B.M. (1977) 'Industrial diversification and internationalisation: Some empirical evidence', *Journal of Industrial Economics* 2: 177–91.

7 Strategic management and transnational firm behaviour

A formal approach

Edward M. Graham

It is largely accepted among economists that analysis of the multinational enterprise (MNE) is an extension of the study of large firms (e.g. see Caves, 1982). Thus this analysis properly belongs in the domain of industrial organization, a field that has witnessed considerable development over the past two decades or so, giving rise to what is often termed the 'new' industrial organization. The 'new' industrial organization is treated comprehensively by Tirole (1988).

A major distinction between industrial organization and traditional microeconomics is the context in which the decisions of the firm are made. Large firms operating in concentrated industries, when formulating decisions with respect to the setting of price or output and how much to invest in new product development, must take into account the likely reactions of their competitors to these decisions, whereas firms operating in competitive industries do not. The distinction can be summarized by saying that the former firms must make decisions 'strategically', whereas the latter do not.

In spite of this distinction, much of the modern literature specific to the multinational enterprise largely ignores the effects of rivalry on MNE decision-making. Thus, for example, the 'internalization' theories of Buckley and Casson (1976) and Rugman (1986) and the 'eclectic' theory of Dunning (1988) focus largely on factors internal to the firm in analysing why MNEs make the decisions they do. There have indeed been some efforts to account for inter-firm rivalry in this literature (e.g. Casson, 1987; Flowers, 1976; Graham, 1978; Knickerbocker, 1973; Veugelers, 1995; Yu and Ito, 1988). But on the whole the literature has concentrated on explanations other than rivalry.

The intent of this chapter is to bring some concepts from the 'new industrial organization to bear upon the multinational enterprise. Much of the 'new' industrial organization is derived from modern game theory, and the aim in this chapter is to apply certain concepts from non-cooperative game theory to the understanding of MNE rivalry.

The chapter is divided into three sections. The first presents some basic concepts. Two firms, each a monopolist in a national market, are considering entering each other's home market. Given certain simplifying assumptions, under what circumstances will entry take place, and what then will be the reaction of the other firm? The second section extends this analysis to the case where one firm is subject to economies of learning and each firm possesses incomplete or imperfect information. The third section attempts to draw some conclusions relevant to the real world from the results of the first two.

Some basic considerations

In this section, rivalry between two multinational firms operating in two markets is examined. In order to keep the formal analysis tractable, a number of simplifying assumptions are made. These assumptions are relaxed in the following sections. where more realistic considerations are discussed.

Let us consider a world consisting of just two firms operating in two national markets. Each firm enjoys a monopoly in its home market. The firms are named A and B, with home markets market A and market B respectively. There are insurmountable barriers to trade between the two markets, and hence, if either firm wishes to participate in the market of the other, it must do so by means of investment. The firms produce a single undifferentiated good. Each firm knows both its own and the other firm's cost structure, and each firm can observe the other firm's past strategy. We will further assume that each firm's strategy is based on a Cournot conjecture, that is, each firm sets its quantity of output in the current period on the assumption that rival firms will not change their output. Thus, regarding the other firm's strategy, what is important is that each knows the quantity of output produced in any market period by the other. These assumptions can be summarized by saying that each firm works with complete and perfect information.

In order to prevent confusion, let us introduce the following conventions. Variables having a single subscript pertain to a market. For example, the variable P_A is the price of the good in market A. Variables with double subscript pertain to a firm in a market. The first subscript identifies the market, and the second the firm. For example, Q_{AB} indicates the quantity produced by firm B in market A.

Suppose that the total demand in market A (for the product produced by both firm A and firm B) is given by the following inverted demand function: $P_A = D_A - m_A Q_A$. (The underlying demand function $Q_A = 1/m_A (D_A - P_A)$ clearly can be inverted because it is continuous, strictly decreasing and everywhere differentiable.) Here m_A and D_A are constants and Q_A is the total amount of the product demanded. Likewise, suppose demand in market B can be written as $P_B = D_B - m_B Q_B$. Each firm will of course price monopolistically in its home market as long as the other firm remains outside that market, but if either market is entered by the outside firm, the two firms will initially compete with one another, following Cournot conjectures. so that the outcome will be a Cournot equilibrium. We further assume that the equilibrium is reached instantaneously after entry, and that there are no costs associated with entry. We first ask, given these assumptions, under what conditions will the lower-cost firm – we will arbitrarily designate it firm A – choose to enter market B? (For reasons that follow, the higher-cost firm B does not consider entry of market A unless its home market has already been entered by firm A.)

To keep things interesting but manageable, let us assume further that firm A produces at constant marginal cost C_A and that firm B produces at constant marginal cost C_B, where, as noted, $C_A \leq C_B$. If firm A stays at home, it will retain a monopoly there and can garner a monopoly profit per period π_A^m equal to $(D_A^2 - C_A^2)/4m_A$, assuming of course that the firm chooses to produce at all (which happens if $D_A > C_A$). One further assumption will be made in the name of tractability: neither firm discounts future profits. The profit earned by firm A in market B will then be:

$$\pi_{BA} = (D_B^2 - 4C_A D_B + 2C_B D_B + 4C_A^2 + C_B^2 - 4C_A C_B)/9m_B \qquad (1)$$

subject to the constraint that the quantity produced by firm A in market B is positive. This quantity is given by:

$$Q_{BA} = (D_B - 2C_A + C_B)/3m_B$$

It will be positive if firm B produces in market B prior to the entry of firm A, because for firm B to do so it is necessary that $C_B < D_B$, and by assumption $C_A < C_B$. The reader can easily verify if $C_A = C_B = C$ then the expression for π_{BA} reduces to the more familiar result for the Cournot duopoly equilibrium

$$\pi_{BA} = (D_B - C)^2/9m_B$$

The reader can also easily verify that π_{BA} is always positive if firm B produces in market B (again because $C_A < C_B$). Finally, the reader can verify that if C_B is sufficiently high and C_A sufficiently low, after the entry of firm A into market B, firm B would operate at a loss at the Cournot equilibrium and hence would choose to withdraw from the market. In what follows we shall assume that this lattermost does not in fact happen.

Even so, we would be near the end of our story if it were not for the reaction of firm B to firm A's entry into market B. If there were no counter-entry, then under our assumption that firm A's entry into market B is costless, firm A would surely enter in order to garner $\pi_{BA} > 0$. Obviously, if there were some cost of entry K_{BA}, then the entry would occur only if the expected present value of profits from the entry exceeded this cost. (Under our assumption of no discounting, this would always be met if $\pi_{BA} > 0$. But of course the story would be different if firm A discounted future profits.) The following proposition then is straightforward: firm B's best response to firm A's entry into market B is to enter market A if it can achieve positive profit from doing so.

We remind ourselves that a best response is a strategic move by a firm that maximizes its pay-off in the current period on the condition that its rival(s) continue to play the same strategic move in the current period as they played in the period immediately preceding. Because the Cournot duopoly equilibrium is a Nash equilibrium in market B, firm B maximizes its profits in that market by continuing to hold to this equilibrium in market B (on the assumption, of course, that firm A will continue to hold to the same strategy). But if firm B can achieve positive profits by entering market A, it will increase its total profits by doing so. By assumption, the outcome there will also be a Cournot duopoly equilibrium, and by the Nash property no strategy of firm A can reduce firm B's profits in market A. Hence if $\pi_{AB} > 0$, entry of firm B into market A is a best response to the entry of firm A into market B.

Again, this proposition depends upon the assumption that there is no entry cost to firm B in entering market A. If there were to be such a cost, entry would be a best response only if the expected present value of the entry exceeded that cost. These considerations again figure, of course, only if firm B discounts future profits, which by assumption it does not.

Firm B will not necessarily be able to garner a profit by entering market A. The profit to firm B from doing so is equal to:

$$\pi_{AB} = (D_A^2 - 4C_B D_A + 2C_A D_A + 4C_B^2 + C_A^2 - 4C_A C_B)/9m_A$$

subject to the constraint that Q_{AB} is positive. There is a C_B sufficiently high and a C_A sufficiently low that firm B would operate at a loss were it to enter market A at any (positive) level of output by firm A there.

But if this does not happen, then, by entering market B, firm A faces the loss of profit in its home market as a result of the subsequent entry of firm B. Continuing with the assumption that firm A does not discount its future profits, and firm B does respond by entering market A when firm A enters market B, firm A's criterion for entry of market B is thus that:

$$\pi_{BA} + \pi_{AA} > \pi_A^m \tag{2}$$

where π_{BA} and π_{AA} are respectively the Cournot duopoly profits to firm A in markets B and A respectively and π_A^m is the monopoly profit to firm A in market A.

Under what conditions will this last inequality hold? If one writes out the inequality in its entirety, the only thing that is immediately clear is that the expressions are not easy to evaluate. Let us assume for the moment that the slopes of the demand curves in the two markets are equal. Then the following can be said, defining $\pi_A^C = \pi_{BA} + \pi_{AA}$:

$$\frac{\partial \pi_A^C}{\partial C_A} > 0 \tag{3a}$$

In other words, the lower C_A relative to C_B the more likely firm A will choose to enter market B. It should be noted that this result is completely consistent with the early theory of the MNE, dating to Hymer (1960), wherein it has been held that a firm must hold a cost advantage relative to its overseas rivals before it makes sense for that firm to extend its operations multinationally.

Let us now drop the assumption that $C_A < C_B$. We then find that:

$$\frac{\partial \pi_A^C}{\partial D_B} > 0 \tag{3b}$$

In other words, the larger market B is relative to market A, the more likely it is that firm A will enter market B, irrespective of the relative costs of firms A and B. Indeed, for any D_A, C_A and C_B there is a D_B sufficiently large that $\pi_A^C > \pi_A^m$, so that it would pay firm A to enter market B.

This result is consistent with the observation that multinational firms from smaller countries do exist. However, it is fair to note that these firms are typically very efficient producers (i.e. something like our assumption $C_A \leq C_B$ also holds true).

It intuitively makes sense that if

$$\frac{1}{D_B} \frac{dD_B}{dt} > \frac{1}{D_A} \frac{dD_A}{dt}$$

(that is, if market B were growing faster than market A), *ceteris paribus*, this would lead to a higher likelihood that firm A would enter market B than if

$$\frac{1}{D_B} \frac{dD_B}{dt} \leq \frac{1}{D_A} \frac{dD_A}{dt}$$

This is consistent with inequality 3b above.

Following entry of each firm into the other's home market, there are circumstances under which it would pay for both firms to collude in both markets to appropriate and share full monopoly rent (e.g. this would be the case if $C_A = C_B$ and the sharing rule were to be that each firm received half the rent in each market). Under these circumstances the Friedman version of the 'folk theorem' for infinitely repeated non-cooperative games holds: the strategy of appropriation and splitting of monopoly rents, under the assumptions that both firms intend to participate in the markets in perpetuity and that the rate at which the firms discount future profits is below sonic threshold level, is a sub-game perfect Nash equilibrium. This 'repeated game' Nash equilibrium will Pareto-dominate the Cournot equilibrium, and hence the new equilibrium will be preferred by both firms to the Cournot equilibrium. (See Friedman, 1971; Graham, 1990.)

It should be noted, however, that this holds only so long as the underlying circumstances continue to hold. If the costs of the two firms are too disparate, no repeated game Nash equilibrium will exist. Thus, if collusion is initiated at a time when $C_A = C_B$ and the sharing rule is that rents in both markets are divided equally, but in some subsequent time interval one firm succeeds in lowering its costs faster than the other, it is possible that the lower-cost firm could eventually prefer to revert to the Cournot duopoly equilibrium in the two markets rather than continue to appropriate and split monopoly rents equally. This possibility could give both firms an incentive to continue to reduce costs even while they were colluding to appropriate monopoly rents.

Even so, if one firm did succeed in reducing its costs relative to the other, both firms would always prefer to collude to maximize total rents under some unequal sharing rule (for example, a rule to split profits according to market share under the Cournot equilibrium) than to revert to the Cournot equilibrium.

A variant on this theme can come about if we drop our initial assumption that upon the entry of one firm into the other's home market, the outcome (without collusion) is an immediate Cournot equilibrium. Suppose instead that for some reason (customer loyalty?) it takes time for the new entrant to build market share. Suppose further that $C_A = C_B - C$. Then there is a share of market below which the new entrant (again, assume it is firm A in market B) would prefer the Cournot equilibrium to collusion to maximize total profits and to split them on the basis of market share. The condition is that:

$$[(S_{BA}/4)\,(D_B^2 - C^2 < (D_B - C)^2/9]$$

where S_{BA} is the share of firm A in market B, $0 < S_{BA} < 1$. Thus it is possible that a new entrant into the market will choose to compete rather than collude until it achieves a certain threshold share of the market, whereupon it will be willing to consider a more co-operative approach to things than it had previously been willing to.

Before closing this section, one should note that significant policy and welfare implications follow from the preceding discussion. Many are self-evident. But to give a synopsis none the less, let us begin by summarizing our main result: (1) under reasonable assumptions, entry by a firm from one country into the market of another country already served by a local firm can, under plausible circumstances, trigger entry of the second firm into the home market of the first but (2) the cross-entry will not necessarily lead to price competition by the two firms in the two markets. The dynamics of the entry and cross-entry as described (in the admittedly very simplified and stylized analysis of this section) might help explain such phenomena as the increasing propensity of major industrial countries to be both home and host to foreign direct investment to and from other such countries (see, for example, Graham and Krugman, 1995). Even though cross-entry could result in collusion of the cross-entrants to appropriate jointly monopoly rents, other forms of rivalry could prevail; we have discussed the possibility of continuing cost-reducing efforts. Were the discussion to be extended to allow for product differentiation, the rivalry could be manifested in product improvement and new product innovation.

Does this help us to explain firm behaviour in the real world? This issue is taken up in the third section of this chapter, but here let us rule simply that price collusion among oligopolists combined with rivalry with respect to cost reduction and new product development can be demonstrated in fact to occur in real life. The best example with which the author is familiar is that of the semiconductor producers in Japan, who, according to many accounts, enjoyed a closed home market for their products during the 1980s.

These producers seemed to collude to hold domestic prices high, but to price competitively in external markets. Also, they competed vigorously in both the development of new products and the reduction of cost of existing products. The latter behaviour was possibly motivated by competition from strong non-Japanese rivals in markets external to Japan. Thus it can be claimed that these producers acted jointly as a monopoly at home but as oligopolists in external markets, along the lines postulated by our model. But a fuller accounting of the behaviour of these firms must also take into account economies of learning, introduced in the next section.

Two-market duopoly where firms are subject to learning and where information may be incomplete or imperfect

Two restrictive and unrealistic assumptions in the previous section's analysis were that firms operated with constant marginal costs and complete and perfect information. In this section we attempt to extend the analysis by relaxing these assumptions (but retaining the equally unrealistic and restrictive assumptions of a two-firm, two-market world, a completely homogeneous product and costless entry which leads immediately to a new equilibrium). Even so, a full analysis of the two-market. two-firm situation where returns to scale are not constant and information is incomplete and imperfect would be a considerable task, beyond the scope of this section. Here the analysis is limited to a first pass.

To begin, let us consider the case where firms, rather than having constant marginal costs, instead are subject to economies of learning (dynamic scale economies). That is, the marginal cost is a declining function of the total accumulated production volume of the firm. A special case of economy of learning has been extensively analysed by Spence (1981). The marginal cost at time t of a firm (call it $C(t)$) decomposes into a constant M and a component which declines exponentially with respect to total accumulated production $Q(t)$:

$$C(t) = M + A_0 \exp(-bQ(t))$$

$$Q(t) = \int_0^t q(r) dr$$

and $q(r)$ is the instantaneous rate of production of the product.

Spence uses the calculus of variations to show that the firm will maximize profits (under an assumption of no discounting of future profits) not by setting current marginal revenue equal to current marginal costs but by setting current marginal revenue equal to marginal costs as they will be at the end of the life-cycle of the product. This result is difficult to operationalize, because, in general, firms do not know what their marginal costs will be at the end of the life-cycle of the product. (Spence gets around this by assuming that the firm faces a known stationary demand curve and a tractable exponential learning curve given by the equations above, and knows exactly the life span of the product; but the first and the last of these assumptions are clearly unrealistic.) The practical result of the Spence analysis is that a firm subject to economies of learning will set prices lower than will a monopolist or a colluding oligopolist in order to maximize profits by 'sliding down' the learning curve faster than would be possible at a higher price and lower per period volume of output.

What effects will this have on the decision of firm A with respect to entry to market B? If firm A recognizes that it is subject to economies of learning, so that its marginal costs at future time t will behave according to some relation of the form $C(t) = C(0)\exp - rQ(t)$, it will want to increase its total per period volume of output over the optimal volume, given constant marginal costs $C(0)$. This will imply that it will price in its home market at a level below the static monopoly price, offering a higher volume of output to the market.

This will lead to a different situation from that considered in the previous section, but the mechanics of the analysis will none the less remain largely the same. What changes is the algorithm by which the firm maximizes its profits.

A full-blown analysis of the dynamics of duopoly with complete and perfect information where each firm is subject to economies of learning is beyond the scope of this chapter and is not attempted here. We focus instead on the situation where information is incomplete and imperfect. Imperfect information implies that each firm is missing information with respect to exactly what are some of the fundamental characteristics of its competitor (e.g. is it subject to economies of learning?). Incomplete information means that some aspect of the information needed by a firm to determine an optimal strategy is missing and that the firm knows that the information is not available (e.g. what is the value of the parameter m_A or m_B?). We content ourselves here with some relatively qualitative observations pertaining to this situation.

We noted in the previous section that the propensity of firm A to enter market B depends in part upon the relative costs of firms A and B. But suppose that firm A does not really know for sure the costs of firm B, but can observe that market A is growing faster than market B and hence believes that it is moving down a learning curve faster than firm B. The decision of firm A to enter market B would clearly be influenced by whether or not the learning garnered in market A was transferable by firm A to market B, and vice versa. If the learning were to be transferable, firm A might bet that it would eventually produce in both markets at lower cost than firm B. And if participation in market B enabled firm A to accelerate its own learning, it would then reduce the (profit-maximizing) price it charged in its home market. This reduction in price would serve to deter the counter-entry of firm B into market A.

So would firm A enter market B? The answer also depends in part upon firm A's estimates of the cost structure of firm B. Again, this information is imperfect and incomplete. Information that firm A does have is the price being charged and the level and rate of growth of equilibrium demand in market B. Firm A must infer the costs of firm B from these price and quantity data. Entry will occur only if firm A calculates that at the post-entry equilibrium it will achieve marginal revenue equal to or greater than marginal cost. But marginal cost here is long-run marginal cost after all learning has taken place. If this cost is low relative to current marginal cost, it is possible that firm A would enter even if it were to incur a current operating loss.

It is worth asking, under circumstances as above but where firm A has not entered market B, would firm B be likely to enter market A? Market B, we recall, is the relatively slow-growth economy. It is thus likely that firm B is moving much more slowly down a learning curve than is firm A. Firm B can also observe the rate of growth of realized demand in market A and from it infer that firm A is likely on a faster learning curve. But failure of firm A to enter market B might be taken by firm B as an indication that firm A was currently a high-cost producer; further information would be given by the current price in market A. Also, firm B must consider whether it could accelerate its own learning by entering market A. Obviously, if it believed that it could, it would be more likely to enter than if it felt otherwise.

Of course, each firm is uncertain with respect to how much information is in the hands of the other. Hence, from the perspective of either firm, failure of the other to enter could simply be the product of uncertainty.

So exactly what can be said about entry and counter-entry under these circumstances? The following proposition seems safe enough. If the first firm to enter the other's market has as its home the faster growing market, so that the entering firm is on a faster learning curve in its new market than is the firm already established there, it is less likely that the established firm will counter the move by entry into the first firm's home market than if both firms were to have constant marginal cost. It is tempting to say also that the faster learning firm will be more likely to enter in the first place. But, absent further information, it is truly difficult to say under what circumstances an initial entry would take place and by whom.

It is quite clear that there is considerable room for more research into the dynamics of firm rivalry when firms are subject to economies of learning and when information is incomplete or imperfect. Indeed, little research has been attempted in this area. Thus this section does little more than raise some issues without really resolving them.

Can any of this be applied to the real world?

The real world, of course, consists of more than two countries, and in each country there are typically to be found more than one industry and more than one firm in each industry. Do any of the observations offered in this chapter, other than ones of the order of 'the world is complex and it is hard to know', have any bearing upon actual corporate strategy?

The main theme of this chapter is, of course, that the conduct of multinational firms depends in part upon inter-firm rivalry, and that such rivalry has been largely ignored in the literature on these firms. One point worth making is that just as two firms operating in a rarified two-market duopoly, as posited in the first two sections of this chapter, must take into account the likely reactions of the other in making strategic moves, so must firms operating in multiple markets with multiple rivals be conscious of the consequences of their strategic moves upon rivals' behaviour. In the real world, multinational firms do indeed tend to watch their rivals' moves closely and to react to them.

This truism aside, there are points from the earlier sections of this chapter that do generalize to multinational corporate strategy in the world as we know it. A best response to the new entry into a national market by a firm already established in some other market can indeed be counter-entry into that firm's established market by its rival. It has already been suggested that this counter-action may account for the very marked propensity for large firms from most of the industrialized countries to cross-penetrate each other's home markets. (See, for example, Graham, 1978; Yu and Ito, 1988.)

Such cross-entry is indeed observable, with one notable exception: Japan. Although this might be changing, Japan has been an outlier with respect to the proportion of its economic output that is accounted for by local subsidiaries of foreign-controlled firms (see Graham and Krugman, 1996; Julius and Thomsen, 1988). For many reasons, Japan has been a mystery in this regard. During the 1980s and early 1990s, Japanese multinationals were particularly aggressive with respect to entry to other industrial countries' markets. In particular, both the EC countries and the United States witnessed massive rates of new entry by Japanese-based firms.

Japan's outlier status may be accounted for by reasons hinted at in the previous section: Japan's firms, during the 1980s, tended to be subject to rapid economies of learning, and their resulting cost advantages presumably both were transferable to other economies and served as entry barriers to Japan itself. But other factors doubtless contributed to Japan's outlier status. These would almost surely include the virtual prohibition of foreign direct investment in Japan that was in effect from the end of the Allied occupation in the early 1950s until the late 1970s (but why has there been so little entry by multinationals into Japan following termination of official barriers to entry?). Cultural factors, including the noted propensity of Japanese firms within Keiretsu groups to buy only from other Keiretsu members, doubtless also have played a role.

Certain other aspects of the conduct of new Japanese entrants, if the accounts of this conduct that have appeared in the business press are accurate, may be explainable via arguments put forward in the previous sections of this chapter. The business press has noted that Japanese new entrants into non-Japanese markets often underpriced the established firms in order to build market share. It was claimed that the underpricing is often such that the Japanese firms sustain current operating losses. A possible explanation centres on the argument in the first section of this chapter that a firm which is a new entrant to a market is likely to behave rivalistically as long as its market share is low; it will prefer a Cournot equilibrium to joint appropriation of monopoly rent and sharing of that rent according to market share. But at some threshold level of market share its preferences will change. The joint appropriation and sharing will at this threshold be preferred to the Cournot equilibrium, and the firm will then be willing to enter into co-operative strategies with rival firms. According to this argument, Japanese firms would then cease underpricing once a threshold market share had been attained. In some industries this seems in fact to have happened e.g. in the US automobile industry, once the firms became firmly established.

It may be noted (and the reader can easily verify) that under the assumptions of the first section above a firm will prefer a co-operative strategy at a much lower threshold market share in a new market if its home market is counter-entered than if it is not. (That is, if the rival firms enter the home market of the new entrant, and then offer to co-operate there in exchange for the new entrant's entering into a co-operative arrangement in their home markets, the new entrant is more likely to do so at a low market share than if no counter-entry takes place.) Thus one reason for the reported continued aggressive pricing of Japanese firms in markets outside Japan even after substantial market share has been gained could very well be the failure of non-Japanese firms to penetrate the Japanese home market.

An alternative explanation of the same phenomenon (aggressive price competition by Japanese firms that are new entrants into a market outside Japan) rests on arguments offered in the second section, notably that a firm subject to economies of learning may sustain current operating losses upon entry into a new market if the additional volume of output attained in that market enables the firm to accelerate its overall rate of learning. And, as noted previously, this acceleration of learning will in fact serve as a barrier to entry to the Japanese market itself.

The issue of Japan as an outlier aside, arguments presented in previous sections suggest that multinational firms that have cross-penetrated each other's home markets may collude to hold prices high (i.e. at monopoly levels) but may none the less engage in rivalistic behaviour along other dimensions (e.g. cost reduction, product improvement, new product innovation, marketing, etc.). The major reason for this behaviour is actually defensive, e.g. if one firm were to lower its costs relative to all others, it might pay that firm to initiate price competition, whereas if all firms were to lower their costs in tandem the conditions for a repeated game, sub-game perfect Nash equilibrium (which Pareto-dominates a one-period Nash equilibrium) would be maintained. Thus the dynamics of rivalry can help to explain why multinational firms often seem to compete more on a nonprice than on a price basis.

The author hopes that the main point of this chapter, that inter-firm rivalry must be part of any explanation of multinational firm behaviour, is adequately demonstrated, even if some of the details are missing. Indeed, the missing details suggest that there is much work yet to be done on the dynamics of rivalry of these large firms. Until this work is carried further it must be said that the theory of the strategic behaviour of the multinational firm is incomplete.

References

Buckley, P.J. and M.C. Casson (1976) *The Future of the Multinational Enterprise*, London: Macmillan.

Casson, M.C. (1987) *The Firm and the Market*, Cambridge, Mass.: MIT Press.

Caves, R.E. (1982) *Multinational Enterprise and Economic Analysis*, Cambridge: Cambridge University Press.

Dunning, J.H. (1988) 'The eclectic paradigm of international production: a restatement and some possible extensions', *Journal of International Business Studies* 9, 1: 1–31.

Flowers, E.B. (1976) 'Oligopolistic reactions in European and Canadian direct investment in the United States', *Journal of International Business Studies* 7, 3: 43–55.

Friedman, J.W. (1971) 'A noncooperative equilibrium for supergames', *Review of Economic Studies* 38, 1: 1–12.

Graham, E.M. (1978) 'Transatlantic investment by multinational firms: a rivalistic phenomenon?', *Journal of Post-Keynesian Economics* 1, 1: 82–99.

—— (1990) ' "Exchange of threat" between multinational firms as an infinitely repeated noncooperative game', *International Trade Journal* 4, 3: 259–77.

Graham, E.M., and P.R. Krugman (1995) *Foreign Direct Investment in the United States*, 3rd edn, Washington, DC: Institute for International Economics.

Hymer, S.H. (1960) 'The international operations of national firms', Ph.D. dissertation, Massachusetts Institute of Technology, published by MIT Press in 1976.

Julius, D. and Thomsen, S. (1988) *Foreign-owned Firms, Trade, and Economic Integration*, Tokyo Club Papers, No. 2, London: Royal Institute of International Affairs.

Knickerbocker, F.T. (1973) *Oligopolistic Reaction and the Multinational Enterprise*, Cambridge, Mass.: Harvard University Press.

Rugman, A.M. (1986) 'New theories of multinational enterprise: an assessment of internalisation theory', *Bulletin of Economic Research* 38, 2: 101–18.

Spence, A.M. (1981) 'The learning curve and competition', *Bell Journal of Economics* 12, 1: 49–70.

Tirole, J. (1988) *The Theory of Industrial Organization*, Cambridge, Mass: MIT Press.

Veugelers, R. (1995) 'Strategic incentives for multinational operations', *Managerial and Decision Economics* 16, 1 (Jan./Feb.): 47–57.

Yu, C.J. and K. Ito (1988) 'Oligopolistic reaction and foreign direct investment: the case of the US tire and textile industries, *Journal of International Business Studies* 19. 3: 449–60.

8 Divide and rule by transnational corporations

James Peoples and Roger Sugden

Why are there transnational corporations? For example, supposing firm A initially produces in country X, why should it acquire production facilities in country Y? Similarly, if it initially produces in X and Y, why should it acquire further facilities in Y? In answering this question, analysis has traditionally followed the general rule of economics, to be obsessed with (Pareto) efficient outcomes. However, this chapter is more unusual: it pursues an analysis emphasizing distribution.

More specifically, our concern is transnationals' use of divide and rule strategies towards labour.[1] We argue that there is an asymmetry of power between labour and the transnational corporation. This asymmetry derives from the corporation's transnationality, which may be exploited by playing on the locational rigidity of labour. We suggest that by producing in various countries firms may divide their workforce, thereby reducing labour's bargaining power and consequently obtaining lower labour costs.

Our discussion considers theoretical analysis and empirical evidence. It follows a line of literature that views firms' costs as dependent upon the bargaining power of labour and its employers where this power is endogenous to firms' decisions (see, for example, Marglin (1974) on the introduction of factories, Edwards (1979) on hierarchy in the workplace and the review by McPherson (1983)). Our theoretical analysis is implicit in such earlier works as Fröbel *et al.* (1980) but we at least add more detail. As for the empirics, we focus on divide and rule as a contributory reason for production in various countries. This is limited in so far as it does not attempt to establish the exact influence of divide and rule. Yet it is a valid and useful beginning because many have been very quick to dismiss the explanation on the basis of allegedly widespread evidence that transnationals pay wages at least as high as their rivals.

Theoretical analysis

A firm's labour costs depend upon such factors as wage rates, the effort labour puts into its assigned tasks, the time allowed for tea breaks, and so on. There is a conflict over these costs in that employers and labour have different optima. This can be seen very clearly in the case of wage rates: for example, with all else being the same – and this includes having a job! – a worker will prefer higher wages than his or her employer is willing to pay. In a perfect labour market this conflict is resolved by competition. For instance, any attempt by a firm to depress wage rates and thereby increase profits would be met by other firms entering the market, paying higher wages and obtaining normal profits. However this is an unrealistic scenario. Industry entry barriers limit the set of potential employers, who can also be expected to avoid competition for labour that pushes wages to the point where only normal profits are obtained. That is, employers can be expected to collude over wages.[2] Furthermore, if there is an excess supply of labour, collusion is unnecessary because there will be enough labour for all firms. Thus, in reality the concept of a perfect labour market is a red herring. What happens is that the outcome of their conflict is determined by the bargaining power of labour and employers.

In its turn bargaining power depends very much on the ability of labour to act collectively (see Burkitt and Bowers, 1979, for instance).[3] If there is no collective action, labour tends to have a weaker bargaining position. This results from various factors, such as:

- employers being allowed to replace specific workers by rearranging the activities of others, thereby offsetting any loss of profit resulting from failure to settle the conflict;
- increased competition for jobs, greater competition implying a weaker bargaining position;
- labour having reduced information on its value to particular employers.

Against this background of labour/employer conflict, what is the importance of transnationals? Suppose individual I is a typical worker in country X, employed by firm A. Consider the case where A can choose between two methods of production: it can either produce only in country X or it can produce in countries X and Y. Define the labour costs associated with I in these two situations as w^n and w^t, respectively. Because the choice affects the ability of labour to act collectively, in general there is a tendency towards $w^t < w^n$. That is, by choosing to be a transnational corporation, firm A may *increase its profits* by decreasing the labour costs associated with I, hence *decreasing I's utility*.

The reasons for collective action being at best very difficult and at worst impossible when people work in different countries are manifest and well documented (see, for example, ILO, 1976 and Helfgott, 1983). They include such organizational problems as devising institutional arrangements for international trade unions and also more deep-rooted cultural factors such as different languages, xenophobia, and different religions. For instance, CIS (1978) refers to the problems faced by Ford workers in Europe, let alone the world:

> It's difficult enough for Ford workers in one country, sharing a common language and separated by comparatively small distances, to organize effectively against the company on anything more than a local plant or shop level. Even here, major problems of communication, sectionalism, and

cumbersome national union machinery arise. On a European scale the problems are multiplied many times. Workers in France, Germany, Belgium, Spain and the UK use six different languages plus those of the immigrants. It means much greater distances – over a thousand miles from Halewood to Valencia, with disproportionately large travel and telephone costs as a result. There are that many more unions – and another layer, the international union organisation on top.

In principle it should be possible to overcome the purely organizational problems without too much difficulty. After all, transnational corporations provide an indication of how activities can be organized where large distances are involved. But cultural factors pose fundamental problems for which there is no easy solution. Indeed, they reveal a basic asymmetry between labour and its employers at the international level. Labour tends to be locationally rigid, often having close human and physical ties to a particular region's history and culture. This can raise major barriers to collective action, because such action requires a considerable amount of cooperation. In contrast, employers have by no means as many problems in operating successfully across national borders. First, wherever a firm operates, employers talk a common language and have a common religion: profit. Second, simply pursuing profits across the world does not require the same level of cooperation by people from different countries that would be demanded of labour for it to act collectively. Rather, pursuing profits essentially requires an appropriate hierarchical organization into which people can be slotted. This is more a problem of coordination than of cooperation.

All of this clearly suggests that a firm may produce in various countries so that it can face a more fragmented workforce, with the consequent advantages of reducing labour's bargaining power and labour costs.

To illustrate, suppose a firm manufactures shirts in two stages: cutting and then the sewing of cloth. Assume that initially all of its manufacturing facilities are in Britain and that its workforce is united, quick to seize the opportunity to act collectively to maintain working conditions. For example, if the firm tries to reduce the quality of working life for the cutters, the entire workforce is prepared to strike, completely halting production. The firm can respond to this in various ways. One possibility is to transfer part of both its cutting and sewing operations to, say, the Philippines. Then, even if its workforce in Britain has a grievance which leads it to strike, while work continues in the Philippines the firm can indefinitely maintain at least partial supply to its customers.[4] A second option is to divide its workforce by transferring the sewing operations to the Philippines. A case when this might be preferable is if the firm doubts the skill of the Filipino workers to do the cutting. The transfer will still reduce labour's bargaining power in certain circumstances. For instance, if the firm now tries to reduce the quality of working life for cutters, production will not stop as long as there are stocks of cut cloth to supply sewers in the Philippines and those sewers are willing to work.[5]

This is not to deny that even without transferring any production outside Britain the firm could undermine strikes. For example, it could build up stocks of finished goods to enable supplies to customers to continue at least for a while. But the critical point is that the possibilities for reducing labour's bargaining power by producing in various countries give added degrees of freedom – more room to manœuvre. Nor are the possibilities of transferring operations to the Philippines the firm's only options; it has many others. It could transfer activity to somewhere other than the Philippines, or divide its work-force amongst three, four, five, or even more countries.

The choice it makes will depend upon many factors, such as the skill of workers in one part of the world versus those elsewhere, and its expectations of labour 'militancy' in Europe as compared to Asia. Also important will be the attitudes of governments in different locations and the extent to which these can be influenced by the firm. Governments can directly influence labour costs – by such obvious means as legislation affecting working hours or the right to strike, but also by more subtle ways such as encouraging greater effort from labour. Moreover, the attitudes of governments are not independent of firms' wishes, rather they are endogenous to firms' activities.

Another important factor will be the types of organizational form at the firm's disposal. The significance of organizational form to firms producing in more than one country was recognized in general by Hymer (1972). Using the United States as an illustration, he noted the growth of Marshallian firms into large corporations requiring completely different forms of organization, especially the so-called multi-divisional form. He argued that this helped to provide the 'power to go abroad' because it gave firms an appropriate administrative structure. However, with the more specific issue of divide and rule leading to production in various countries, we suggest that the choice between market and non-market activity is especially interesting.

Following Cowling and Sugden's (1998) view that a firm is the means of coordinating production from one centre of strategic decision-making and that this coordination can include both market and non-market activity, suppose the shirt manufacturer in our example decides to respond to a militant work-force by dividing its sewing operations between the Philippines and Britain. One possibility is to set up factories in both countries and have relatively little to do with the market until the final goods are sold to the consumers. Another may be to subcontract the sewing to small workshops dotted throughout Britain and the Philippines. This would involve market exchanges because the workshops would be contracted to do sewing in consideration for a specified sum of money. But provided production was being coordinated from one centre of strategic decision-making, there would still be only one firm. Moreover the subcontracting option may be particularly appealing to a firm because it can provide an extreme division of a militant work-force. For instance, whilst those Ford workers employed in huge plants clearly identified with the Ford Motor Company find organizing collective action very difficult, imagine the problems of workers dotted across the world in small work-shops operating under completely different names. How many would even begin to recognize that they work for the same firm? Simply attempting to organize collective action would be a nightmare. Actually doing so might be impossible.

Having said this, a firm will not necessarily use the subcontracting option. It may be impossible because of limitations in available technology; some production activity cannot be carried out in small workshops. Perhaps there is neither a system of small workshops readily available nor the possibility of establishing such a system in an appropriate time period. Furthermore it may be simply unnecessary, for example because a workforce can be broken into a very weak body with no real bargaining power without resort to such extreme division. It may be sufficient to locate one plant in the Philippines, another in Britain and rely on (or perhaps promote) racial tension to keep labour in the two completely alienated.

Our analysis thus far also points to a second, closely related explanation for the existence of transnationals. Suppose, for instance, firm A decides to establish production facilities to manufacture a particular good. *Ceteris paribus*, it will employ the labour that accepts the lowest wages. This is again determined by bargaining. If all potential employees act collectively, employers will have to settle for the best they can negotiate with, for example, the trade union. However, if workers do not act collectively, employers can play off one group against another – bearing in mind the factors weakening the workers' position when they are divided – and thereby secure lower wages. For instance, having asked workers in country X their price, firm A can tell workers in Y that if they accept lower wages, they get the jobs. When workers in Y are about to concede, firm A can return to workers in X and seek still more gains. On some occasions A will produce in just one country because workers in that country always accept the lowest wages. But this will not always be so, in which case transnationals arise.

Thus we have two specific reasons for the existence of transnationals. An appropriate description covering either of these bargaining situations is 'divide and rule' (see Marglin, 1974): by dividing labour into country-specific groups, employers improve their bargaining position, thereby gaining *at the expense* of labour. A possible criticism of this is as follows: 'If workers are better off when a firm produces in one country, why do they not offer their services more cheaply to the firm if it continues to produce solely in one country and thereby avoid its acquiring production facilities elsewhere?'[6] This criticism can be countered.

Consider first the case of bargaining when a firm establishes new production facilities. The argument here recognized that a firm may in fact locate in one country. But with a workforce divided into groups that can be played off against each other, a game involving bluff and counter-bluff, threat and counter-threat is played; perhaps, for example, labour in country X simply does not believe that its failure to accept lower wages will lead to a firm producing elsewhere. As a result, transnationals may arise. The criticism is therefore not valid.

Whereas this aspect of divide and rule concerns bargaining over new investments in, say, period t, the first case outlined earlier examines the wage conflict in periods $t + 1$, $t + 2$ and so on, albeit still referring to a decision to become a transnational in period t. Compare now two situations. In the first, firm A produces solely in country X, where it faces workers acting collectively. In the second, A is a transnational producing in X and Y, and facing two groups of workers. Consider again the three aforementioned factors illustrating the importance of collective action. If A chooses the first situation rather than the second it might face a workforce that could in fact: (1) inflict greater loss of profits on the firm if the wage conflict is not settled; (2) compete less – indeed, not at all – within itself for jobs; (3) obtain greater information on the value of particular workers to A. So will A choose to produce in one country because the workforce will restrain itself by not attempting to use factors like these? Yes, if workers: (a) can accurately assess employers' beliefs regarding workers' increased bargaining power when production is in just one country; (b) choose not to use that power; and (c) convince employers that this is the case. But (a) and (c) again involve a game of bluff, and accordingly transnationals will sometimes arise. The criticism is not valid.

Even more to the point, why should workers choose to restrain themselves in periods $t + 1$, $t + 2$, ... simply because the firm could have chosen to produce elsewhere in period t? If workers ignore future investments, they will make full use of factors like (1)–(3), simply because what happened in the past is in the past. If they do not ignore future investments, fear that the firm will subsequently become a transnational may temper their behaviour. But as this is again a game of bluff, there will be times when employers believe that if they do not produce in various countries, workers may use their full collective strength, at least on some occasions. For example, workers may seek as much as possible immediately because they are unsure whether A will make more new investments. Thus, whether or not workers ignore future investments, transnationals arise. The crucial point is that any improvements in a firm's bargaining power as a result of its ability to become a transnational are *guaranteed* only by its actually being a transnational. Again, the criticism is not valid.

This can be simply illustrated. Define π_a^T as firm A's profits if it produces in countries X and Y; π_a^{N1} as A's profits if it produces only in X, and workers use their full collective strength; π_a^{N2} as A's profits if it produces only in X and workers do not use their full collective strength; p as the probability employers attach to workers using their full collective strength when A produces only in X. (If workers ignore future investments, $p = 1$; if they may use their full collective strength, $0 < p < 1$.) Then, if A is a risk-neutral profit maximizer, it will become a transnational if: $\pi_a^T > p\, \pi_a^{N1} + (1 - p)\, \pi_a^{N2}$. If the only effect on A's profits from becoming a transnational is this wage effect, $\pi_a^T = \pi_a^{N2} > \pi_a^{N1}$ and $p > 0$ means A will become a transnational.[7]

Accordingly, we have presented a theoretical analysis showing that firms' attempts to dominate labour markets may lead to production in various countries.[8] In a moment we will consider empirical evidence concerning the divide and rule hypothesis but, before turning to this, it is worth emphasizing two points about our theoretical argument. First, as an explanation for why firms produce in various countries its focus is distribution and not Pareto efficiency; distribution is the very essence of the bargaining analysis. This compares starkly with mainstream economic approaches to why firms produce in various countries. The thrust of our argument is that a firm may produce in different countries to weaken the bargaining power of its work-force and thereby to *increase profits at the expense of that work-force*. A second point worth emphasizing concerns the international division of labour. The divide and rule analysis implies the spreading of production activity throughout the world. The exact locations firms use will depend upon the sorts of factors we have mentioned, but firms will establish production sites in many places. For example, unskilled activity knows few geographical bounds. Moreover production technology is endogenous to the wishes of firms, which therefore seek the technology they find most desirable (see Marglin, 1974). Over time, for example, firms will develop technology which deskills more and more activity, thereby opening more and more of the world to their production activity. We suggest that the benefits to firms of dividing and ruling labour are an incentive for such changes. The implication is that the desire to divide and rule undermines the 'old' international division of labour. The old division saw the countries of the world split into industrial and primary producers, international trade being carried out between the two. The industrial countries bought raw materials and agricultural products from the primary producers, who in return imported manufactured goods. However, the 'new' division cuts through this simple dichotomy (see the evidence and discussion in Adam 1975; Cowling 1986; Fröbel *et al.* 1980; Hymer 1972).

These are significant implications. However, and *not* to undermine the theoretical analysis developed in this chapter, the value of further theoretical discussion is limited; no matter how detailed theoretical arguments become, without supporting empirical evidence they tend to be accepted at best with scepticism. The concern of the remainder of this chapter is therefore to examine empirical evidence related to the divide and rule concept.

Some empirical evidence

In any particular case there are likely to be a number of reasons contributing to a firm's decision to produce in more than one country. It is with this in mind that we shall focus on the following hypothesis: an at least contributory reason for the existence of some transnationals is the division of workers into country-specific groups, enabling a firm to lower its labour costs when it is a transnational compared to when it produces in just one country. To explore this hypothesis we shall discuss some of the empirical evidence in the existing literature, looking in turn at results for Britain, the US, and Canada.

British experience

A usual reaction to the divide and rule hypothesis is to reject it on the basis of evidence on wage levels in different types of firm. The argument is that transnationals appear to pay wages at least as high as their rivals and that therefore production in various countries cannot be founded on a division of the work-force to lower labour costs. The apparent evidence for this comes from many studies covering many countries (see, for example, the survey in Dunning, 1993). Typical is the analysis in Buckley and Enderwick (1983) and Blanchflower (1984). This examines senior management's estimates of employees' average weekly gross pay in British manufacturing plants using data from the 1980 *Workplace Industrial Relations Survey*. The conclusion is that, in general, non-UK-owned plants offer comparable or higher wages than UK-owned plants. However, we suggest that in fact this is consistent with divide and rule.[9]

First, no distinction is drawn between transnationals and their rivals. Correspondingly there is no relevant evidence of relative wages. The difficulty here is in part one of definition; reference to plant ownership does not and cannot capture the full extent of a transnational's activities. What is likely to be especially important is that the data ignore subcontracting arrangements. Moreover the difficulty is also because a UK-owned plant could be as much a part of a transnational as a non-UK-owned plant; the distinction therefore fails to pick out transnationals. Thus if UK-owned transnationals are particularly successful at dividing their work-force across the world, they can pay sufficiently low wages to allow non-UK-owned plants to pay more than UK-owned plants, whilst transnationals pay less than their rivals.

Second, the data ignore such factors as effort. This is a crucial omission. The hypothesis centres on labour costs. Ignore for the moment the wages that transnationals pay. What about the effort put into jobs, the time allowed for lunches, and the conditions in which work is carried out? Even if transnationals do pay higher wages than their rivals, it is clear that their labour costs may nevertheless be lower.

Third, even if all transnationals pay more than all firms producing in just one country, the existence of a transnational paying higher wages may nevertheless be explained by the divide and rule concept. Suppose firm A is a wage leader in country Y and that, dividing workers into country-specific groups in order to pay less wages, it acquires production facilities in country X. In X, A can be a high-payer – for example, because it feels this brings forth better workers, or because it faces workers well organized within X. Yet it can still pay less than if it produced entirely in Y, facing a workforce acting collectively. For instance, A may use its X production to undermine a strike by workers in Y and thereby secure lower wages in Y; and/or, in making its initial investment in X, A may play off two separated yet individually well-organized workforces to obtain lower wages. In addition, even though A uses its production base in X to undermine workers in Y, it can remain a wage leader in Y – for example, because it continues to face the best organized workers in Y, or because of historical inertia. In short, firm A can be a high-payer in X *and* Y, even though divide and rule is a reason for its producing in both countries. The critical factor in our hypothesis is simply that a firm's labour costs are less when it divides workers across countries than when it produces in only one country. Whether the firm is a high-payer or a low-payer relative to rivals is irrelevant.

To argue successfully that divide and rule is an important reason for firms to produce in more than one country, however, we must be more positive. It is not enough simply to refute the wages view because this only removes an obstacle from our path. What is needed is evidence that goes to the heart of the hypothesis. Unfortunately this is not easy to come by, because divide and rule is not an issue that has occupied researchers' attention to any substantial degree.

Nevertheless some evidence is available, and especially interesting is that relating to specific situations. For example, ILO (1976) mentions the case of labour unrest in Britain leading the Chrysler Corporation to contemplate the transfer of production to sister operations in France and/or Japan. Also Gennard (1972) refers to the antics of the Goodyear Tyre Company in using supplies from elsewhere to undermine industrial action in Britain. See also Harte and Sugden (1990) on the dealings of General Motors with Vauxhall workers over the siting of a new engine plant, and the claims in early 1993 that Hoover played off workers in France and Scotland.[10] Strictly speaking, this sort of evidence does not show firms becoming transnationals because of divide and rule opportunities, but it is strongly suggestive.

Comparatively well documented are the activities of Ford. Indeed, the clearest possible case of divide and rule is provided by the CIS (1978) report of Ford's decision deliberately to dual-source components for its Fiesta model to reduce labour's bargaining power. This is shown by its engines policy:

> In the event of a shutdown of the Dagenham Fiesta engine line, the company's aim would be to boost output of the Valencia engine line to supply extra units to the Dagenham and Saarlouis assembly lines. With a higher output of the Valencia engined cars from these two plants, stocks of the Dagenham engines could be stretched out to minimise interruptions in supply of any model. Similarly if the Valencia engine plant were shut down.

More subtle is the continuous barrage of threats Ford has hurled at its workforce over the years. One of the bargaining strategies commonly used by all firms is to argue that unless labour costs are lowered immediately, the prospects for future investment are bleak. A firm certainly need not be a transnational to do this. But when it is, it has the added ability to threaten workers convincingly in any one country that failure to accept lower labour costs now will mean future investment elsewhere. Ford's use of this strategy is clearly felt by Friedman (1977) to be an important feature of its industrial relations: 'One of the most significant features of industrial relations in the UK motor industry from the mid-1960s has been the ever-present threat, particularly coming from Chrysler and Ford, to shift operations to other countries.'

More specifically, it is shown in Steuer and Gennard's (1971) report that in February 1970 Henry Ford was questioned by Halewood shop stewards. They were concerned about rumours of new investment going to Germany rather than Britain, it being known that Detroit was unhappy with British industrial relations. This story is taken up by ILO (1976). In 1971 there was a strike at Ford in Britain:

> While this dispute was underway . . . Henry Ford . . . was reported to have declared that parts of the Ford Escort and Cortina models . . . would in future

no longer be made in the United Kingdom but would be manufactured in Asia ... Mr Ford came to London shortly thereafter, and in a meeting with the [then] British Prime Minister Heath, he is reported to have let it be known, with regard to the company's labour difficulties, that if improvements were not forthcoming, the company would take its business elsewhere.

Furthermore, it would seem that the threats have not been empty:

In 1973 when the company decided to locate the bulk of its small car engine production in the United States [for the Pinto model, sold largely in the United States], the *Financial Times* (22 June) reported: 'It is no secret that industrial disputes in Britain priced the United Kingdom out of the market ...'. The same paper added, 'There was, of course, no guarantee that Britain would ever have been selected for such a major development but the comments of Henry Ford ... [in] the early part of the year made it clear that the United Kingdom had dropped out of the running ...'. The same report added, 'the fear of similar labour unrest in Germany in the future may have entered into the company's decision to locate the plant in the United States.'

Meanwhile, coming more up to date, it is clear from *Financial Times* reports that the threats at Ford were continuing. Ford's employee relations director, Paul Roots, is said to have told British unions in 1983 that labour cost were too high:

'This year, to date, we have achieved only 62 to 64 per cent of capacity at Halewood and Dagenham against 100 per cent at Saarlouis in West Germany and 96 percent at Valencia, Spain,' he said. 'If we do not get our costs down we cannot compete and if we cannot compete we will not survive in Britain as a manufacturing company.'[11]

The following year Ford of Europe's then vice-president for manufacturing, Mr Hayden, delivered the same message to those in dispute with the company over investment plans:

Although Mr Hayden denied that Ford was running down its British plants, he gave a stiff warning that the consequences for future investment would be serious if the productivity gap with European plants was not closed.[12]

And coming into the 1990s, the saga continues. For example, in February 1992 the workforce at the Dagenham and Halewood assembly plants was warned in no uncertain terms that it should catch up with performance at Ford's equivalent operations elsewhere in Europe. The chairman of Ford of Europe argued:

It isn't the facilities that are different [to those in continental Europe], there is not a damn thing wrong with the Halewood facility. It is the way labour is organised and the way labour functions ... You have to close the gap [with continental Europe] eventually or you will have to shift capacity – because otherwise you will have to say to hell with it.[13]

This followed a warning to Dagenham workers earlier in 1992 that improved productivity in Fiesta production was needed if they were to be sure of their role in producing the model's successor.[14] Clearly, little has changed over the years.

This leaves us with a catalogue of instances that can permit little doubt that divide and rule is important to understanding the activities of one of the largest companies in the world. The difficulty with this sort of evidence is that it is uncertain just how typical Ford is, but it seems extremely unlikely that it is very unusual. Rather, we can reasonably expect Ford to be typical. So this is also clear evidence that more generally divide and rule of labour is an important reason for production in more than one country.

US findings

Concern over the possibility of divide and rule tactics by transnationals is not limited to Europe, as North American unions claim that the growth of these types of companies has led to significant job displacement. Indeed, the AFL-CIO's Industrial Union Department calculated that 900,000 jobs had been lost in the US between 1966 and 1971 as a result of the expansion of US transnationals abroad.[15] Using data from the US Bureau of Labour Statistics and the US Department of Labour, this job displacement figure was derived by estimating the number of jobs required to produce the increase in imports to the US for US-owned subsidiaries from abroad and subtracting this from the estimated number of jobs generated from the increase in US exports from these transnationals. Such employment patterns associated with the growth of transnationals are consistent with the divide and rule hypothesis, since job displacement reflects the ability of transnational employers to use alternative sources of production. Job displacement associated with the expansion of US transnationals, however, might arise owing to reasons other than employers' use of divide and rule tactics. For instance, transnationals might expand their overseas operations in an attempt to locate in low-wage markets. Furthermore, transnationals might eliminate entire production lines at some locations to avoid unnecessary duplication of operations across plants. While these alternative reasons for increased job displacement suggest using caution when identifying divide and rule tactics, the organisational structure of the transnational may none the less be considered to allow employers to exercise options that threaten the job security of workers.

Further evidence of the enhanced ability of transnational employers to engage in divide and rule tactics is reported by Greer and Shearer (1981). This study uses survey information on 50 US unions, 13 having experience with non-US-owned companies. Table 8.1 reproduces some results. These again raise the dual-sourcing issue, and the use of threats is revealed by the actual 'use of foreign production to undercut US unions' bargaining position' and to 'undercut US unions' position during a strike'. This still does not establish conclusively that

Table 8.1 Number of unions reporting on the use of multinational bargaining tactics by foreign-owned US firms

Company tactic	Firms frequently use	Firms seldom use	Firms never use
Use of foreign production to undercut US union's bargaining position:			
Threatened	0	1	7
Actual	0	2	4
Use of foreign production to undercut US union's position during a strike:			
Threatened	1	1	5
Actual	1	1	4
Movement of US production facilities abroad or new investments abroad to strengthen US bargaining position:			
Threatened to move/ invest abroad	0	2	6
Actually moved/ invested abroad	0	2	5

Source: Greer and Shearer (1981)

a reason for 'foreign production' is to undercut US unions, but it does add to the suggestion. Even more persuasive is the claim from two unions (out of seven) that firms do move their US production facilities elsewhere or do make new investments abroad to strengthen their US bargaining advantage. These results are clear evidence favouring our hypothesis.

In addition, Greer and Shearer (1981) report a survey of 29 US companies, each non-US-owned. Seven out of 26 firms agreed they would consider using production in various countries to discourage US strikes, while one out of 28 agreed they had actually done so. Again, while this does not say firms become transnationals to improve their bargaining advantage, it is suggestive; if firms recognize a means by which they can benefit from being a transnational, then it is likely to be a contributory factor explaining their becoming a transnational.

These results are also supported by Craypo's (1975) examination of the overseas transfer of US domestic production of the Royal typewriter division of Litton Industries. Craypo reveals that Litton's consummation of the German-owned Triumph-Adler Typewriter Company opened the way for overseas production of Royal typewriters. Immediately following the acquisition, union representation of workers employed at the Royal's Springfield Missouri plant imposed a strike in response to the refusal of the company to renegotiate the expiring labour contract with Local 469 of the Allied Industrial Workers. Craypo reports that Royal's decision was based on the fact that the company could not legally bargain with the union pending the outcome of a motion filed with the National Labor Relations Board by a dissident group inside the plant requesting the decertification of the union as the bargaining agent. Sixty days following the union's actions Royal announced the planned shutdown of the Springfield plant with part of the production temporarily moved to Hartford Connecticut and the rest assigned overseas in Portugal. Eventually, Triumph-Adler expanded its German facilities which allowed it to replace Hartford's remaining manufacturing responsibilities.

Craypo argues that this transnational employer's ability to exploit national differences in wages when bargaining with US unions was demonstrated at Springfield and Hartford. Indeed, the company's director of labour relations acknowledged greater incentive to reach a settlement if the wages of these US workers matched that of their counterparts performing the same task at Litton's overseas locations.[16] Thus, whereas claims of dual sourcing and so on were examined earlier as evidence favouring the divide and rule hypothesis, the Litton acquisition of Triumph-Adler is an actual example providing likewise evidence. Furthermore, Litton's willingness to close the high-wage US operations strengthens the credibility of future company threats of plant closures when negotiating with labour at the remaining locations. All in all, there is strong empirical evidence for accepting our hypothesis. It is reasonable to claim that at least one contributory reason for the existence of some transnationals is the division of workers into country-specific groups, allowing a firm to obtain lower labour costs when it is a transnational than when it produces in just one country.

It should be noted, however, that the notion that the threat of job displacement is enhanced when workers are employed by a transnational is not universally accepted. Other research of US transnationals suggests the possibility of a net employment gain associated with the growth of transnationals. For example, Hawkins and Jedel (1975) argue that while overseas production allows the transnational to substitute US jobs with low-wage foreign jobs, demand for US workers might increase if greater demand for the final good produced overseas actually generates greater demand for US capital goods and raw materials. Citing findings from Hirsch (1975), Horst (1974), and others, Hawkins and Jedel conclude that, assuming the same average labour productivity, the number of US jobs eliminated by US transnationals' substituting foreign production for exports is less than the number of US jobs required to support the exports stimulated by that foreign activity. However, those workers who are displaced are less skilled workers who face a more elastic labour supply schedule than their more skilled counterparts. As Hawkins and Jedel state, 'these differing probabilities of displacement across skill levels creates a domestic conflict of interest between groups of workers with respect to transnational expansion.'

In addition, their findings suggest that less skilled workers are susceptible to divide and rule tactics by transnationals, since these workers are more easily substitutable than highly skilled workers. Hence, past work that compares wages paid by transnational and national firms may mask the complete wage effect of transnational firms by failing to control for differences in worker skill levels.

Canadian results

Research on transnational and labour activity in Canada uses an alternative approach for examining this type of firm's influence on labour markets. These studies investigate strike activity at transnationals as a way of indicating worker dissatisfaction.[17] For instance, Ng and Maki (1988) use an ordinary least squares (OLS) technique to estimate a strike activity equation. Canadian sales accounted for by US-controlled transnationals as a share of total industry sales are included as a determinant of strike activity. This variable allows for an examination of the influence of US transnational activity on the frequency of labour strikes in Canada. A positive association of these variables might reflect US transnationals' ability to use divide and rule tactics to negotiate lower wages and benefits, if workers exhibit their dissatisfaction over these issues by engaging in a labour strike. However, it is not clear that unions would necessarily respond in this manner. Unions facing transnational employers might try to avoid labour strikes because they recognize the inherent bargaining advantage that this type of company derives from its ability to use divide and rule tactics.

Another strike determinant included in the strike equation specified by Ng and Maki is the ratio of Canadian worker representation by international unions and total Canadian membership as a way to investigate the influence of international unions on strike activity. These authors report that this ratio equalled 44.2 per cent for their study's 1983 observation period. This clearly suggests that international unions represented a nontrivial portion of total union members in Canada. The inclusion of this strike determinant is significant because international unions might have greater bargaining strength than national unions when negotiating with a transnational corporation. For instance, these authors observe that since international unions in Canada also have access to US funds, these 'deep pockets' enhance these unions' chances of commanding the support of their members in the event of a strike. Compared to their national counterparts, the effect of the international union striking is potentially more damaging to the transnational because the union can disrupt operations at multiple locations. Apparently, then, the ability to exercise divide and rule tactics may be reduced if transnational corporations are more likely to negotiate with international than national unions. However, as mentioned earlier in the theory section, organizational problems such as communication, sectionalism, and cumbersome national union machinery weaken the ability of international unions to act collectively. Ng and Maki also caution that the bargaining advantage of international unions is dependent on the negotiation strength of the bargaining units representing members employed at plants in the US transnational's home country. These companies may experience a negotiation advantage if US bargaining units are in a much weaker bargaining position than their Canadian counterparts. The US transnational can target these union representatives to set the wage pattern for multiple plant negotiations. Indeed, this is a common practice of US transnationals negotiating with international unions comprised of Canadian and US bargaining units.

Ng and Maki do not find evidence of a significant association between the prevalence of transnational corporations and the frequency of strike activity. While this does not seem to reveal strong support for the divide and rule hypothesis, Ng and Maki do find that strike activity is significantly and negatively associated with the membership share of international unions. For example, they predict that a 9.5 per cent increase in international unions' share of total membership is associated with a 10 per cent reduction in the number of workdays lost due to a strike. This result is consistent with the notion that these unions have greater negotiation leverage than their national counterparts, and thus should be better able to contend with divide and rule tactics. This, combined with the possibility that international unions are more prevalent at transnational plants, might partly explain evidence revealing the lack of a significant association between strike activity and the growth of transnational corporations.

Subsequent work by Budd (1994) also reveals a lack of association between the prevalence of transnational corporations and the frequency of strike activity. However, he does examine the probability that the workforces of transnational corporations are more likely to be represented by international unions than by their national counterparts.[18] He finds that 78.41 per cent of the organised workforce of foreign-owned corporations in Canada are represented by international unions. This is statistically significantly higher than the 70.8 per cent representation rate he finds for domestic corporations in Canada. Budd also maintains that the mean duration of strikes is significantly lower when firms negotiate with international unions. While these findings seem to support the notion that the increased likelihood of negotiating with international unions could partly explain the lack of significant strike activity at transnational corporations, Budd does reveal that workers represented by international unions receive statistically significantly lower wages than workers represented by national unions. Hence, the lower duration of strikes experienced when facing an international union apparently does not suggest enhanced bargaining strength since companies' ability to negotiate lower wages is actually enhanced when bargaining with these unions.

In sum, Canadian evidence on strike activity is consistent with the notion that transnational corporations are well positioned to practise divide and rule tactics, *even when confronting an international union*. This may be due in part to the ability of these corporations to target weak union bargaining units to set the labour wage pattern when negotiating with international unions. In addition, the organizational problems faced by international unions when attempting to act collectively possibly contributes to the transnational's bargaining advantage. However, there has not been a direct test of this hypothesis. This suggests a path for future research that addresses the possibility that transnational corporations' whipsawing advantage over international unions influences the wage level and strike activity at these Canadian corporations.

Conclusion

In analysing the 'why transnationals?' question, this chapter has rejected the traditional obsession with (Pareto) efficient outcomes and has instead emphasized distributional considerations. It has done so by exploring in some detail a divide and rule analysis.

Our overall conclusion is that it is undoubtedly the case that divide and rule occurs. Moreover it would be surprising to the point of incredulity if the possibility and practice of divide and rule were not a significant contributory factor underlying firms' choosing to produce in more than one country. Nevertheless, it is also the case that the empirical evidence is typically unclear, capable of interpretation in various ways. Hence we cannot be certain of the precise significance of divide and rule by transnationals. Progress in that regard continues to await further research.

Acknowledgements

We would like to acknowledge the support of the University of Birmingham and the University of Wisconsin-Milwaukee in enabling us to cooperate on this project.

Notes

1 See also Sugden (1991, 1993) and Cowling and Sugden (1994); this chapter draws heavily on these earlier works.
2 See the evidence of collusion over wages in Forsyth's (1972) survey of Scottish firms.
3 It is not only collective bargaining that is at issue. For instance, contacts by workers to foster information sharing are important (see, for example, Enderwick 1985).
4 In his 'eclectic theory', Dunning (1980) suggests that transnationals may be able to 'reduce the impact of strikes or industrial unrest in one country by operating parallel production capacity in another'.
5 The comparison being made here is a firm manufacturing shirts by cutting and sewing cloth in Britain versus a firm doing the same thing but in Britain and the Philippines. This is not to deny that different comparisons could be made – for example, between the bargaining power of labour when it is employed by a firm whose sole activity is to cut cloth in Britain and when it is employed by a firm which cuts cloth in Britain and sews this into shirts in the Philippines. Then labour in Britain may have more bargaining power when it is part of the wider operation encompassing the Philippines, other things being equal (for example, because a strike in Britain would cause disruption in the Philippines by stopping work there once any stock of cut cloth is exhausted). But introducing these other comparisons does not undermine our divide and rule analysis; the point of our analysis is to focus on the activities of a particular firm and compare labour costs when *those* activities are carried out in one versus more than one country.
6 This would not necessarily increase workers' utility but would mean that 'divide and rule' does not answer the question 'why transnationals?'.
7 Observe how this analysis of bargaining in periods $t + 1, t + 2, \ldots$ is closely linked with the bargaining over new investments. When firms bargain with workers over new investment in period t, they will bear in mind how those workers have behaved in the past.

8 See also Carmichael (1992), developing an approach derived from Ashenfelter and Johnson (1969), and Hollingsworth (1996), which explores a formal theoretical analysis using a bargaining model derived from Nickell and Andrews (1983), Zhoa (1995), and Naylor (1995).

9 See also Carmichael (1992). Although seeing both the earlier literature on wages and her own estimations as inconclusive, she concludes: 'What can be stated with a fair degree of confidence is that, even though multinationality confers a potential bargaining advantage on firms . . . this potential is not realised to any great advantage.'

10 *Financial Times*, 5 March 1993.

11 *Financial Times*, 29 October 1983.

12 *Financial Times*, 23 February 1984.

13 *Financial Times*, 17 February 1992.

14 *Financial Times*, 14 January 1992.

15 Subcommittee on International Trade of the Committee of Finance on the US Senate, 'An American Trade Union View of International Trade and Investment, AFL-CIO, in Transnational Corporations', (Washington, DC, 1973), pp. 59–86.

16 Craypo reports that cost data provided by Litton suggest that average hourly earnings were five times greater for workers employed at the Hartford plant than at the plant in Hull, England.

17 This interpretation glosses over the possibility that a strike may be engineered by employers; it focuses only on strikes as actions by employees in response to their grievances.

18 Information on union affiliation and international status was taken from *Labour Organisation in Canada* (Ottawa: Labour Canada) and *Collective Bargaining Review* (Ottawa: Labour Canada).

References

Adam, G. (1975) 'Multinational corporations and worldwide sourcing', in H. Radice (ed.), *International Firms and Modern Imperialism*, London: Penguin.

Ashenfelter, 0. and G.E. Johnson (1969) 'Bargaining theory, trade unions and industrial strike activity', *American Economic Review*: 35–49.

Blanchflower, D. (1984) 'Comparative pay levels in domestically-owned and foreign-owned manufacturing plants: A comment', *British Journal of Industrial Relations* XXII: 265–267.

Buckley, P.J and P. Enderwick (1983) 'Comparative pay levels in domestically-owned and foreign-owned plants in UK manufacturing – Evidence from the 1980 Workplace Industrial Relations Survey', *British Journal of Industrial Relations* XXI: 395–400.

Budd, J. (1994) 'The effect of multinational institutions on strike activity in Canada', *Industrial and Labour Relations Review*, April: 401–16.

Burkitt, B. and D. Bowers (1979) *Trade Unions and the Economy*, London: Macmillan.

Carmichael, F. (1992) 'The impact of multinational enterprise on wages: Theory and evidence', *International Journal of Manpower* 13, 2: 27—40.

Counter Information Services (1978) *Anti-report: the Ford Motor Company*, Anti-report no. 20. London: CIS.

Cowling, K. (1986). 'The internationalization of production and deindustrialization', in A. Amin and J. Goddard (eds), *Technological Change, Industrial Restructuring and Regional Development*, London: Allen & Unwin.

Cowling, K. and R. Sugden (1994) *Beyond Capitalism. Towards a New World Economic Order*. London: Pinter.

—— (1998) 'The essence of the modern corporation: Markets, strategic decision-making and the theory of the firm', *The Manchester School*, 66, 1: 59–86.

Craypo, C. (1975) 'Collective bargaining in the conglomerate, multinational firm: Litton's shutdown of Royal Typewriter', *Industrial and Labour Relations Review*: 3–25.

Dunning, J.H. (1980) 'Toward an eclectic theory of international production: Some empirical tests', *Journal of International Business Studies* 11: 9-31.

—— (1993) *Multinational Enterprises and the Global Economy*, Wokingham, England and Reading, Mass.: Addison-Wesley.

Edwards, R. (1979) *Contested Terrain*, London: Heinemann.

Enderwick, P. (1985) *Multinational Business and Labour*, London: Croom Helm.

Forsyth, D.J.C. (1972) *US Investment in Scotland*, New York: Praeger.

Friedman, A.L. (1977). *Industry and Labour: Class Struggle at Work and Monopoly Capitalism*, London: Macmillan.

Fröbel, F., J. Heinrichs and O. Kreye (1980) *The New International Division of Labour*, Cambridge: Cambridge University Press.

Gennard, J. (1972) *Multinational Corporations and British Labour: A Review of British Attitudes and Responses*, British–North American Committee, n.p.

Greer, C. and J. Shearer (1981) 'Do foreign-owned U.S. firms practice unconventional labour relations?', *Monthly Labour Review*: 44–48.

Harte, G. and R. Sugden (1990) 'A proposal for monitoring transnational corporations', in K. Cowling and R. Sugden (eds), *A New Economic Policy for Britain: Essays on the Development of Industry*, Manchester: Manchester University Press.

Hawkins, R. and Michael J. (1975) 'U.S. jobs and foreign investment', in D. Kujawa (ed.) *International Labour and the Multinational Enterprise*, New York: Praeger.

Helfgott, R.B. (1983) 'American unions and multinational companies: A case of misplaced emphasis', *Columbia Journal of World Business* 18: 81–86.

Hirsch, S. (1975) 'An international trade and investment theory of the firm', *Economica*.

Hollingsworth, C.K. (1996) 'Bargaining in the value chain. Two examples'. Paper presented at the *EUNIP* Turku Workshop, Finland, 19–20 July.

Horst, T. (1974) *American Exports and Foreign Direct Investments*, Harvard Institute of Economic Research, Discussion Paper no. 362.

Hymer, S.H. (1972) 'The multinational corporation and the law of uneven development', in J.N. Bhagwati (ed.), *Economics and World Order*, London: Macmillan.

International Labour Office (1976) *Multinationals in Western Europe: The Industrial Relations Experience*, Geneva: ILO.

McPherson, M. (1983) 'Efficiency and liberty in the productive enterprise: Recent work in the economics of work organisation', *Philosophy and Public Affairs* 12: 354–68.

Marglin, S.A. (1974) 'What do bosses do? The origins and functions of hierarchy in capitalist production', *Review of Radical Political Economics* 6: 60–112.

Naylor, R. (1995) 'International trade and economic integration when labour markets are generally unionised', mimeo, University of Warwick.

Nickell, S. and M. Andrews (1983) *Workers, Real Wages and Employment in Britain, 1951–1979*, Oxford Economic Papers, Oxford: OUP.

Ng, I. and D. Maki (1988) 'Strike activity of U.S. institutions in Canada', *British Journal of Industrial Relations*, March: 63–73.

Steuer, M. and J. Gennard (1971) 'Industrial relations, labour disputes and labour utilisation in foreign-owned firms in the United Kingdom', in J.H. Dunning (ed.) *The Multinational Enterprise*, London: Allen & Unwin.

Sugden, R. (1991) 'The importance of distributional considerations', in C. Pitelis and R. Sugden (eds) *The Nature of the Transnational Firm*, London: Routledge.

—— (1993) 'Why transnational corporations? The significance of divide and rule', in G.R. Krishnamurthy (ed.) *Human Resource Management in Multinationals*, Delhi: Kanishka Publishing House.

Zhoa, L. (1995) 'Cross-hauling, direct foreign investment and unionised oligopoly', *European Economic Review* 39: 1237–53.

9 The TNC: An all-weather company

Christos N. Pitelis

Introduction

The idea that demand-side deficiencies can provide an inducement for outward investments by transnational corporations (TNCs) has never acquired much currency. This is despite its long history and the fact that existing theories often have implications supportive of it. Arguably, a reason for this is that the idea had never been subjected to rigorous empirical testing. In this chapter we report some econometric evidence in favour of this view. The next section critically surveys and attempts to synthesize the mainstream microeconomic or supply-side theories of the TNC. The subsequent section examines the case for a demand-side perspective, links this to the supply side and discusses some existing indirect evidence in support of this perspective. The discussion then focuses on direct evidence in favour of the demand-side perspective. The final section presents conclusions and policy implications.

Supply-side theories of the TNC

The first serious attempt to analyse the TNC within the broad mainstream tradition is Stephen Hymer's doctoral thesis completed in 1960, but first published in 1976. Hymer recognized three main factors pertaining to a firm's decision to become a TNC: the possession of ownership or monopolistic advantages;[1] the removal of conflict, and the internalization of market imperfections. Regarding the latter, and despite a reference to Coase's classic 1937 article on the nature of the firm (see Yamin, this volume), Hymer emphasized structural market imperfections rather than transactional ones (see Dunning and Rugman, 1985).

Three main traditions subsequently developed within the mainstream research programme. Kindleberger (1969, 1984) and Caves (1971) expanded the monopolistic advantage aspect of Hymer's theory. The main idea is that there exist natural disadvantages for a foreign firm operating outside its country of origin: language, cultural and other related problems. For a firm to be able to undertake overseas activities through direct foreign investment (DFI), it must possess an advantage that indigenous firms do not. Technology, know-how, management, and liquidity-related advantages could be exploited in order to overcome the inherent disadvantages of DFI and make contemplated overseas operations more attractive.

An implication of this Hymer–Kindleberger–Caves (HKC) tradition is that TNCs need not be Pareto-efficient.[2] Their monopolistic advantages may facilitate a process of monopolization abroad, thus potentially reducing the welfare of the 'host' countries.[3] Although proponents of the theory (for example, Kindleberger, 1969), express the belief that the long-run benefits of TNCs will offset any short-run costs, the HKC tradition recognizes the possibility of the existence of both efficiency and inefficiency aspects of TNC operations. The possibility that TNCs will consciously monopolize global markets so as to obtain monopoly profits, and that in so doing they will tend to behave collusively (eliminate conflict), has been developed by the 'global reach' variant of Hymer's theory (see Jenkins, 1987). Vaitsos (1974) and Newfarmer (1985) are important contributions along this line of thought, as is a good part of Cowling and Sugden (1987).[4] Unlike Kindleberger, this line of thought emphasizes the (Pareto) inefficiency aspects of TNC operations.

The case with 'internalization' is different. Affiliates of this school emphasize the internalization of market imperfections. It is suggested that TNCs internalize 'cognitive' or natural' market imperfections, defined as those arising out of excessive market transaction costs (see Dunning and Rugman, 1985). The basic notion that the firm exists in order to reduce the costs associated with the operation of the price mechanism dates back to Coase (1937). The forceful reintroduction and extension of Coase's insight is due primarily to Williamson (1975, 1981). For Williamson, three main factors – bounded rationality, opportunism, and asset specificity – give rise to high market transaction costs, such as the costs of searching, contracting, negotiating and policing agreements. These costs can often be reduced if the market is superseded by a hierarchy, such as the firm. The existence of firms can thus result in decreased transaction costs.

While most proponents of this perspective would agree with the above statement, not everybody would agree with the reasons why. In Williamson (1981), for example, the driving force behind the emergence of excessive trans-action costs leading to internalization is ex-post hold-ups due to asset specificity. Buckley and Casson (1976) on the other hand, have focused on appropriability problems of intermediate products (usually intangible assets) such as technology, know-how, managerial skills, etc. All these are claimed to exhibit 'public goods' characteristics, giving rise to excessive transaction costs of markets, thus to integration (the choice over DFI to, for example, licensing). Another view is that of Hennart (this volume). Hennart in effect goes back to Coase's focus on the employment contract. He claims that internalization requires not just market failure but also firm success. The later is attributed to the ability of (foreign) hierarchies to co-ordinate, more efficiently than indigenous firms, employees in the 'host' country. In addition, Hennart's approach focuses on the internalization of markets, not just advantages, in apparent contrast to other transaction costs-related perspectives.

A synthesis of the HKC and the internalization/transaction costs tradition has been offered by Dunning's (1981, 1988) 'eclectic theory' and, more recently, his 'Ownership, Location, Internalization' (OLI) paradigm (Dunning, 1991, 1998, and this volume). In Dunning's theory, ownership advantages and the internalization of market transactions are reasons for TNCs as well as 'locational factors'. Dunning's (1958) early work on the TNC explained US TNC activities in Europe in terms of such locational factors (see also Fieldhouse, 1986). The role of such factors has received little attention from other authors, partly owing to the belief that locational differences between developed countries are of no importance (see Gray, 1985). Rugman (1986) has suggested that Dunning's ownership advantages need to be internalized before TNCs can result. Accordingly, the eclectic theory can be seen as internalization-cum-locational factors, which is internalization only if the latter factors are not important.

In a more radical vein, Marglin (1974) focused attention on the labour market. Starting from the classic dichotomy between capital and labour, Marglin suggested that the emergence of the factory system from the putting-out system was more likely to have been due to the desire of capitalists to increase their control over the workforce than to any alleged technological superiority of the factory system. Accordingly, the emergence of the more hierarchical structure from the more decentralized, market-based one need not necessarily be associated with exclusively (Pareto) efficiency attributes. Labour, for example, may not perceive the change of institutional form as an improvement.

Sugden (1991) has extended Marglin's analysis to the TNC. According to Sugden, the TNC allows capital to increase its control over global labour, which thus allows it to pursue 'divide and rule' policies in order to reduce further the power of trade unions by playing off country-specific worker groups against each other. The potential mobility of TNC operations, as compared to the inherent immobility of country-specific labour groups, increases TNCs' bargaining power, allowing them to derive distributional gains from labour. This redistributional aspect of TNCs definitionally implies Pareto inefficiency (see also Peoples and Sugden, this volume).

To summarize, supply-side theories of the TNC tend to emphasize the exploitation of monopolistic advantages by firms (the HKC tradition and 'global reach' theories), the internalization of market transaction costs, an eclectic synthesis cum locational factors (the OLI paradigm), or the increased power over labour markets ('divide and rule' theory). In principle, all these theories can be integrated within the general concept of internalization. TNCs can be argued to arise in order to reduce 'natural' and structural market failures (as suggested by Rugman, 1986) as well as what they view as labour market imperfections, an extended internalization view (see Pitelis, 1991a). The problem for the internalization theory, resulting from this integration, is that the efficiency-only property fades away. The internalization of monopolistic advantages may result in the restriction of competition, which need not be Pareto-efficient or socially beneficial despite its private gains to the TNC itself.[5] This is clearer in the case of the internalization of 'labour market inefficiencies'.[6]

There are various problems with the aforementioned theories. Williamson's almost exclusive focus on hold-up problems due to specific assets has been criticized widely (see, in particular, Kay (1991), Demsetz (1995), and, more recently, Holmström and Roberts (1998)). Kay was among the first to observe that TNCs internalize both specific and nonspecific assets; indeed, that the 'other' internalization theorists' focus (i.e. Buckley and Casson's) was mostly on non-specific assets. On the other hand, Buckley and Casson's focus on the alleged 'public goods' nature of the TNC has been criticized by Kogut and Zander (1993). Building on work by Teece (1977), Kogut and Zander observed that much of knowledge-related (intangible) assets involve tacit knowledge, thus are hard to transfer across markets. The differential ability of firms to transfer these assets internally may explain the TNC. This need not require market failure; only differential ability *vis-à-vis* the market and other firms. In addition to the above, it is now widely recognized that the internalization perspective is a comparative static one, basically underplaying dynamics. This old criticism (see, for example, Pitelis, 1991b) is acknowledged by Buckley and Casson (1998b) themselves, who call for a dynamic theory, based on the concept (and need for) flexibility.

There are additional and related concerns. First, the issue of motivation for growth; second, the acquisition of advantages; lastly, the direction of expansion. In all theories the profit maximization concept is maintained, or at least not challenged. In Hymer, this is pursued by, among others, monopolizing markets; in the internalization school, by reducing transaction costs. In both cases, the inducement to expansion is external opportunities (monopoly or transaction cost reductions, respectively). No internal inducements to growth are recognized, whilst it remains unclear whether reference is made to short-term or long-term profit maximization.

Coming to the advantages (including intangible assets), it is not always clear how they are derived. In Hymer's work taken as a whole (see the collection of his papers in Hymer, 1979), advantages derive from a process of expansion motivated by external market opportunity. Building on Chandler (1962), Hymer suggests the existence of a 'law of increasing firm size' in four stages: (1) small, owner-managed firms; (2) public limited national companies, with limited liability; (3) M-form firms; (4) TNCs. Hymer claims that advantages are derived in the very process, while the TNC is unique in having access to all these in a package. These are not limited to technology, know-how, marketing and distribution and (retained) profits, but include organizational form (e.g. the M-form) and even expanded horizons. In the internalization school, advantages are taken to be either inherited or the result of the very action of internalization. In neither case are advantages derived through a process of internal inducements to growth.

Concerning the direction of expansion, this is unclear. In the monopolistic advantage perspective, one could suggest that diversification would take place where 'attractive markets' exist, domestically and/or abroad. This would be very much in line with Porter's (1980) five-forces analysis, whereby attractive industries are chosen on the basis of the lack of competitive forces within them.

A push factor in Hymer is the product life cycle, which induces domestic diversification so as to create what has been known in the strategic management literature as 'all-weather company'. However, this does not suffice to distinguish between domestic diversification and expansion abroad. So, why the latter? Does the profit motive *à la* Hymer or Coase suffice?

To summarize, existing work fails adequately to address the issues of motivation, internal inducements, and direction of expansion. In view of the wide recognition of dynamics, this is the issue to be addressed. In addition, there is scope for refining the distinction between domestic diversification and expansion abroad.

Some of the above issues are dealt with in the work of Penrose. In her, now classic, *The Theory of the Growth of the Firm* (1995: first published 1959), Penrose defined the firm as a bundle of resources under administrative coordination. From these, human resources and especially managerial ones are seen as crucial. The main reason is *learning* and *knowledge creation* within the cohesive shell of an organization. This results from specialization, division of labour and teamwork, generally a process of learning. This releases resources which, alongside resource indivisibility, induce internal (endogenous) expansion and (through) continuous innovation to make use of these resources. The search for long-term profits motivates entrepreneurs to exploit internal resources and perceived external opportunities. Crucially, competitive advantages are generated within the firm. They are often unavailable in the spot market, notably managerial skills. This generates a limit to the rate of growth, albeit not to the size of the firm *per se*.

It is not possible to provide a full account of the Penrosean contribution here; see for more details Pitelis and Wahl (1998) and Pitelis and Pseiridis (1999). Suffice it to observe that within her theory we have an explanation for internal growth that supplements existing theories. Moreover it explains the process of generation of internal competitive–firm specific advantages, which is in accord with, and supplements, Hymer's view. Last but not least, Penrose's is the only theory which provides a hint as to the *direction* of expansion. This should, in the first instance, be in activities where firms have already developed a resource base, what in today's parlance is called a competence (see e.g. Prahalad and Hamel, 1990). Importantly, as Penrose explains in what is arguably the best case study of all times, the Hercules Powder Company (Penrose, 1960), the intra-firm innovation process may well be the result of quasi-chance. To that extent the direction of diversification is only partially predictable. Importantly, the internally generated resources may well be firm specific and an ownership or monopolistic advantage, but need not be specific assets in the Williamsonian sense. Some may be, some others may not. In the latter case the fundamental issue returns: why not sell these?[7] Fundamentally there are only two generic reasons: inability and/or unwillingness. Inability could be the result of failing and/or missing markets. Unwillingness can be the result of expectations for higher profits, and/or lower losses. The former case is, for example, that of differential efficiency; the latter can be the avoidance of creating a competitor. There can simply not be a general answer to all cases. Each case should be reviewed individually by the actors involved.

The above analysis, however, does allow scope for synthesis. Penrose supplements Hymer in explaining endogenous growth, the internal generation of advantages, and partially the direction of expansion. Hymer discusses pull and push factors for diversification. The various versions of transaction costs analysis explain the choice of mode. Dunning's OLI addresses the issue of location. Throughout, the pursuit of long-term profit through innovation and/or monopoly restrictions and oligopolistic interaction motivates and shapes decisions and choices. It is worth pointing out that despite widespread recognition of difficulties associated with a 'general theory' in the 1990s, an increasing number of leading scholars have pointed out that the desirability and usefulness of synthesizing different pairs of the above pieces of the puzzle.[8] This, we believe, supports our case for a synthesis. In addition to the aforementioned, this synthesis should consider labour. Both in terms of the Marxian notion of intra-firm competition between capital and labour,[9] now widely acknowledged as the agency issue – see Alchian and Demsetz (1972), Jensen and Meckling (1976), Grossman and Hart (1986) – and in terms of the Marglin and Sugden focus on divide and rule strategies to reduce labour costs. Indeed, a synthesis along the above lines is not only possible but also suggested by the widely used assumption of 'profit maximization'. Once this is accepted as an aim, it becomes difficult to explain why a firm should stop short of redeploying its whole arsenal to achieve it. This can include the reduction of market transaction costs and also of labour and other costs, and/or the increase of prices through, e.g., the monopolization of markets.[10] The ability of a TNC to achieve all the above may, in fact, be viewed as a supply-side reason *per se* why firms choose to become TNCs (see also Dunning, 1992).

However, still missing from this synthesis are factors differentiating domestic from foreign diversification – a gap in the literature noted by Dunning (1998). As already mentioned, in Hymer (and others) a push factor for domestic diversification is the product life cycle. Here we suggest that extending this reasoning, a push factor contributing to foreign diversification can be (is) the 'business cycle' and, more specifically, differential effective demand growth-related (locational) factors among countries. This need not be the only such factor, but we claim it to be an important one. Following an account of the history of such arguments in the existing literature, we elaborate and discuss evidence in support of this view in the rest of this chapter.

The demand-side perspective

In this section we suggest that demand-side, effective demand-type reasons have a useful role to play in providing a general framework within which firms' decisions concerning the choice between existing alternatives are taken.

A long tradition of 'theories of imperialism', dating back to Luxemburg (1963), Hilferding (1981, first published in 1910), and Lenin (1917), among others, regarded 'imperialism' as the result of the inherent tendency of capitalist economies to crisis – usually of the effective demand type (underconsumption and realization crises) and/or the increasing organic composition of capital/ declining rate of profit type. Extensive surveys of these theories can be found in, for example, Bleaney (1976), Brewer (1980), and Hood and Young (1979). In this framework, the suggestion is that the underlying crisis is a reason for firms to undertake overseas investment, so as to relieve their profitability pressures, be they due to supply-side problems, demand-side problems, or a combination of the two. The TNC is seen as the institutional manifestation of the crisis-induced international production, and an 'agent of imperialism'.

The potential importance of effective demand on firms' decisions to seek 'external' markets has also been acknowledged by Kalecki (1971) in a critique of Rosa Luxemburg. Based on this and other contributions by Kalecki, Steindl (1952), and earlier work on their own, Baran and Sweezey (1966) generated a revival of interest in such ideas. Their main point was that most domestic industries of advanced industrial countries today are dominated by giant firms, which jointly attempt to charge the joint profit-maximizing (monopoly) price. This pricing policy generates a tendency for deficient effective demand by reducing consumers' expenditure. This in turn reduces the incentive for domestic investment, leaving outward investment as a distinct possibility.

Baran and Sweezy's theory attracted both interest and substantial criticism (see Pitelis, 1987). Their main point, however – that oligopolistic pricing can lead to an increasing share of gross profits to income – has been supported formally by Cowling (1982), under the assumption of successful strategic entry deterrence (of the excess capacity investment type) by incumbents. Moreover, the emergence of the joint stock company may provide another independent source of demand-side deficiencies in market economies. A way for firm growth is through the socialization of ownership by joint stock companies, through direct or indirect (often compulsory) shareholding, in particular through occupational pension funds. This socialization process increases the internal finances of joint stock firms but simultaneously may reduce the share of income available for consumption. Given evidence on less than perfect substitutability between different types of saving, the result is a tendency towards declining consumer expenditure (see Pitelis, 1987 for such evidence). *Ceteris paribus*, this leads to effective demand pressures, combined with the availability of 'excess' liquidity, in terms of corporate retentions and pension fund surpluses in the hands of the corporate sector. The two, combined, could be seen as a factor contributing to the tendency for the internationalization of production.

A serious attack on the Baran-Sweezy theory of international production has come from the marxist tradition, mainly from the proponents of the 'internationalization of capital' school; see the collection in Radice (1975) and Jenkins (1987). The main arguments are as follows. First, Baran and Sweezy's focus on monopoly is based on a neoclassical-type 'quantity theory of competition', which regards competition and monopoly as polar opposite types of market structure. In fact, competition should be viewed as a process which dialectically links competition and monopoly, as Marx argued. Accordingly, increasing concentration need not imply monopoly power, given actual and potential competition by rival firms. Baran and Sweezy's theory also fails to explain the direction of DFI from capital-exporting countries, such as the US. to other capital-exporting countries, such as those in Europe.

The 'internationalization of capital' theorists' alternative is to explain the emergence of the latter in terms of the inherent competition in capitalist economies between capital and labour for the generation of 'surplus value' (potential gross profit) on the one hand and intercapitalist differences on the other (for the appropriation of such profit). This competitive process suffices to provide a supply-side incentive for the internationalization of capital; where labour power exists, so does profit potential, and the first to exploit it will do better in the competitive struggle.

Accepting that supply-side considerations are important in motivating international production, it does not follow that demand-side issues cannot play a role. Demand-side factors can be of the push type or of the pull type, or both. On the push side, declining domestic effective demand, low expected rates of profitability and growth can play a role. From the pull side, faster expected growth rates and/or profits abroad can be seen as locational advantages (see Dunning, 1998).[11] When the two are combined, with demand declining at home alongside accumulated retained profits and other ownership or monopolistic advantages, there remains almost no other choice. It follows that a demand-side argument can legitimately be made. Interestingly, and despite the fact that such factors are often underplayed in the literature, demand-side considerations are often implicit in other theories, notably in Dunning, and they usefully complement Hymer's explanation of product life cycle-based domestic diversification. Demand-side questions from the point of view of the firm also enter Vernon's (1966) 'product cycle' hypothesis.

In Vernon's approach, products are seen to have a life cycle with three main phases: introduction and growth; maturity; and decline. In the first phase production takes place at home, for various reasons, such as the need for careful control and monitoring of the market. In the second phase the product becomes standardized, and given that it is already somewhat known abroad through exports, DFI is contemplated. In the third phase, DFI becomes inevitable, as tariffs tend to constrain further exports. Scale economies tend to be exhausted at home and servicing foreign markets becomes very difficult.

Vernon's theory has been attacked as an inadequate account of post Second World War TNC activities, notably by Buckley and Casson (1976) on grounds such as the difficulty the theory has in explaining non-export substituting investments, the appearance of non-standardized products being produced abroad, and the case of carefully differentiated products to suit the local market. Another potential criticism of the theory is that the decline in the rate of growth of demand in the maturity phase can be avoided through unrelated diversification to products at a different phase of their cycle. In this sense, conglomeration can be seen as an answer to the vagaries of the product cycle, as in Hymer (1979).

All the aforementioned criticisms derive from the focus of Vernon's approach to demand for the individual product, not aggregate demand. The aggregate demand deficiency argument applies to all firms, at all phases of their products, albeit with different degrees of severity, depending among other things, on the phase of the product cycle. DFI, in our framework, can be seen as firms' reply to the vagaries of the 'business cycle', thus giving rise to a genuinely 'all-weather company'. In conclusion, the aggregate demand argument both goes beyond, and survives the criticisms of the product cycle theory, while however retaining the important role of demand considerations.

To summarize, demand-side factors can be said to be a reason (incentive to firms) for the internationalization of production. This argument helps to counter-balance the focus on the supply side. However, it fails to address directly the issue of the choice between institutional modes. It provides a partial answer to the question 'Why internationalization?' but has little to say on 'Why TNCs?' as opposed to exporting, licensing and/or subcontracting. To answer these questions, it is necessary to go back to the supply-side theories.

As already noted, the above criticism applies also to supply-side theories. To explain fully the choice of institutional mode, one needs failing markets and/or differentially efficient firms and/or oligopolistic interaction, or all these together. Transaction costs associated with internalizing (internally generated) specific or non-specific assets (as the case may be) alongside differential firm efficiency in using (rather than selling) these resources-advantages (as the case may be), in the context of oligopolistic interaction, can explain the choice of institutional mode in specific cases by specific firms. All other factors that reduce unit costs (including labour ones) and/or increase value (added) (quality, differentiation, brand name) can also be of relevance. Alongside our account of endogenous growth advantages, the direction of expansion and the choice of location, we have most elements of the puzzle. The desire to have a genuine 'all-weather company' can add an extra, mostly demand-side, factor to explain internationalization. All these provide not a general theory, but the main elements of a framework and tools to be applied in specific cases in order to explain and/or predict specific strategies by specific firms.[12]

Some evidence for the demand-side theory

Some evidence for the demand-side theory is in Pitelis (1987, 1996) and is reported here. Pitelis (1987) is concerned with the issue that a stylized fact of TNC operations in the 1950s and 1960s is that such firms were US-based and undertook operations in the main in other developed countries (see Casson, 1987). Why should firms suffering from demand-side problems domestically choose to expand to other countries that were potentially suffering from similar problems?

There are a number of reasons answering the above and also some empirical evidence. First, a firm may have a different (sufficiently differentiated) product to offer. Given similarities in tastes or needs in other developed countries, they would be the obvious choice. Second, the proximity of other developed countries to sources of cheap labour and raw materials, in this case, for example, the proximity of northern European countries to southern Europe and North Africa. Developed countries can be the base through which easier access to less developed countries can be achieved. The infrastructure of developed countries makes them a good base, as does their politico-economic stability. Third, the acquisition of a stronghold within the emerging common European market and the associated avoidance of tariffs and other such barriers to firms' operations. Fourth, there are the advantages of being transnational *per se*, with the resultant reduction in labour and other costs and the increase in market power. Fifth, and important in our framework, the time and/or severity of demand-side problems may differ among developed countries.

Given this latter possibility, we examine the demand/profit share/liquidity situation of the US economy in the period preceding the growth of TNCs and DFI. Starting from the post-1929 Depression period, consumer expenditure as a percentage of after-tax gross private (personal and corporate) income declined from 96.24 per cent in 1930–34 to 90.01 per cent in 1935–39 and 82.64 per cent in the 1945–49 period. Corporate retentions in the same periods increased from a mere 1.63 per cent to 5.85 per cent and to 9.16 per cent respectively. The profit share increased from 7.23 per cent to 11.24 per cent and 12.42 per cent respectively. All three measures became relatively stable up to the mid-1960s. It is in the period during and following the dramatic decline in consumer expenditure and increase in profit share and liquidity that US DFI took off— nearly tenfold between 1946 and 1969 (see Tugendhat, 1971).

Much of this investment was directed to the UK. This renders interesting an examination of the UK data for the period. The share of consumer expenditure was far more stable than in the USA. From 92.99 per cent in the 1930–34 period, it declined to 89.24 per cent in the 1935–39 period and to 88.23 per cent in 1945–49. Consumer demand, therefore, was not as bad in the UK at the time, a point also supported by Cantwell (1988, 1991). More interestingly, following US DFI to Europe, the US consumer expenditure share effectively stabilized. The UK share declined dramatically, by nearly 10 per cent from the mid-1940s to the mid-1960s. This coincided with a dramatic increase in UK DFI (see Stopford and Dunning, 1983).

The above does not provide conclusive evidence for the demand-side argument, but it provides an explanation of the direction of DFI which is consistent with it. Given this, it is logical, we believe, to suggest that demand-side considerations may be of use.

The 'evidence' discussed so far fails to test directly whether aggregate effective demand problems can be an inducement to outward investment from a country. The *direct* way to test the hypothesis is by econometric estimation of the relationships involved. Below we report some findings from such an investigation, in Pitelis (1996).

We have treated the following relationship:

$$ODI_t = f(ED_t, Z_t) \tag{1}$$

where ODI = outward direct investment,
  ED = effective demand,
  Z = other explanatory variable(s),
  t = a time subscript

For estimation purposes, (1) can be written as

$$ODI_t = \alpha_0 + \alpha_1 ED_t + \alpha_2 Z_t + u_t \tag{2}$$

where α_0 = a constant term
  u_t = NID $(0, \sigma^2)$, is an error term assumed to satisfy the usual requirements

ED is defined in standard Keynesian terms to be the sum of aggregate consumers' expenditure (C) plus investment expenditure (I) plus the export surplus (ES) plus the budget deficit (BD), i.e., $ED = C + I + BD + ES$. We used UK data for the 1963–92 period, obtained from the *Economic Trends Annual Supplement* (ETAS, 1994). In line with our earlier discussion, it is expected that in (1) α_1 should be negative, implying that when aggregate effective demand decreases, outward direct investment increases and vice versa.

We pursued a 'general to specific' methodology in line with prevalent practice (see Harvey, 1981), namely we started with a general estimated equation in line with our propositions and gradually imposed parameter restrictions in order to find our 'preferred' equation, namely one that describes our data generation process most parsimoniously. Obvious explanatory variables besides ED are lagged ED, the lagged dependent variable (LDV) and the profit rate.

An important reason for including the above variables is that we need as general as possible an equation, subject to satisfying theoretical expectations and to keeping sufficient degrees of freedom, so as not to undermine the validity of our results. In the above framework, the three chosen explanatory variables satisfy these requirements. The domestic profit rate is likely to affect ODI negatively for evident reasons. Firms faced with a low domestic profit rate are likely to seek investments in overseas markets where profit rates may be higher. The profit rate is measured as gross trading profits, minus interest payment by manufacturing firms, divided by gross fixed capital formation. Data are from ETAS, 1994.

It is widely believed that firms' investment decisions are influenced by the *expected* profit rate (see Pitelis 1987 for a discussion). It is common to proxy 'expected' variables with the past values of the variable in question. If we assume that expected profit rates can be approximated by a geometrically declining distributed lag of the current variable, we have one justification/reason for also including the lagged dependent variable, (ODI_{t-1}) through the 'Koyck transformation'. There are other reasons justifying the inclusion of the LDV (see Wallis,

1979) including the conceptual possibility that it has a role to play in explaining ODI_t. Lastly, we have included lagged ED as an additional variable (ED_{t-1}). The reason is the need to seek a general equation, but also the possibility that ODI is influenced by *changes* (not levels) of ED. If so, this should be shown to be true by the data itself.

Given the above, our general equation took the form

$$ODI_t = \alpha_0 + \alpha_1 AD_t + \alpha_2 AD_{t-1} + \alpha_3 PROR_t + \alpha_4 ODI_{t-1} + u_t. \tag{3}$$

On estimation, with Ordinary Least Squares (OLS) we obtained the following 'preferred' equation

$$ODI_t = 7051.6* \quad -0.08* \ \Delta AD_t - 12.96* \ PROR_t + 0.83* \ ODI_{t-1}, \tag{4}$$
$$2.03 \qquad 2.15 \qquad\quad -2.38 \qquad\quad 9.11$$

$$\bar{R}^2 = 0.767, DW = 2.17$$

*denotes significances at the 5 per cent level of a 't' test.

According to (4), ODI is affected negatively and significantly by the change in effective demand and also by the profit rate. This is in line with our theoretical propositions. Moreover, the explanatory power of the equation is high and the equation is free of *all* conventional econometric problems (serial correlation, functional form, normality, multicollinearity, heteroscedasticity) as shown by the standard tests provided by the Mfit package.

It is worth noting that the effect of effective demand on ODI is independent of that of the profit rate. This is important given the potential theoretical link between AD and the profit rate, whereby the latter could be seen as a proxy for the former. As it turns out, the impact of AD is independent of that of the profit rate, which supports our theoretical propositions. In order to check whether AD affects ODI even in the absence of the profit rate, we have also run a regression where the latter was excluded. (Evidently, this is equivalent to imposing an already known to be invalid zero parameter restriction on [4].) On estimation this gave

$$ODI_t = -831.65 \ -0.85* \ \Delta AD_t + 0.82* \ ODI_{t-1} \tag{5}$$
$$0.70 \qquad 2.04 \qquad\quad 8.30$$

$$\bar{R}^2 = 0.720, DW = 1.95$$

As in (4), the impact of ΔAD on ODI is negative and significant, in line with our expectations. The equation is free of all conventional econometric problems. However, the explanatory variable of the equation is now lower and the constant term insignificantly different from zero. One would expect this to be positive and significant to indicate that some ODI would be expected even in the absence of AD and profit rate decreases. However, the fact that AD is still as expected and significant points to the robustness of our result. This was reinforced by numerous other regressions, in all of which the coefficient of AD never failed to be negative and significant.

To conclude, we have found support for the hypothesis that effective demand is inversely linked to outward investment. We also found support for the proposition that the domestic profit rate affects negatively outward investment. The equation was robust and of high explanatory power. This provides us with some confidence for its validity. This is not to underestimate the various problems of econometric estimation, including that our relationships do not prove any causal links. In this sense, our results are taken as failing to disprove a long existing, yet highly controversial and surprisingly disregarded proposition: that effective demand problems can be a stimulus to outward investment by TNCs.

Conclusions and policy

We discussed existing, mainly supply-side, theories of the TNC. We pointed out various deficiencies and tried to rectify this by building on developments on the Penrosean perspective. We moved on to suggest the elements of a synthesis of supply-side theories, to account for (endogenous) growth, motivation, direction of expansion, and choice of institutional mode. We observed the lack of considera- tion for demand-side issues in the theory of international production and the TNC, and went on to suggest that demand-side considerations can be an additional reason for geographical diversification, leading to a genuine 'all-weather company'. We suggested that a synthesis of supply-side considerations can explain the choice of institutional mode, when carefully applied in specific cases of specific firms. Last, but not least, we have suggested that the only generalization from the literature and our analysis is that one cannot generalize. All theories can be of use in certain cases, but no theory in all cases and all of the time. This applies equally to the demand-side arguments we have suggested in this chapter.

Acknowledgements

The author is grateful to Hugo Radice, Roger Sugden, Mo Yamin, and participants in numerous workshops for comments and discussion on earlier versions of this paper. Also, the author is grateful to George Argitis for research assistance.

Notes

1 See Cantwell (this volume) and Dunning (this volume) for a discussion of differences in the use of the terms.
2 It is worth noting that Caves' later work (1982, 1996) is in line with the transaction costs perspective and arguably a dynamic version of it, akin to resource-based ideas (see Pitelis and Sugden, this volume).
3 This need not be the case if markets are perfectly contestable; see Baumol (1982). Pitelis (1991b) has a critique pertaining to the actions of TNCs.
4 Besides extending Hymer's contribution, Cowling and Sugden also discuss 'divide and rule' ideas, as well as demand-side incentives.

5 It is possible, for example, that the social costs from internalization may exceed the private benefits (see Dunning, 1992).
6 Dunning (1989) traces the origin of internalization of Coase-type costs as well as the internalization of labour markets to Marx (1959), first published in 1867! A similar claim is made by Bowles (1985).
7 Penrose (1955) herself raised this question but, intriguingly, throughout the full length of her article, failed to return to the question.
8 See, for example, for resources and oligopolistic interaction, Cantwell (this volume); for location and ownership advantages, Dunning (1998); for transaction costs plus knowledge benefits, Kogut and Zander (1993), for Penrose and Hymer in the light of Kogut and Zander, Buckley and Casson (1998b); for ownership advantages and capabilities, Kogut and Zander (1993); for transaction costs and oligopolistic inter-action, Buckley and Casson (1998a); for transaction costs and ownership advantages, Cantwell (this volume). For a recent survey, see Caves (1996). For new developments, see Buckley and Casson (1998b).
9 While widely recognized in the 'agency' literature, in Marx this intra-firm struggle provides an inducement for endogenous technological developments (of the labour-saving type). This is akin to, and complements, the Penrosean endogenous growth theory, and is to our knowledge the only (along with Penrose's) theory of endogenous innovation.
10 In our framework 'profit maximization' is seen as the pursuit of maximum *possible*, long-term profitability (see below). It is questionable whether the profit maximization assumption of neoclassical price theory is compatible with bounded rationality (see Kay, 1984).
11 Such advantages could provide an answer to the other critique of the Baran–Sweezy tradition, regarding the direction of DFI. To the extent that the United States, for example, faced demand-side problems before, for example, Europe, the latter could be seen as an attractive location in which to invest for US firms. Moreover, monop-olization and socialization of capital tendencies need not be the only reasons for demand-side deficiencies. In the Keynesian and neoclassical tradition, for example, such differences can arise for reasons related to changes in consumers tastes, investor attitudes and/or monetary policies such as increases in interest rates.
12 A further factor leading to internationalization and TNCs can be international competition between nation states.

References

Alchian, A. and H. Demsetz (1972) 'Production, information costs and economic organization', *American Economic Review* 62, 5, December: 777–95.
Baran, P. and P. Sweezy (1966) *Monopoly Capital*, Harmondsworth: Penguin.
Baumol, W. (1982) 'Contestable markets: An uprising in the theory of industry structure', *American Economic Review* 72: 1–15.
Bleaney, M. (1976) *Underconsumption Theories: A History and Critical Analysis*, London: Lawrence & Wishart.
Bowles, J. (1985) 'The production process in a competitive economy', *American Economic Review* 75.
Brewer, A. (1980) *Marxist Theories of Imperialism*, London: Routledge & Kegan Paul.
Buckley, P.J. and M.C. Casson (1976) *The Future of Multinational Enterprise*, London: Macmillan.
—— (1998a) 'Analyzing foreign market entry strategies: Extending the internalization approach', *Journal of International Business Studies*, 29, 3: 539–62.

—— (1998b) 'Models of the multinational enterprise', *Journal of International Business Studies* 29, 1: 21–44.

Cantwell, J. (1988) 'Theories of international production', University of Reading Discussion Papers in International Investment and Business Studies, no. 122.

—— (1991) 'Theories of international production', in C.N. Pitelis and R. Sugden (eds) *The Nature of the Transnational Firm*, London: Routledge.

Casson, M.C. (1987) 'Multinational firms', in R. Clarke and T. McGuiness (eds) *The Economics of the Firm*, Oxford: Blackwells.

Caves, R.E. (1971) 'International corporations: The industrial economics of foreign investment', *Economica*, 38: 1–27.

—— (1996) [1982] *Multinational Enterprise and Economic Analysis*, Cambridge: Cambridge University Press.

Chandler, A.D. (1962) *Strategy and Structure*, Cambridge, Mass.: MIT Press.

Coase, R.H. (1937) 'The nature of the firm', *Economica* 4: 386–405.

Cowling, K. (1982) *Monopoly Capitalism*, London: Macmillan.

Cowling, K. and R. Sugden (1987) *Transnational Monopoly Capitalism*, Hemel Hempstead: Wheatsheaf.

Demsetz, H. (1995) *The Economics of the Business Firm: Seven Critical Commentaries*, Cambridge: Cambridge University Press.

Dunning, J.H. (1958) *American Investment in British Manufacturing Industry*, London: Allen & Unwin.

—— (1981) *International Production and Multinational Enterprise*, London: Allen & Unwin.

—— (1988) 'The eclectic paradigm of international production', *Journal of International Business Studies* 19: 1–31.

—— (1989) *Explaining International Production*, London: Unwin Hyman.

—— (1991) 'The eclectic paradigm in international production', in C.N. Pitelis and R. Sugden (eds) *The Nature of the Transnational Firm*, London: Routledge, 116–36.

—— (1992) 'The competitive advantage of countries and the activities of transnational corporations', *Transnational Corporations* 1, 2: 135–68.

—— (1998) 'Location and the multinational enterprise: A neglected factor?', *Journal of International Business Studies* 29, 1: 45–66.

Dunning, J.H. and A. Rugman (1985) 'The influence of Hymer's dissertation on the theory of foreign direct investment', *American Economic Review* 75: 228–39.

Economic Trends Annual Supplement (1994), London: HMSO.

Fieldhouse, D. (1986) 'The multinational: A critique of a concept', in A. Teihova, M. Levy-Leboyer and H. Nussbaum (eds) *Multinational Enterprise in Historical Perspective*, Cambridge: Cambridge University Press.

Gray, H.P. (1985) 'Macroeconomic theories of foreign direct investment: An assessment', in A. Rugman (ed.) *New Theories of Multinational Enterprise*, London: Croom Helm.

Grossman, S. and O. Hart (1986) 'The costs and benefits of ownership: A theory of lateral and vertical integration', *Journal of Political Economy* 94: 691–719.

Harvey, A.C. (1981) *The Econometric Analysis of Time Series*, London: Philip Allan.

Hilferding, R. (1981) [1910] *Finance Capital*, London: Routledge & Kegan Paul.

Holmström, B. and J. Roberts (1998) 'The boundaries of the firm revisited', *Journal of Economic Perspectives* 12, 4: 73–94.

Hood, N. and S. Young (1979) *The Economics of the Multinational Enterprise*, London: Longman.

Hymer, S.H. (1976) *The International Operations of National Firms: A Study of Foreign Direct Investment*, Cambridge, Mass.: MIT Press.

—— (1979) *The Multinational Corporation*, ed. R.B. Cohen *et al.*, Cambridge: Cambridge University Press.

Jenkins, R. (1987) *Transnational Corporations and Uneven Development*, London: Methuen.

Jensen, M.C. and W. Meckling (1976) 'Theory of the firm: Managerial behaviour, agency costs and ownership structure', *Journal of Financial Economics* 3: 304–60.

Kalecki, M. (1971) *Dynamics of the Capitalist Economy*, Cambridge: Cambridge University Press.

Kay, N. (1984) *The Emergent Firm: Knowledge, Ignorance and Surprise in Economic Organization*, London: Macmillan.

—— (1991) 'Multinational enterprise as strategic choice: Some transaction cost perspectives', in C. Pitelis and R. Sugden (eds) *The Nature of the Transnational Firm*, London: Routledge.

Kindleberger, C.P. (1969) *International Business Abroad*, New Haven, Conn.: Yale University Press.

—— (1984) *Multinational Excursions*, Cambridge, Mass.: MIT Press.

Kogut, B. and U. Zander (1993) 'Knowledge of the firm and the evolutionary theory of the multinational corporation', *Journal of International Business Studies*, 4th quarter: 625–45.

Lenin, V.I. (1917) *Imperialism: The Highest State of Capitalism*, Moscow.

Luxemburg, R. (1963) *The Accumulation of Capital*, London: Routledge & Kegan Paul.

Marglin, S. (1974) 'What do bosses do? The origins and functions of hierarchy in capitalist production', *Review of Radical Political Economics* 6, Winter: 60–112.

Marx, K. (1959) *Capital*, vol. I, London: Lawrence & Wishart.

Newfarmer, R. (1985) (ed.) *Profits, Progress and Poverty: Case Studies of International Industries in Latin America*, Notre Dame, Ind.: Notre Dame University Press.

Penrose, E.T. (1955) 'Research on the business firms: Limits to growth and size of firms', *American Economic Review* XLV, 2.

—— (1995) [1959] *The Theory of the Growth of the Firm*, Oxford: Oxford University Press.

—— (1960) 'The growth of the firm – A case study: The Hercules Powder Company', *Business History Review* XXXIV: 1–23.

Pitelis, C.N. (1987) *Corporate Capital: Control Ownership, Saving and Crisis*, Cambridge: Cambridge University Press.

—— (1991a) 'The transnational corporation: Demand-side issues and a synthesis', in C. Pitelis and R. Sugden (eds) *The Nature of the Transnational Firm*, London: Routledge.

—— (1991b) *Market and Non-Market Hierarchies: Theory of Institutional Failure*, Oxford: Basil Blackwell.

—— (1996) 'Effective demand, outward investment and the (theory of the) transnational corporation: An empirical investigation', *Scottish Journal of Political Economy* 43, 2: 192–206.

Pitelis, C.N. and A.N. Pseiridis (1999) 'Transaction costs versus resource value?', *Journal of Economic Studies*, 26, 3: 221–40.

Pitelis, C.N. and M. Wahl (1998) 'Edith Penrose: A pioneer of stakeholder theory', *Long Range Planning*, May.

Porter, M.E. (1980) *Competitive Strategy*, New York: Free Press.

Prahalad, C.K. and G. Hamel (1990) 'The core competence of the corporation', *Harvard Business Review*, May–June: 79–91.

Radice, H. (ed.) (1975) *International Firms and Modern Imperialism*, Harmondsworth: Penguin.

Rugman, A.M. (1986) 'New theories of the multinational enterprise: An assessment of internalization theory', *Bulletin of Economic Research* 38: 101–8.

Steindl, J. (1952) *Maturity and Stagnation of American Capitalism*, Oxford: Oxford University Press.

Stopford, J.M. and J. Dunning (1983) *Multinationals: Company Performance and Global Trends*, London: Macmillan.

Sugden, R. (1991) 'The importance of distributional considerations', in C. Pitelis and R. Sugden (eds), *The Nature of the Transnational Firm*, London: Routledge, 168–93.

Teece, D. (1977) 'Technology transfer by multinational firms: The resource costs of transferring technological know-how', *Economic Journal* 87: 242–61.

Tugendhat, T. (1971) *The Multinationals*, London: Penguin.

Vaitsos, K. (1974) *Inter-country Income Distribution and Transnational Enterprises*, Oxford: Clarendon Press.

Vernon, R. (1966) 'International investment and international trade in the product cycle', *Quarterly Journal of Economics* 80: 90–207.

Wallis, K. (1979) *Topics in Applied Econometrics*, Oxford: Basil Blackwell.

Williamson, O.E. (1975) *Markets and Hierarchies*, New York: Free Press.

—— (1981) 'The modern corporation: Origins, evolution, attributes', *Journal of Economic Literature* 19, 4: 1537–68.

Name index

Subject index

Printed in the United Kingdom by
Lightning Source UK Ltd., Milton Keynes
137068UK00001B/94-96/A